KABUKI GREATS

Dramatic Dances

歌舞伎名演目 ── 舞踊

監修　松竹株式会社

Supervised by SHOCHIKU

はじめに

　このたび、弊社の監修により「歌舞伎名演目」が出版される運びとなりました。
　現在でもしばしば上演されている人気演目のあらすじ、登場人物、見どころなどを3巻にわたり、写真とともに紹介する企画です。

　本書はその第三巻で、「舞踊」の作品20演目を紹介します。
　「歌舞伎おどり」から現在に至るまで、舞踊はレパートリーの大きな位置を占め、俳優は踊りの修練が欠かせません。もとは女方の専門領域でしたが、やがて立役も踊るようになり、伴奏音楽の発展とともにレパートリーが広がりました。音楽に乗せ躍動的な動きを見せる舞踊の魅力に溢れる作品に加え、演劇的な構成と内容を持ち、かつ音楽的、舞踊的な見せ場もある「舞踊劇」ともいうべき演目もあり、長さも小品から大作まで多彩です。
　それらの中から、現在でもしばしば上演されている演目を選定いたしました。

　劇的な内容を持つ一部の作品を除き、舞踊を言葉で説明するのは難しく、また、振付や上演時の都合により、適宜カットが行なわれることも多いのですが、ここでは、現在上演される振付・演出をもとに説明をすることにいたしました。
　また、歌詞・詞章の一部を、適宜漢字をあて、現代仮名遣いで掲載しました。

　本書でも、前二巻と同じく、演目の魅力や内容を数行で表す、いわばキャッチコピー的な文章を冒頭に据え、演目のイメージを大づかみでつかんでいただくと同時に、簡潔なあらすじとコラム、写真などの多彩な切り口で全体像を伝えることを主眼といたしました。

　歌舞伎の魅力は舞台にあり、書物ではなかなか伝えきれませんが、お読みになった後でその演目をご覧になった際、演技や舞台がよりお楽しみいただけるような実用にも役立つ一冊を心がけました。
　本書が歌舞伎ご愛好の方々のご観劇のよき手引きとなることはもとより、本書で歌舞伎に初めて触れる方々が劇場に足をお運びいただくきっかけとなれば幸いでございます。

松竹株式会社

Foreword

We are pleased to present the next volume in the *Kabuki Greats* series. The goal of this three-part project is to compile synopses, character profiles, and highlight notes of some of the most oft-performed kabuki plays, along with pictures to aid in understanding and visualization.

Dramatic Dances, the third and final volume of the series, introduces twenty buyo dances.

The style of dance known as "buyo" has been an integral part of the kabuki repertoire from the early *"kabuki-odori"* to the modern buyo dances of today. Because of this, mastering buyo is a natural requirement of any aspiring kabuki actor. In the past, buyo was performed exclusively by *onnagata* actors, but with time *tachiyaku* leads were required to dance as well, expanding the repertoire both of actors and the accompaniment musicians and singers.

The genre of buyo is a rich one, ranging from simple rhythmic dances set to music to dances with intricate stories that may more accurately be referred to as "dance dramas." The length of buyo dances varies greatly, some lasting a mere twenty minutes and still others ninety or more. For this book, we took care to select only the most popular and oft-performed buyo pieces to introduce.

Other than the more dramatic dances that have strong plotlines, buyo plays are incredibly difficult to describe in words. What's more, it is common for buyo dances to be abridged and edited to fit with a given performance schedule. Here, we have based our synopses and explanations on the most recent versions of the plays introduced. We have also included portions of the song lyrics and scripts.

In this volume, like the last two, we strove to convey the charms of the works introduced in appealing language by including impactful headings that give readers a birds-eye view of the piece before presenting photographs and highlight columns written in concise and easy-to-understand language to help readers gain a balanced view of kabuki from different vantage points.

The delights of kabuki are something that can only be seen on the stage. Even so, we hope that this book may offer a practical understanding of the fundamentals of kabuki, allowing readers to enjoy this unique artform more fully.

This book is not only meant to be a guide to kabuki lovers, but also an introduction to the theater for those who have never experienced it for themselves. It is our sincere hope that this book inspires newcomers to make their way to the theater and experience the fascinating world of kabuki for themselves.

SHOCHIKU Co., Ltd.

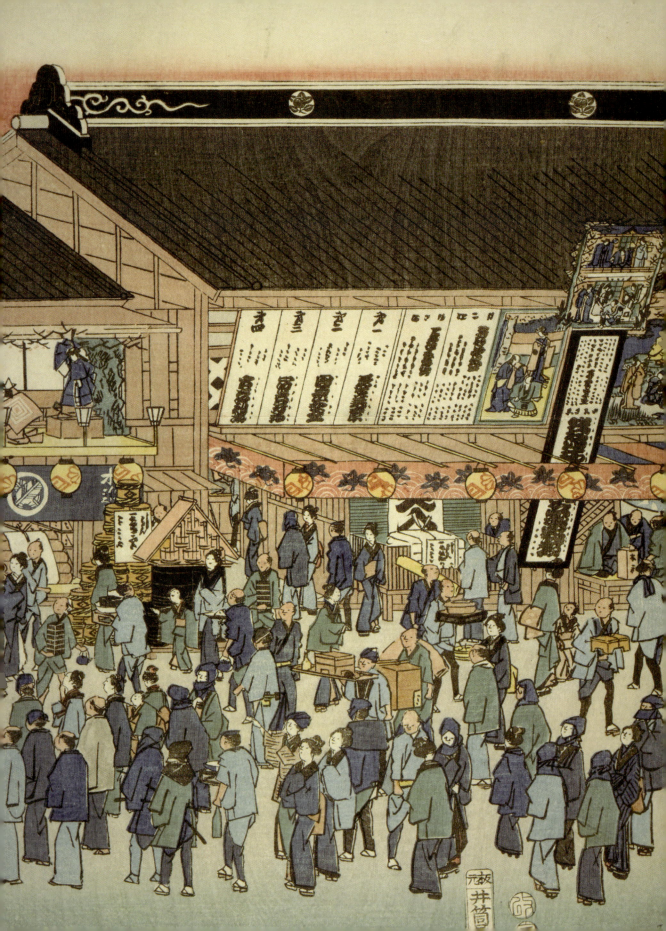

目次

01 京鹿子娘道成寺 きょうがのこむすめどうじょうじ
Kyoganoko Musume Dojoji —— 10

02 鷺娘 さぎむすめ
Sagimusume —— 18

03 積恋雪関扉 つもるこいゆきのせきのと
Tsumoru Koi Yuki no Sekinoto —— 26

04 保名 やすな
Yasuna —— 34

05 藤娘 ふじむすめ
Fujimusume —— 42

06 六歌仙容彩 ろっかせんすがたのいろどり
Rokkasen Sugata no Irodori —— 50

07 寿式三番叟 ことぶきしきさんばそう
Kotobuki Shiki Sanbaso —— 60

08 連獅子 れんじし
Renjishi —— 68

09 春興鏡獅子 しゅんきょうかがみじし
Shunkyo Kagamijishi —— 76

10 船弁慶 ふなべんけい
Funa Benkei —— 84

Contents

11 紅葉狩 もみじがり
Momijigari —— 92

12 身替座禅 みがわりざぜん
Migawari Zazen —— 100

13 土蜘 つちぐも
Tsuchigumo —— 108

14 棒しばり ぼうしばり
Bo Shibari —— 118

15 二人椀久 ににんわんきゅう
Ninin Wankyu —— 126

16 色彩間苅豆 いろもようちょっとかりまめ
Iromoyo Chotto Karimame —— 134

17 忍夜恋曲者 しのびよるこいはくせもの
Shinobiyoru Koi wa Kusemono —— 142

18 黒塚 くろづか
Kurozuka —— 150

19 三社祭 さんじゃまつり
Sanja Matsuri —— 158

20 お祭り おまつり
Omatsuri —— 166

カバーイラストレーション：『連獅子』親獅子の精
Cover illustration: *Renjishi: Parent Shishi Spirit*

KABUKI
PLAYS

演目紹介

Dramatic Dances

舞踊

京鹿子娘道成寺
Kyoganoko Musume Dojoji

『京鹿子娘道成寺』
2010年8月　新橋演舞場
白拍子花子（九代目中村福助）

Kyoganoko Musume Dojoji
(Shinbashi Enbujo Theatre, August 2010)
Shirabyoshi Hanako (Nakamura Fukusuke IX)

あらすじ　　　　　　　　　　Synopsis

「鐘に恨みは数々ござる……」
ここは紀州の道成寺、咲き誇る桜を背に
女心を謳い上げる歌舞伎舞踊の代表作

春爛漫、満開の桜を浴びながら艶やかに舞う花子の姿はこの上なく美しい。あどけない少女の淡い恋への憧れからやがて燃える想いを化粧に託し、気分は高まってゆく。時には男の浮気心に嫉妬も覚えるが、そんな姿もたちまち一変、美しい娘と見えたのは道成寺の鐘にまつわる清姫の怨霊だった。

—————— A representative piece of kabuki buyo that depicts the deeply etched resentments of a woman toward an ancient bell at Dojoji Temple in the province of Kishu.

Hanako's dance among the resplendent cherry blossoms of spring is a sight of unparalleled beauty. Watch as the innocent love of a young girl transforms into a fiery resentment. As the jealousy of a faithless man slowly creeps into her performance, we finally see that she is, in fact, the spirit of Kiyohime, who holds a deep grudge against Dojoji Temple's bell.

幕が開くと桜満開の紀州道成寺。大勢の所化が登場し、寺で鐘の供養があることなどを語る。かつて清姫によって焼かれた鐘が再興され、その供養が執り行なわれているのである。

やがて竹本連中の乗った山台が引き出され、「道行」となり、花道より白拍子花子が登場し踊る。なお、竹本の代わりに常磐津を使うこともある。
鐘供養があることを聞いた白拍子花子が、振袖にびらり帽子という華やかな風情で道成寺に急ぐ踊りである。鐘への執着をところどころ見せつつ、踊り終えた花子は花道から本舞台に来る。

本舞台では所化との問答があり、鐘の供養を拝みたいと願う花子は、舞を舞うことを条件に寺に入ることを許される。所化から借りた金の烏帽子を着けた花子は、中啓（扇の一種）を持ち厳かな舞を見せる。

ここから長唄に合わせての踊りとなる。

　　花のほかには松ばかり
　　暮れ初めて鐘や響くらん

The curtains open, revealing Dojoji Temple in Kishu Province, the cherry blossoms in full bloom. A number of *shoke* monks are chatting about the dedication of the temple's new bell, a reproduction of the bell that was burned down by Kiyohime years ago.

A *takemoto* accompaniment is brought out atop a *yamadai* platform (sometimes a *Tokiwazu* band is used instead).
Shirabyoshi Hanako, who heard about the bell dedication, appears on the *hanamichi* wearing a *furisode* robe and performs an dance that betrays her connection to the bell.

When her dance finishes, Hanako moves to the main stage, where she is interrogated about love by the *shoke* monks. She is eventually allowed into the temple on the condition that she perform a dance in honor of the new bell. Hanako performs a solemn dance, holding a ceremonial fan and donning a golden *eboshi* hat lent to her by the *shoke*.

A new dance begins, accompanied by *nagauta*-style music.

(See Japanese lyrics on left)

京鹿子娘道成寺

あらすじ

花子は能の道成寺にある乱拍子を踏むなど、能を写した舞を荘重に舞うと同時に、鐘への執着を垣間見せる。

鐘尽くしの舞を舞い終わり、烏帽子を取ると、それまでとはがらりと変わり、くだけた曲調で手踊りを見せる。移り気な男の気持ちを嘆く歌詞に合わせて恋の切なさを踊る。

続いて吉原、島原など各地の遊郭を読み込んだ、廓尽くしの唄に合わせ、少女の鞠つきをまねて踊る。

さらに、花子は笠を被り、振出笠を手にして踊る。『わきて節』という曲に合わせての踊りである。花子が一くさり踊って引っ込むと、今度は所化たちが花傘を持って踊る。

その後、花子は手拭いを手にして登場、恋する心の切なさや哀しさを踊る。この部分を「クドキ」といい、踊りの眼目とされる。

恋の手習い
つい見ならいて
誰に見しょとて紅かね付きょぞ
みんな主への心中だて
おおうれし　おおうれし

しっとりと踊った後は、胸に鞨鼓（かっこ）と呼ばれる楽器を付け、撥（ばち）で打ち鳴らしながら各地の山の名を唄い込んだ山尽くしの曲を踊る。

さらに、少女の手踊り、鈴太鼓の踊りと続く。

踊っているうちに花子の形相が変わり、鐘の中に飛び込んでしまう。白拍子と見えたのは、実はかつて鐘に隠れた恋しい男を恨んで蛇体となり、鐘もろともに焼き尽くした清姫の怨霊であった。

この場を「鐘入り」といい、ここまでの上演が多いが、以降の押戻しも時に上演される。なおこの場までも、クドキを中心にして、前後を適宜省略して上演される。

鐘が落ちて花子が鐘の中に入り、所化の祈り。この後、鱗四天（うろこよてん）の捕り手たちが道成にかかり、「とう尽くし」のせりふなどがあり、鐘が引き上げられる。

そこに現れたのは蛇体となった清姫の怨霊（後ジテ）の恐ろしい姿。

そこへ豪傑・大館左馬五郎が現れ、清姫の怨霊を押し戻すのであった。

While emulating the solemn dance of the noh play *Dojoji*, Hanako betrays her attachment to the temple's bell, performing a dance to lyrics that tell of the hardships of love and the fickle hearts of men.

Next, she mimics the poor lot of a young girl used as a plaything, set to a song depicting the famed pleasure quarters of Yoshiwara, Shimabara, etc.

She proceeds to don a *kasa* hat and perform a dance to the tune "*Wakite-bushi.*" After she has finished, the *shoke* monks come on stage and perform a dance with decorative parasols called *hanagasa*.

After the *shoke* monks' dance, Hanako returns with a handkerchief in hand to perform a dance about the hardships of love in the play's focal point, a scene called "*Kudoki*" ("wooing").

(See Japanese lyrics on left)

After this languid performance, she dances while striking a special drum called a *kakko* to a song naming the various famous mountains of Japan.

The *te-odori* and *suzu-daiko* dances follow until Hanako's expression changes mid-dance and she suddenly jumps into the new temple bell.

The dancer Hanako reveals her true identity, the spirit of Kiyohime who burned down the old bell after her fickle lover hid within it, transformed into a great snake.

This section of the play is called "*kane-iri*" ("entering the bell"), and while some performances end here, still others feature an "*oshimodoshi*" scene. Other scenes are often omitted or included at the performer's discretion, but the central "*Kudoki*" scene and the climax remain unchanged.

After the bell falls, the temple *shoke* monks pray as guards called *uroko-yoten* lift the bell up from the *hanamichi* to reveal a ghastly snake, the form taken by Kiyohime's vengeful spirit.

Finally, the great Odate Samagoro appears and fights back the angry spirit of Kiyohime, ending the show.

『京鹿子娘道成寺』
2003年1月　歌舞伎座
白拍子花子（五代目坂東玉三郎）

Kyoganoko Musume Dojoji
(Kabukiza Theatre, January 2003)
Shirabyoshi Hanako (Bando Tamasaburo V)

作品の概要

演目名

京鹿子娘道成寺

作者

作詞＝藤本斗文
作曲＝初世杵屋弥三郎

概要

　女方舞踊の最高峰。能『道成寺』を換骨奪胎した長唄舞踊で、華やかな娘の恋心の様々を踊り抜く長編である。初演時は『男達初買曾我（おとこだてはつがいそが）』三番目として上演され、尾形三郎の妹・横笛が滝口小四郎という若者に片思いして狂乱し、兄に殺され、その亡霊が鐘供養に現れる筋であった。白拍子花子が花道に登場し、義太夫地の道行を踊った後、舞台に入って道成寺の所化との問答。ここまでは省略されることもある。「花のほかには松ばかり」から烏帽子をつけた乱拍子、急の舞。「鐘に恨みは数々ござる」から調子が変わり、しだいに歌舞伎本来の賑やかな舞踊となる。以後引抜きなどで衣裳を変えながら手踊り、鞠唄、花笠踊、所化たちの傘踊り、「恋の手習い」からはくどき、山尽し、手踊り、鈴太鼓と華麗な踊りが続く。最後に蛇の本性を現し鐘に上り幕。押戻しが付く時は、隈取をした後シテに変わり、花道から現れた押戻しと争い、舞台へ押し戻され幕となる。『二人道成寺』『奴道成寺』『男女道成寺』など、脚色を変えた作品も多い。

初演

宝暦3（1753）年3月江戸・中村座で、初世中村富十郎による。作詞は藤本斗文、作曲は初世杵屋弥三郎。振付は中村傳次郎、市川團五郎。

Overview

Title

Kyoganoko Musume Dojoji

Writer

Lyrics: Fujimoto Tobun
Music: Kineya Yasaburo I

Overview

　　The crown jewel of *onnagata-buyo*, *Kyoganoko Musume Dojoji* is a *nagauta* buyo play based on the noh play Dojoji. It features dances depicting the many facets of a young girl's love. Its debut performance was as the third act of *Otokodate Hatsugai Soga*, which depicts the one-sided love of a young girl named Yokobue who is killed by her older brother Ogata Saburo after being driven mad by her love. Her spirit then appears at the dedication of Dojoji's bell. In *Kyoganoko Musume Dojoji*, Shirabyoshi Hanako enters from the *hanamichi*, dancing several *michiyuki* pieces in the *gidayu* style before she is interrogated by the *shoke* monks. The story up to this point is sometimes omitted in performances of this play. At this point, Hanako begins to dance wildly, donning an *eboshi* hat, but with the lyrics, "Many are the grudges held toward a bell," the performance suddenly shifts to the more typical, energetic kabuki-style buyo. From this point onward, an extravagant series of dances are performed one after another, accompanied by a number of costume changes. Finally, Hanako shows her true form: a great snake that climbs up onto the bell, signaling the end of the play. Some performances include the appearance of an *oshimodoshi* character who fights with the angry spirit of Kiyohime on the *hanamichi*, forcing her to return to the stage before the play ends. Other versions of this play include *Ninin Dojoji*, *Yakko Dojoji*, *Meoto Dojoji*, etc.

Premiere

March 1753, Nakamuraza Theatre. Feat. Nakamura Tomijuro I. Lyrics by Fujimoto Tobun. Music by Kineya Yasaburo I. Choreography by Nakamura Denjiro and Ichikawa Dangoro.

登場人物 / Characters

白拍子花子
しらびょうしはなこ

白拍子は宴を歌や舞でもてなす芸人だが多くは遊女。女人の立入りが厳しく戒められている道成寺の鐘供養の日、白拍子花子は所化たちの問答に鮮やかに答え、舞を舞うといって寺の中へと入る。やがて烏帽子姿から様々に姿を変えて、若い娘の恋心や喜びそして嫉妬などを舞に乗せて語ってゆく。しかし鐘を恨めしそうに見上げると本性を現し、蛇体となって鐘に取り付く。実は鐘に恨みを持つ清姫の怨霊であった。

Shirabyoshi Hanako

Shirabyoshi are girls who sing and dance at banquets for entertainment. On the day of the ceremony for the dedication of Dojoji Temple's new bell, Shirabyoshi Hanako comes to perform but is stopped by the young *shoke* monks. Because the temple does not normally allow women into the precincts, the monks interrogate her. She answers their questions with ease, however, and makes her way into the temple saying "I'm going to dance." Hanako then proceeds to dance, changing her appearance many times to depict the story of the joys and pitfalls of young love. Finally, however, Hanako transforms into a snake, showing her true form and possessing the bell. Finally, it is revealed that Hanako is actually Kiyohime's enraged spirit who has a grudge against this bell.

所化
しょけ

所化というのは若い修行僧のこと。幕開きに登場する大勢の所化が「聞いたか聞いたか」「聞いたぞ聞いたぞ」と唱えながら出てくるので「聞いたか坊主」と通称される。道成寺は焼け落ちた鐘が永年再興されず、この日ようやく新しい鐘の供養を迎えるが、所化たちにとってはお師匠様の長い念仏を聞くのが憂鬱。そこへ美しい白拍子がやって来たので、舞を舞うならばと女人禁制の寺へ引き入れてしまう。

Shoke

Shoke are young Buddhist monks. Because of their lines at the beginning of this play ("did you hear, did you hear," / "yes I heard, yes I heard."), they are often referred to as "*kiitaka bozu*" ("did-you-hear monks."). The new bell's dedication is extremely significant, as Dojoji Temple had been without a bell for many years after a fire destroyed the old one. The *shoke* monks, however, are dreading having to listen to their master's long prayers. They are easily distracted when a beautiful *shirabyoshi* dancer comes to dance, and eventually they let her into the temple despite Dojoji's rules against allowing women inside.

大館左馬五郎
おおだてさまごろう

「押戻し」と呼ばれる荒事の役で、顔には勇壮な隈取を施し大きな竹を持って幕切れ近くに登場し、鬼女の姿となった清姫の霊を花道から舞台に押し戻すような形で激しく対峙する。『道成寺』の踊りはこの演出が付かない上演も多い。江戸時代の上演時は役名がその都度様々に変えられていたが、明治以降はこの大館左馬五郎という役名にほぼ統一されるようになった。

Odate Samagoro

A rough *aragoto* role called *oshimodoshi*, Odate Samagoro sports gallant *kumadori* makeup and appears near the end of the performance to confront the angry spirit of Kiyohime. This part is sometimes omitted from performances of *Dojoji*. During the Edo Period, this role was called by many names, but the name Odate Samagoro was fixed in the Meiji Period.

安珍
あんちん

この舞台には登場しないが、紀州の道成寺に古くから伝わる伝説の主人公で、奥州白河からやって来た年若く美しい僧。熊野権現を参詣する途中に紀州田辺で宿を取り、そこの娘・清姫に惚れられてしまう。参詣後に必ず立ち戻ることを約束するが逃げてしまい、気付いた清姫に追いかけられる。やがて道成寺の鐘の中に逃げ込むが、激しい嫉妬から蛇体と化した清姫に鐘もろとも焼き殺されてしまう。

Anchin

Though he doesn't appear in this play, Anchin is a handsome young monk from Mutsu Province who falls in love with Kiyohime in an old legend from Dojoji Temple in Kii Province. He is visiting Kii Province to pay homage at Dojoji Temple but falls in love with Kiyohime whom he meets at the home where he's staying. He promises to return to her after visiting the temple, but Kiyohime realizes he is lying and runs after him. He eventually hides in Dojoji Temple's bell, but Kiyohime, filled with jealousy, transforms into a snake and burns the bell down, killing Anchin along with it.

清姫
きよひめ

安珍と共に道成寺の伝説で知られる女性。紀州の真砂庄司の娘で、この家に宿を取った安珍に一目惚れ。安珍も甘い言葉で参詣帰りに必ず戻る約束を交わしたが反故にされ、嫉妬に狂って安珍を追いかける。逃げる安珍に邪恋は激しく燃え、蛇の姿となって日高川を泳いで渡り、道成寺の鐘に取り付いて口から火を放ち、中に逃げ込んだ安珍を焼き殺してしまう。舞台に登場した白拍子花子はその怨霊。

Kiyohime

Kiyohime is a well-known character from the Dojoji Temple legend. She is the daughter of the Masago Shoji house. She falls in love with a visiting monk named Anchin who promises to return for her after he visits Dojoji Temple, but when he breaks his promise the jealous Kiyohime chases after him. Burning with jealousy, she turns into a snake, crosses the Hidaka River, and finds Anchin hiding in the temple's bell. She spits fire from her mouth, burning the bell and killing Anchin. The *shirabyoshi* dancer Hanako, who appears in *Kyoganoko Musume Dojoji* is actually the enraged spirit of Kiyohime.

みどころ
Highlights

1. 白拍子花子の衣裳 —— Hanako's Costume

白拍子舞の振袖。赤綸子地に、雲霞に枝垂桜柄が刺繍されている。この後に引抜きなどで、浅葱(あさぎ)色、鴇(とき)色、藤色、紫、白地、玉子色の振袖や襦袢へと変わり、本性を見せると銀のウロコ模様の衣裳となる。

Furisode robes worn by *shirabyoshi* dancers, Hanako's costume is made from a figured satin fabric embroidered with a weeping cherry (*shidarezakura*) pattern. As the performance proceeds, she changes costumes many times before showing her true nature with a scale-patterned robe.

2. 女方の卒業論文 —— Final Thesis for *Onnagata*

『京鹿子娘道成寺』は道行から鐘入りまですべてを上演すると1時間を超える大曲。女方の卒業論文といわれるほど大切な曲で、襲名披露の演目に選ばれることも多い。能の『道成寺』は「鐘への恨み」というテーマの比重が大きいが、歌舞伎では、それよりも女性の美しさ・可愛らしさの様々を踊り尽くすことに眼目がある。俳優の系統によって特色の違いも見られるので、長年見比べると面白さが倍加し、歌舞伎観劇の醍醐味が感じられてくる。

Kyoganoko Musume Dojoji is a grand musical piece that takes over an hour to perform from the opening *michiyuki* to the *kaneiri* finale. It is an extremely important piece of the repertoire that is often called the "final thesis of *onnagata* actors." It is also performed as a *shumei-hiro* piece commemorating an actor's succession to a stage name. Though the overriding theme of a woman's resentful feelings toward the Dojoji Temple bell is the focal point of the noh play *Dojoji*, the kabuki version focuses much more on the depiction of womanly beauty and charm. There are distinctive differences between the performances of actors from different traditions, making this show even more interesting when viewed many times over the years. Doing so is sure to reveal something of the true essence of kabuki theatre.

3. 聞いて驚く人もなし
—— Not a soul is surprised...

朝晩に鳴り響くお寺の鐘は、「諸行無常（しょぎょうむじょう）、寂滅為楽（じゃくめついらく）」と響いて世の無常を伝えると、『京鹿子娘道成寺』の歌詞にはある。しかしその後、「（鐘の音を）聞いて驚く人もなし」と受け流すような文句が続いている。要するに、寺の鐘を毎日聞いても、人間そう簡単には悟ることなんかない、というわけだ。真紅の振袖を身にまとった白拍子の舞に始まる本曲は、艶やかな現世謳歌の踊りなのである。

Kyoganoko's lyrics declare the impermanence of all worldly things and exalts the path to enlightenment as the temple bell rings. After this, however, the lyrics proceed to flip this sentiment on its head with the line, "not a soul hears the bell with surprise." In other words, listening to a sacred bell every day is not enough to reach enlightenment. As if to stress this point, the following dance performed by Hanako, who wears deep crimson robes, is a distinctly worldly one.

4. 道成寺二度目の災難
—— The Second Fire at Dojoji Temple

紀州道成寺は、安珍清姫の伝説で知られる。美男の僧・安珍に、ところの庄司の娘・清姫が恋をする。安珍は驚いて嘘の約束をして逃げ、道成寺に隠れる。怒った清姫は蛇に姿を変え、道成寺の鐘の下に潜む安珍を鐘もろとも焼き滅ぼし、日高川に入水。その後清姫の霊は、寺の手厚い供養で成仏したという伝説だ。本作は、やっと鐘が再建された道成寺の鐘供養の庭に、再び清姫の霊が現れる物語。道成寺にとっては二度目の災難を描いている。

Dojoji Temple is known for the legend of Anchin and Kiyohime. Kiyohime of the Shoji house falls in love with the handsome monk Anchin, who is flustered and makes a false promise to appease his unwanted lover. He then flees to Dojoji Temple, where the enraged Kiyohime eventually finds him hidden inside the temple bell. Transformed by her rage into a fearsome snake, she sets fire to the bell, killing Anchin and destroying the bell before drowning herself in the Hidaka River. It is said that afterward, the Dojoji monks made offerings to calm Kiyohime's spirit, but in this play her spirit appears once again at the dedication of the newly-forged bell, causing a second fire at the temple.

鷺娘
Sagimusume

『鷺娘』
2005年5月　歌舞伎座
鷺娘（五代目坂東玉三郎）

Sagimusume
(Kabukiza Theatre, May 2005)
Sagimusume (Bando Tamasaburo V)

あらすじ　　　　　Synopsis

一面の雪景色に映える透き通るような白無垢姿。
綿帽子と傘に隠されたその真の姿は……。
美しい白鷺の幻想舞台

雪がしんしんと降りしきる一面の銀世界、浮かび上がって見えたのは美しく清らかな花嫁姿。娘は思いに耽り恋する女の心を舞に乗せて語ってゆくが、時折見せるのは恋の苦しさと一抹の寂しさ。再び雪は降り続き、娘は地獄の責めに苦しみながら鷺の姿と重なり合い、ついに力尽きてゆく。

—————— The incarnation of a white heron dances in this vivid yet illusory scene, her sheer white *shiromuku* robes nearly transparent among the falling snow...

A beautiful bride dances amid the unceasing snow. Her dances depict reminiscences of love, but soon her focus shifts to the many hardship of romance, ending ultimately in loneliness. As the snow picks up yet again, she expresses deep agony as the image of the girl and that of the white heron overlap until finally she is completely spent.

舞台は一面の雪景色の汀。長唄囃子連中が居並んでいる。

　妄執の雲晴れやらぬ朧夜の
　　恋に迷いしわが心

　長唄の声につれ、白無垢姿の娘が姿を現す。娘は傘を手にしてしょんぼりと佇んでいる。実はこの娘は鷺の精の化身で、人間の男と道ならぬ恋をして思い悩んでいるのである。
　鷺の精は自らの苦しい心の内を踊る。

　吹けども傘に雪持って
　積もる思いは泡雪と
　消えて果敢なき恋路とや

　思い重なる胸の闇
　せめて哀れと夕暮に
　ちらちら雪に濡鷺の
　しょんぼりと可愛らし

　迷う心の細流れ
　ちょろちょろ水の一筋に

The stage is set as a snowscape next to a body of water, the *nagauta* musicians ready to begin.

(See Japanese lyrics on left)

As the song begins, a young woman in a white *shiromuku* kimono appears. She holds an umbrella in a somewhat downhearted stance. She is the incarnation of a heron who had an illicit affair with a man and is greatly troubled.
　The girl begins to dance, her movements depicting her heart's troubles.

(See Japanese lyrics on left)

鷺娘

怨みの外は白鷺の
水に馴れたる足どりも
濡れて雫と消ゆるもの

　やがて、衣裳もガラリと変わり、その男と結ばれた頃の
ことを思い起こし、一転して賑やかに踊り出す。
　そして男心のつれなさを、須磨の汐汲みや、繻子の袴の
襞をとる様子に例えた唄に合わせて踊る。

　　われは涙に乾く間も
　　袖干しあえぬ月影に
　　忍ぶその夜の話を捨てて

　　縁を結ぶの神さんに
　　取り上げられし嬉しさも
　　余る色香の恥かしや

　　須磨の浦辺で汐汲むよりも
　　君の心が汲みにくい
　　さりとは　実に誠と思わんせ

あらすじ

　　繻子の袴の襞とるよりも
　　主の心が取りにくい
　　さりとは　実に誠と思わんせ

　さらに傘を使って艶やかに踊る。

　　傘をや　傘をさすならば
　　てんてんてん日照傘
　　それえそれえ　さしかけて
　　いざさらば　花見にごんせ吉野山

　しかし道ならぬ恋をした地獄の責め苦が鷺の精を襲い始
める。

　　添うも添われず　あまつさえ
　　邪慳の刃に先立ちて
　　此世からさえ剣の山

　　一樹のうちに恐ろしや
　　地獄の有様ことごとく
　　罪を糺して閻王の
　　鉄杖正にありありと

　　等活畜生　衆生地獄
　　或は叫喚大叫喚
　　修羅の太鼓は隙もなく

　鷺の精は地獄の責め苦に息も絶え絶えとなるのであった。

　　　She changes her robes in a flash and recalls the
beginnings of love in a lively, bright dance.
　　　She continues to dance as the lyrics liken the coldness
of a man's heart to drawing water from the sea in the land
of Suma or trying to straighten the pleats of satin *hakama*
trousers.

　　(See Japanese lyrics on left)

　　　She takes up her parasol and begins an entrancing dance.

　　(See Japanese lyrics on left)

　　　In the end, however, the woes of her illicit affair are a
torture worse than hell.

　　(See Japanese lyrics on left)

　　　The heron spirit suffers great agony before finally
breathing her last feeble breath.

『鷺娘』
2009年1月 歌舞伎座
鷺娘（五代目坂東玉三郎）

Sagimusume
(Kabukiza Theatre, January 2009)
Sagimusume (Bando Tamasaburo V)

作品の概要

演目名

鷺娘

作者

作詞 = 不明
作曲 = 富士田吉次、杵屋忠次郎

概要

　鷺の精が人間の娘の姿に変じて踊るというのが本作の趣向である。本名題『柳雛諸鳥囀（やなぎにひなしょちょうのさえずり）』という変化物の一つとして初演された。初演から124年後の明治19（1886）年5月に東京・新富座で九世市川團十郎が復活して、このときは三変化『月雪花三組杯觴（つきゆきはなみつぐみさかずき）』の一つとして上演されている。以来『鷺娘』の部分が再演されるようになり、人気の舞踊作品となった。20分ほどの短い作品ながら、三下りの長唄は名曲である。しっとりした曲調のなか、寂しい雪景色に白鷺の精が娘姿で白無地の着物に黒い帯を締め、綿帽子を被って佇む場面から、引抜きで艶やかな赤地染柄の着物の町娘となる。やがてぶっ返りなどで鷺の本性を顕わにし、地獄のような恋の苦しみに身を焦がすという展開がドラマチックである。大正以降、西洋のバレエ『瀕死の白鳥』の手法を取り入れた演出が生まれ、古風な型と共に行なわれている。

初演

宝暦12（1762）年4月江戸・市村座で、二世瀬川菊之丞による。作詞者不明、作曲は富士田吉次、杵屋忠次郎。

Overview

Title

Sagimusume

Writer

Lyrics: Unknown
Music: Fujita Kichiji, Kineya Chujiro

Overview

　This buyo piece features the spirit of a heron dancing in human form. The formal title of the play is *Yanagi ni Hina Shocho no Saezuri*, *Sagimusume* being one part of the longer *hengemono* piece. It was revived by Ichikawa Danjuro IX at the Shintomiza Theatre in 1886, 124 years after its first performance. At that time it was performed as a part of the *san-henge* play *Tsukiyukihana Mitsugumi Sakazuki*. Since then, *Sagimusume* has become a popular buyo piece that is often performed on its own. Only 20 minutes in length, this short piece features a three-part *nagauta* accompaniment in a quiet mood. Beginning in a sheer white kimono with a black sash, the dancer changes into a beautiful red patterned robe using a technique called *hikinuki*. Finally, using the *bukkaeri* and other techniques, she shows that her true form is that of a white heron, and the dance ends dramatically with the heron writhing in agony. From the Taisho Period (1912-1926) onward, techniques from the ballet piece *The Dying Swan* were incorporated into performances of *Sagimusume*, blending modern elements into the traditional Japanese art of buyo.

Premiere

April 1762, Ichimuraza Theatre. Feat. Segawa Kikunojo II. Music by Fujita Kichiji and Kineya Chujiro. Lyrics, unknown.

登場人物 　　　　　　　　　　Characters

鷺の精
さぎのせい

一面に広がる雪景色の中、白無垢に綿帽子姿の清らかな娘が寂し気に佇む。時折手の仕草で鳥の動きを見せる通り、どうやらこれは鷺の精である。やがて艶やかで可憐な町娘の姿へと変わり、恋の嬉しさ恥ずかしさなど手踊りから傘の踊りへと心の想いを綴ってゆく。最後は再び鷺の姿となり、降りしきる雪の中で責め苦を受け静かに息絶えてゆく。彼女は本当に鳥か？　そこは曖昧さを残したまま。

Sagi Spirit

A woman in a white *shiromuku* robe and silken bridal headdress who dances among the fallen snow. Her birdlike movements hint at her identity--the spirit of the *sagi*, or heron. She eventually transforms into a charming young girl whose dance depicts the many emotions that come with love. Returning to her bird-like form in the end, she breathes her last tormented breath among the unrelenting snow. Leaving a strange warmth behind her, audiences are bound to wonder if this beautiful creature really was a bird.

みどころ
Highlights

1. 娘心は鳥の気持ち
—— A Young Woman's Heart, a Bird's Heart

江戸時代に生まれた歌舞伎舞踊には、鳥の精が主人公になる幻想的でロマンチックな作品がある。西洋のバレエ『白鳥の湖』などにも共通することで、人間は翼のある鳥に仮託して夢を見る存在なのだろう。特に秘めた恋をする若い娘は、その心を鳥に託して羽ばたかせたいもの。『鷺娘』は、苦しい恋をする娘心を鷺の精にかたどった、せつない舞踊で、小曲ながら、極めて人気が高い。日本舞踊の会でも、さかんに上演される。

This is just one of many examples of kabuki buyo that feature a bird spirit as its protagonist. The fantastical idea of a human dancing as a bird is something Western audiences may be familiar with from the famous ballet *Swan Lake*. The expression of a young woman's love expressed through the spirit of a bird is particularly touching. Though *Sagimusume* is a short piece lasting only 20 minutes, the heartbreaking performance has won its immense popularity over the years. It is often played at Japanese buyo events.

2. 絵画のようなラストシーン
—— The Spectacular Finale

古典舞踊のラストは、立役ならば、正面に置かれる「三段」と呼ばれる段に上り、高い位置で大きく極まって幕になることが多い。緋もうせんで覆われた「三段」は黒衣（くろご）がするりと位置に置き、終盤の高揚した気分を損なうことがない。女方の場合には一段低い「二段」に上る決まりで、『鷺娘』も二段に上って美しく終わるのが古来の型。大正以降の、バレエの『瀕死の白鳥』の演出を取り入れた、反り身になって倒れ、幻想的で凄絶な鷺の最期を見せる演出もある。

The final scene of classical buyo pieces often features the lead *tachiyaku* actor climbing onto a three-tiered platform called a *sandan*. This platform is placed on stage by the *kurogo* stagehands in a smooth fashion so as not to break the mood of the performance. Buyo that feature *onnagata* actors feature a two-tiered platform (*nidan*) instead. This is how *Sagimusume* is traditionally performed. From the Taisho Period (1912–1926) onward, some actors incorporated techniques from the ballet piece *The Dying Swan* into performances of *Sagimusume*, strutting about like a bird before expiring in the ghastly, dreamlike final scene.

3. 墨絵、華やぎ、業火 —— A Dance in Three Parts

舞台の重要な道具は「雪」。幕開きの雪景色のなかに、傘を手にした白無垢姿の娘が佇む光景は、静謐な雰囲気で墨絵のような趣だ。それが一転して鮮やかな振袖に身を包んだ町娘の踊りに変わり、舞台には華やぎが充ちる。やがて降りしきる雪のなか、地獄の業火に焼かれるような恋の苦しみに、鳥の本性を現し身もだえする凄烈なラストまで、三様の変化が描かれる。手を隠し、両袖を翼に見立てた振りがまことに優美である。

The most important set piece of *Sagimusume* is snow. The curtains open onto a gorgeous snowy set where a young woman in a *shiromuku* kimono stands with an umbrella in hand. The tranquil scene brings to mind an image from a *sumie* painting. Soon the woman changes into a vibrant *furisode* robe, changing the mood completely. In the end, however, she is revealed to be a bird as she writhes in the terrible agony of her love. These three stages are beautifully performed, and one can't miss the pivotal moment when the actor hides his hands as he spreads wide the sleeves of his robes like a great bird.

4. 絶妙なタイミングで引抜き —— The Perfect Timing of the *Hikinuki*

白無垢姿の娘が、瞬時に鮮やかな振袖姿に変わる。「引抜き」と呼ばれる伝統技法はいつも観客の感嘆を誘う。上に着せた着物の縫い糸を、隠れた黒衣が引き抜いていき、絶妙のタイミングで一気に上の着物を取り去るのだ。黒衣は踊りを熟知して呼吸を合わせて動かなくては勤まらないので、演じる俳優の弟子が担当する。様々な踊りで引抜きを使うが、なかでも短時間に次々と姿を変える『鷺娘』の引抜きは難しいという。

The actor changes from a white shiromuku robe to a vibrant furisode in an instant using a technique called hikinuki. A hidden stagehand (kurogo) deftly removes the stitches that bind the actor's outer robes to his inner ones, allowing him to completely remove the outer robes at just the right moment. For this to succeed, the kurogo must be completely in sync with the actor, so it is common for hikinuki to be performed by the actor's pupil. Various buyo perfomances feature a hikinuki change as well, but the one in Sagimusume is much more difficult.

積恋雪関扉
Tsumoru Koi Yuki no Sekinoto

『積恋雪関扉』
2015年2月　歌舞伎座
関守関兵衛実は大伴黒主（九代目松本幸四郎）

Tsumoru Koi Yuki no Sekinoto
(Kabukiza Theatre, February 2015)
Sekibei (Otomo no Kuronushi) (Matsumoto Koshiro IX)

あらすじ　　　　　　　　　　　Synopsis

雪が積もり桜は満開と、まさしく夢の世界。
逢坂山で桜の精と天下の謀反人が繰り広げる
恋の因縁、うごめく野望

人が行き交う逢坂山の関、広がる雪景色の中で小町桜が満開の花を咲かせている。関守の関兵衛はどこか怪しさを秘めた人物で、ここに隠遁する良峯少将も気付き始めた。やがてしばしの眠りから覚めた関兵衛の前に現れた傾城墨染は小町桜の精、そして関兵衛こそ天下を狙う大伴黒主だった。

—————— A cherry tree in full bloom amid the sheer white snow. Watch as the karmic bonds between a tree spirit and an evil usurper are revealed.

The celebrated Komatsuzakura tree is in full bloom in the snowy months of winter near the Mt. Osaka Barrier along a bustling road. The barrier guard is hiding a terrible secret, and Major General Yoshimine has his suspicions. When the beautiful courtesan Sumizome appears before Sekibei, she reveals that Sekibei is actually the treacherous Otomo no Kuronushi, who is plotting to seize power.

　場面は 逢坂山の関所。常磐津の浄瑠璃のあと、浅葱幕の振り落とし（またはせり上げ）にて、関守である関兵衛の姿が現れる。

　雪景色の中、満開の小町桜。その前で居眠りをする関兵衛。この桜は、仁明天皇の愛樹の古木である。仁明帝の崩御を悲しみ、薄墨色の桜を咲かせたが、小野小町が詠んだ歌の徳によって花の色が元通りになったところから、墨染桜を改め小町桜と呼ばれるようになったという不思議な木である。
　関所には関兵衛と共に良峯少将宗貞が住んでいる。宗貞は先帝の愛樹の桜を、逢坂山に移し植え、みずからは先帝の菩提を弔うため侘び住まいをしているのである。

　宗貞が琴を弾くところへ、三井寺へ参詣に向かう小野小町姫が関所を通りかかる。
　関兵衛と小町の問答の末、小町は関の内に入り、かねて恋仲の宗貞と再会する。
　久しぶりの再会を喜ぶ二人に、関兵衛は二人の恋の馴れ初めを聴きたいと所望。これに応じて宗貞と小町が二人の馴れ初めを語る。

Mt. Osaka Barrier. After a *joruri* narration in the *tokiwazu* style, the barrier keeper Sekibei appears with the falling away of an *asagimaku* curtain (sometimes a *seri* lift is used instead).

The famed Komachizakura is in full bloom amid the fallen snow. The tree had begun to decay, turning a sickly color after Emperor Ninmyo's death, but through the power of Ono no Komachi's poetry, the beautiful hues of its flowers miraculously returned. This mysterious tree was thereafter called Komachizakura.
Gatekeeper Sekibei and Yoshimine Shosho Munesada both live near the barrier. After the beloved Emperor Ninmyo's death, Munesada moved to Mt. Osaka, where the emperor's favorite tree (Komachizakura) was moved so that it be near the imperial tomb.

As Munesada plucks at his *koto*, his lover Ono no Komachi happens by on her way to Miidera Temple. After being questioned by Sekibei, she passes through the gate and is reunited with her beloved Munesada.
As the two rejoice to see one another, Sekibei asks them about how they met each other. Thus Munesada and Komachi begin their story.

As the two are talking, Sekibei accidentally drops two

やがて関兵衛は、懐から二つの品物を取り落とす。一つは勘合の印で、もう一つは割符であった。慌てて勘合の印を取り戻すが、割符は小町姫の手に渡る。怪しむ小町と宗貞、怪しまれた関兵衛の三人の手踊となる。

関兵衛は「仲人は宵の口」と、急ぎこの場を立ち去る。

折からここへ血潮で文字が書かれた片袖を足に付けた白鷹が飛来する。宗貞は書かれた「二子乗舟(じしじょうしゅう)」という言葉から、弟・五位之助安貞が兄の身替りに命を落としたことを悟る。嘆き悲しむ宗貞が片袖を取り落とすと、庭先の石の下から鶏の鳴き声が聞こえる。不審に思い石の下を掘り起こすと、大伴家の重宝・八声(やこえ)の名鏡が埋まっていた。血潮の汚れで声がしたのである。

また、関兵衛が落とした割符は、小町が小野篁(おののたかむら)から預かった割符と合致し、鏡山という文字になった。宗貞は小町姫に、これらの経緯と、さらに合図をしたら関所に討手を向かわせるよう小野篁に伝えるべく小町を立ち去らせる。

宗貞は片袖を琴の中へ隠し、さらにほろ酔い加減で現れた関兵衛の懐を探ろうとするが拒まれ、奥に入る。

関兵衛がさらに大盃を重ねていると、酒に星影が映る。その星の配置は、今宵 三百年の樹齢を保つ桜の古木を護摩木として祈念すれば大願成就するということを告げている。関兵衛は小町桜を切ろうと斧を研ぎ、試しに琴を切り、中に入っていた片袖を手にする。すると懐に入れておいた勘合の印が桜に飛び去ってしまう。

やがてその桜に傾城の姿が浮かび上がる。桜から現れた傾城は墨染と名乗り、関兵衛に会いに来たと明かす。

墨染は関兵衛の望みにまかせ、間夫と傾城の話などの廓の様子を語って聞かせる。

やがて、墨染は関兵衛の取り落とした片袖を見て涙に暮れる。不審に思う関兵衛に、墨染は正体を明かすように迫る。実は関兵衛は天下を望む大伴黒主であった。傾城墨染も実は小町桜の精で、安貞と夫婦となっていたのであった。

互いに本性を現した小町桜の精と黒主は、激しく立ち回るのであった。

suspicious items: an official seal and a tally. Though he quickly retrieves the seal, Komachi picks up the tally. The three begin a *teodori* dance, Munesada and Komachi eying Sekibei suspiciously.

Sekibei eventually hurries away with the words, "a go-between works until nightfall."

Just then, a hawk arrives with a bloody shirtsleeve. The words "two children in a boat" is written on this sleeve in blood, revealing to Munesada that his brother Goinosuke Yasusada has died. As Munesada drops the bloody sleeve in sorrow, a rooster begins to cry from a nearby rock. Suspicious, Munesada digs the rock up and finds beneath it a mirror known to be a family treasure of the Otomo House.

Meanwhile, Komachi checks the tally she picked up with one she received from Ono no Takamura, finding them to be a set. Munesada then tells Komachi to go and tell Ono no Takamura that they must have a unit come to the barrier.

Munesada hides the bloody sleeve in his *koto* and attempts to reach into Sekibei's robes when he stumbles drunkenly by. Sekibei, however, stops him and he is forced to move on.

Sekibei continues to drink and, looking at the starry reflection of the night sky in his glass, he declares that using wood from a 300-year-old cherry tree as offerings is sure to lead to his success. He sharpens an ax to cut down Komachizakura and proceeds to test its cutting edge by cutting Munesada's *koto*. When he does so, the sleeve placed inside is revealed, and suddenly the seal Sekibei had in the breast of his robes flies out into the cherry tree.

Soon after, a beautiful woman emerges from the tree, calling herself Sumizome and claiming to have come to see Sekibei.

Sekibei asks her to teach him about the pleasure quarters, which she seems happy to do.

Finally, Sumizome sees Yasusada's bloody sleeve, accidentally dropped by Sekibei. Tears come to her eyes and she pressures Sekibei to reveal his true identity. It is thus revealed that he is, in fact, the treacherous Otomo no Kuronushi who plans to take over the country. Sumizome is likewise revealed to be the spirit of Komatsuzakura, who had been Yasusada's wife.

Having both revealed their true identities, Kuronushi and the spirit of Komachizakura engage in an intense fight.

『積恋雪関扉』
2008年2月　歌舞伎座
(左から) 傾城墨染実は小町桜の精 (九代目中村福助)、
関守関兵衛実は大伴黒主 (二代目中村吉右衛門)

Tsumoru Koi Yuki no Sekinoto
(Kabukiza Theatre, February 2008)
(from left) Sumizome / Komachizakura tree spirit
(Nakamura Fukusuke IX), Sekibei / Otomo no
Kuronushi (Nakamura Kichiemon II)

作品の概要

演目名

積恋雪関扉

作者

作詞＝宝田寿来
作曲＝初世鳥羽屋里長、二世岸沢式佐

概要

　常磐津舞踊劇の大曲。初演は、顔見世狂言『重重人重小町桜（じゅうにひとえこまちざくら）』の大切（おおぎり）浄瑠璃。初世中村仲蔵が活躍した天明期のこってりした味わいを伝える名作で、すべて上演すると一時間半となる。舞台は桜満開の逢坂の関。時ならぬ大雪で一面銀世界である。その桜の下で繰り広げられる不思議なファンタジーは、日常を忘れさせるのに十分な色濃さ。複雑な物語は甘美で夢幻的である。登場人物は四人で、うち一人は桜の精。関の庵に住む良峯少将のもとへ恋人・小町姫が雪中に振袖姿で登ってくる。良峯と小町、そして怪しい関守関兵衛と、三人の腹の探り合いが前半の見どころ。後半は桜の精が撞木町の傾城姿で出現して関兵衛に絡む。初世仲蔵の芸風を伝える関兵衛は、実は天下を狙う大伴黒主というスケールのある役どころ。朴訥にも見えた関兵衛がぶっ返りで黒々とした貴族の装束に変わると、桜の精と争いとなる。大まさかりを手にした黒主と、髪を振り乱した桜の精とが対峙する見得は最大の見どころ。

初演

天明4（1784）年11月江戸・桐座で、関兵衛が初世中村仲蔵、小町・墨染が三世瀬川菊之丞、宗貞が二世市川門之助。作詞は宝田寿来、作曲は初世鳥羽屋里長、二世岸沢式佐。振付は二世西川扇藏。

Overview

Title

Tsumoru Koi Yuki no Sekinoto

Writer

Lyrics: Takarada Jurai
Music: Tobaya Richo I, Kishizawa Shikisa II

Overview

An epic piece of *Tokiwazu buyo* first performed as a *joruri* at the *kaomise-kyogen* play. At the time it was titled *Junihitoe Komachizakura*. The play lasted an hour and thirty minutes when performed in its entirety, and it perfectly displayed the rich style of Nakamura Nakazo I who performed during the Tenmei Era (1781–1789). The stage is set at the Osaka barrier, where the cherries are in full bloom. An unusually large snow has fallen, making for a dazzling silver spectacle. A fantastical story unfolds involving only four characters, one of whom is actually the spirit of a cherry tree. Komachi climbs up the frigid mountain to visit her lover Yoshimine in the first half of the play. The play between the barrier keeper, Komachi, and Yoshimine who slowly come to know more about each other, is the biggest highlight of this portion of the show. In the latter half, the cherry tree spirit appears in the form of a beautiful woman and, in accordance with the style of Nakazo I, we find out that Sekibei is actually the evil usurper Otomo no Kuronushi. The humble-looking Sekibei suddenly changes, using a technique called *bukkaeri*, into dignified black robes that reveal his true identity. The cherry spirit and Kuronushi face off. The final *mie* poses here are the ultimate highlight of the play.

Premiere

November 1784, Kiriza Theatre. Feat. Nakamura Nakazo I as Sekibei, Segawa Kikunojo III as Komachi / Sumizome, and Ichikawa Mon'nosuke II as Munesada. Lyrics by Takarada Jurai. Music by Tobaya Richo I and Kishizawa Shikisa II. Choreography by Nishikawa Senzo II.

登場人物　Characters

関守関兵衛 実は 大伴黒主
せきもりせきべえ じつは おおとものくろぬし

都の東、逢坂山の関所の関守だが実は謀反を企てる大伴黒主、雪深い山中で身をやつしている。近隣に住まう良峯宗貞にとっては敵側にあたるが、偶然訪ねてきた宗貞の恋人・小町姫を快く迎え入れて仲を取り持つ。しかし証拠の品を二人に見破られ、次第に嫌疑をかけられる。さらに眠りについているうち墨染と名乗る美しい遊女が現れ、ついに正体を明かされる。本来の大伴黒主は平安時代の名高い歌人。

Sekimori Sekibei / Otomo no Kuronushi

Otomo no Kuronushi, disguised as the keeper of the barrier at Mt. Osaka, is hiding deep in the snowy mountains as he plots to seize control of the country. His political enemy Yoshimine Munesada lives nearby, and when his lover Princess Komachi happens to visit, Kuronushi welcomes her happily. Later, however, he drops an item that betrays his true identity, making both Komachi and Munesada suspicious. A mysterious but beautiful courtesan named Sumizome appears while Kuronushi sleeps and uncovers his true identity. Historically, Otomo no Kuronushi was a famous poet of the Heian Period of Japan.

小野小町姫
おののこまちひめ

これも歌人として名高い小野小町に由来する登場人物。先帝の菩提を弔うため遁世している宗貞を慕い旅姿でやってくるが、宗貞の奏でる琴の音に誘われて巡り合うことができる。関兵衛が落とした割符を素早く取り上げ、宗貞が見届けた勘合の印と考え合わせてどうやらその正体を察する。さらに大伴家の重宝・八声の鏡を見つけ、関兵衛が政敵の大伴黒主と知るや、急ぎ都へと向かう。

Princess Ono no Komachi

Komachi, like many of the other characters, is also a famous poet of the Heian Period. Drawn by the sound of his *koto*, she visits her lover Munesada, who is mourning the late emperor in the mountains. There, she finds a document dropped by Sekibei and shows it to Munesada, who realizes that Sekibei is not who he claims to be. After finding a treasured mirror of the Otomo family, Komachi realizes that Sekibei is the treacherous Otomo no Kuronushi and rushes back to the capital.

良峯少将宗貞
よしみねのしょうしょうむねさだ

仁明天皇の信の厚かった宗貞は、天皇の菩提を弔うため逢坂の関に隠遁している。自らの奏でる琴の音を頼りに愛する小町姫がやって来ると、互いに再会を喜び合うが、関兵衛が落とした二つの品を見てその素性を怪しむ。そこへ飛んで来た鷹が血染めの片袖を運んでいたので弟の死を察するが、その敵こそ関兵衛すなわち大伴黒主と見極め、小町姫を都へと走らせる。宗貞は後に六歌仙の一人・僧正遍照となる。

Yoshimine no Shosho Munesada

Munesada has retired to Mt. Osaka in mourning for the late Emperor Ninmyo. His lover Princess Komachi comes to him one day, drawn by the sound of his *koto* playing, and the two rejoice at their reunion. The two become suspicious of the barrier keeper Sekibei when he drops an item that betrays his true identity. Adding to their troubles, a hawk flies overhead, dropping a bloody shirt sleeve informing them of the death of Munesada's younger brother. Realizing that Sekibei may, in fact, be the one responsible for his brother's death, he sends Komachi back to the capital. Munesada eventually becomes one of the famous Six Sages of Song (*rokkasen*), Sojo Henjo.

傾城墨染 実は 小町桜の精
けいせいすみぞめ じつは こまちざくらのせい

雪の降りしきる逢坂の関で満開に咲く桜は樹齢三百年の名木で、先帝崩御により薄墨色に沈んでいたところ小町の歌の色を増し小町桜と名付けられている。その桜の中から現れた女性は撞木町の遊女で墨染と名乗った。関兵衛と何やら色っぽい廓話などをするうち、安貞の形見の片袖を見つけ、恋しい安貞の敵と関兵衛に激しく迫る。その墨染の正体は生身の人間ではなく小町桜の精だった。

Keisei Sumizome / Spirit of Komachizakura

The great cherry tree is in full bloom amid the snow near Osaka Barrier. This 300-year-old tree had lost its color after the late emperor's passing but was revived through the masterful poetry of Princess Komachi. Therefore the tree was named Komachizakura. A woman claiming to be a courtesan named Sumizome emerges from this tree and begins to tell the barrier keeper Sekibei about the pleasure quarters. As they are talking, she discovers the robe-sleeve of her dear Yasusada and accuses Sekibei of his murder. In the end, it is revealed that Sumizome is, in fact, the spirit of the Komachizakura tree.

みどころ
Highlights

1. 逢坂関と墨染桜
—— Osaka Barrier and the Sumizomezakura Tree

「逢坂の関」は山城（京都府）と近江（滋賀県）の境にあったという。百人一首にも「知るも知らぬも逢坂の関」「世に逢坂の関はゆるさじ」の2首があり、文芸史上にロマンチックな印象を残す関だ。悲しみで薄墨色に咲いたという伝説の桜は、現在岐阜県にある樹齢1500年の淡墨桜（うすずみざくら）とは別物。謡曲『墨染桜』にも登場する、深草の仁明天皇陵に薄墨色に咲いたという桜が題材だ。本作は、桜を逢坂山に移し、雪景色に置くという贅沢な設定である。

Osaka Barrier is said to have been located along the border between present-day Kyoto and Shiga Prefecture. Mentioned in two of the famous *Hyakunin Isshu* poems, it is a rather romantic location in the world of Japanese letters. The Usuzumizakura featured in this play is not the same one as the 1500-year-old tree in Gifu Prefecture. The tree was said to have produced sickly gray petals after the death of Emperor Ninmyo. This spectacular buyo play moves the tree to Mt. Osaka where it blooms among the fallen snow.

天明文化はこってり系 — The Extravagant Culture of Tenmei

明和から天明頃(18世紀後半)は、いわゆる田沼時代。江戸の庶民文化が花開き、洒落や機知が好まれて黄表紙や狂歌、川柳などが流行し、『助六』の「通人」のような人物がもてはやされたらしい。歌舞伎でも華やかな芝居が流行り、常磐津などを使った大仕掛けな舞踊劇も生まれていった。一代で上り詰めた初世中村仲蔵が活躍した時代で、天明4(1784)年初演の『積恋雪関扉』は代表作。こってりした「天明ぶり」があふれている。

The Tenmei Era (late 1700's), also called the Tanuma Era, saw a blossoming of popular culture among the lower classes of society. It was an era of style and wit that saw a proliferation of dime novels, comic songs, and characters such as the worldly Sukeroku. During this time the world of kabuki, too, saw the birth of buyo dramas in the *tokiwazu* style featuring extravagant stage mechanisms. The first performance of this play in 1784 featured Nakamura Nakazo I, the premier actor of his time. It is a representative piece from the Tenmei Era that showcases the extravagant culture of the time.

桜の精が男をくどく — A Tree Spirit Wooing a Man

歌舞伎には鳥や獣の精の他、花や木の精も登場する。森林に恵まれた日本らしい趣向だろう。桜の精が傾城(遊女)に化け桜の幹から出現する。居眠り中の関守は知らず、観客には最初から正体が判っている展開で、傾城が初対面の関守に不思議な恋を仕掛ける。以下二人の会話はこんな様子。「何をしに来た」「逢いに」「誰に」「あなたに」「何俺?」「恋人になって下さい」。花の精と悪人の奇々怪々の恋模様は童話のよう。

Kabuki often features spirits not only of birds and beasts, but also those of flowers and trees. One might say this is a very Japanese idea, as our country has an abundance of forests. In this play the tree spirit emerges from a tree while the barrier keeper is asleep. Thus, the audience may revel in knowing the secret of her identity as she proceeds to seduce him. Their flirtatious conversation is like something out of a fairytale.

本性が顕れるぶっ返り — Bukkaeri – A Revelation of a Character's True Nature

「ぶっ返り」とは、上着の肩の縫い糸を瞬時に抜き去って、裏側に隠れていた異質な衣裳が現れる衣裳の仕掛。秘めた本性を顕わにする場面で効果を発揮する。朴訥な関兵衛がぶっ返ると、黒々とした貴族の衣裳に変じ、髪も逆立った大悪人の恐ろしい形相になる。傾城墨染もぶっ返り、髷をほどいて桜の精の本性を現し、桜の枝を手に宙を飛ぶような派手な争いになる。ぶっ返りで、舞台のテンションが一瞬でアップするのだ。

"*Bukkaeri*" is a technique by which shoulder stitches of an actor's jacket are removed in an instant to reveal a vastly different pattern hidden in the inner lining of his robes. This technique is often used to reveal a duplicitous or disguised character's true nature. In this play, the simple barrier keeper Sekibei shows his clothes to be the elegant black robes of an aristocrat as he is revealed to be the fearsome villain Kuronushi. The beautiful courtesan Sumizome also utilizes the *bukkaeri* technique to reveal her true identity as the tree spirit. Letting her hair loose and grasping a cherry branch, she engages Kuronushi in a rather nimble fight. *Bukkaeri* is thus used to raise the tension on stage in an instant.

保名
Yasuna

保名
2005年3月 歌舞伎座
安倍保名(十五代目片岡仁左衛門)

Yasuna
(Kabukiza Theatre, March 2005)
Abe no Yasuna (Kataoka Nizaemon XV)

あらすじ　　　　　　　　　　Synopsis

今は亡き恋人・榊の前を追い求める安倍保名。
心は宙を飛び、菜の花咲き乱れる春の野に彷徨う、
その姿は哀しい

「恋や恋、われ中空になすな恋」、榊の前は今いずこに……　髪も乱れ心も乱れた安倍保名は、
恋人の榊の前が自害するのを目の当たりにして以来、気がふれてこのようにひたすら野を彷徨い歩
くばかり。頭には紫の病鉢巻、身にまとうのは形見の小袖、しかしその姿はどこまでも気高く美しい。

—————— The pitiful Abe no Yasuna yearns and yearns for his lost love Sakaki. Wandering aimlessly through a field of rape blossoms, his grief-stricken heart flies from the stage, entrancing audiences.

"Love, oh Love, stop boring this hole in my heart!" Ever since witnessing Sakaki kill herself before his very eyes, the despondent Yasuna wanders this lonely field, his hair disheveled and his heart in shambles, wondering where his love has gone. He wears a purple *yamai-hachimaki* (headband of sickness) and a *kosode* kimono he keeps as a memento of his lost love. He strikes a deeply melancholy yet elegant, sophisticated figure befitting his noble pedigree.

清元につれ、舞台は徐々に明るくなる。背景は一面の菜
畑である。

　　恋や恋
　　われ中空になすな恋

やがて安倍保名が登場する。
　保名は陰陽師であるが、勢力争いに巻き込まれ婚約者で
ある榊の前を眼前で死なせ、正気を失い、恋人の形見の小
袖を肩に野辺を彷徨っている。

　　姿もいつか乱髪
　　誰が取上て言うことも
　　菜種の畑に狂う蝶
　　翼交わして美し
　　野辺の陽炎春草を
　　素袍袴に踏みしだき
　　狂い狂いて来りける

幻であろうか、恋人があちらにいるという声を聴くが、
行ってみるとやはりいない。

As the *kiyomoto* music progresses, the stage slowly brightens revealing a vast meadow.

**Love, oh Love,
stop boring this hole in my heart!**

Abe no Yasuna finally makes his entrance.
Yasuna is a diviner of high social standing, but he lost his mind when, due to a political power struggle, he witnessed his beloved fiancée Sakaki's death. Now he wanders this field with Sakaki's *kosode* robe, his only memento, draped over his shoulders.

(See Japanese lyrics on left)

A mysterious voice is heard telling Yasuna that his love is close by, but when he goes to look he finds no one.

やがて曲は、「小袖物狂い」の世界を離れ、江戸時代の小西来山という俳人のことを語る。この人は生涯独身で、土で作った人形を愛したという。

あれを今宮の
来山翁が筆ずさみ
土人形のいろ娘
高嶺の花や折ることも
泣いた顔せず　腹立てず
悋気もせねば　おとなしう
あらうつつ無の妹背中

続いて、吉原の様子を歌った浄瑠璃に合わせての振りとなる。

主は忘れてござんしょう
しかも去年の桜時
植えて初日の初会から
逢うての後は一日も
便り聞かねば気も済まず
うつらうつらと夜を明し

さらに曲は鼓に合わせたものになり、小袖を恋人と思っての振りとなる。

夜さの泊りは何処が泊りぞ
草を敷寝のひじ枕
ひとり明すぞ悲しけれ

やがて曲は再び、「小袖物狂い」の世界に戻る。

葉越しの葉越しの幕の内
昔恋しき面影や移香や
その面影に露ばかり
似た人あらば教えてと

保名は恋人の幻を追い、形見の小袖を抱きしめて泣き沈むうちに幕となる。

The lyrics change here, leaving the sad world of Yasuna and Sakaki and instead telling a tale of the haiku poet Konishi Raizan who is said to have lived alone until he died, with only an earthen figurine to love.

(See Japanese lyrics on left)

The lyrics next sing of the Yoshiwara pleasure quarters in a *joruri* style.

(See Japanese lyrics on left)

The tune changes again to a more rhythmic melody in time with the drums, and Yasuna pretends that his *kosode* robes are his lost love.

(See Japanese lyrics on left)

Finally the tune returns to the world of *"Kosode Monogurui."*

(See Japanese lyrics on left)

Yasuna chases after the specter of his lover, clutching Sakaki's *kosode* robe and crying pitifully as the curtains close.

『保名』
2005年3月　歌舞伎座
安倍保名（十五代目片岡仁左衛門）

Yasuna
(Kabukiza Theatre, March 2005)
Abe no Yasuna (Kataoka Nizaemon XV)

Yasuna

保名

作品の概要

演目名

保名

作者

作詞＝篠田金治
作曲＝清沢万吉（初世清元斎兵衛）

概要

　清元地の舞踊。文化15※（1818）年3月、江戸・都座で三世尾上菊五郎が踊った四季の七変化舞踊『深山桜及兼樹振（みやまのはなとどかぬえだぶり）』の春の部の一節。作詞篠田金治、作曲清沢万吉（初世清元斎兵衛）、初演の振付は藤間新三郎・藤間大助（二世勘十郎）。

　義太夫節『芦屋道満大内鑑』の二段目「小袖物狂」の場を清元による舞踊にしたもので、清元の名曲として伝わったが、振は幕末に絶えていた。

　明治に入り九世市川團十郎が復活。さらに大正11（1922）年、六世菊五郎が田中良による幻想的な舞台装置の新演出で上演し、人気演目となった。恋人を失ったがゆえ正気を失った貴公子の姿を美しく描き出している。

　掲載のあらすじは菊五郎の演出によるものであるが、別に古風な演出として、後半に奴が登場し立ち回り風になることもある。

　歌舞伎舞踊には「狂乱物」と呼ばれる一群があり、これもその一つ。歌舞伎は先行芸能である能の狂乱物を様々に取り入れ、歌舞伎舞踊の一大系統をなしている。女性・男性それぞれの狂乱物がある。

※文化15年は4月に文政に改元

初演

文化15（1818）年3月江戸・都座で、三世尾上菊五郎による。作詞は篠田金治、作曲は清沢万吉（初世清元斎兵衛）、振付は藤間新三郎、藤間大助（二世勘十郎）。

Overview

Title

Yasuna

Writer

Lyrics: Shinoda Kinji
Music: Kiyozawa Mankichi
　　　（Kiyomoto Saibei I）

Overview

　Yasuna is a buyo piece in the *kiyomoto* style. It is the spring section of the play *Miyama no Hana Todokanu Edaburi* as performed by Onoe Kikugoro III in March 1818 at the Edo Miyakoza Theatre. The lyrics were written by Shinoda Kinji, music by Kiyozawa Mankichi (Kiyomoto Saibei I), and the original choreography by Fujima Shinzaburo and Fujima Daisuke (Kanjuro II). *Yasuna* is essentially the *"Kosode Monogurui"* scene from the puppet play *Ashiya Doman Ouchikagami* set to *kiyomoto* music. It has come to be known as a masterpiece of *kiyomoto* but had actually gone out of fashion by the end of the Edo Period. It was later revived by Ichikawa Danjuro IX in Meiji (1868–1912), and became a hit after Kikugoro VI's performance on a magnificent new set designed by Tanaka Ryo in 1922. The dance beautifully depicts the story of a young noble driven mad after the death of his lover.

Premiere

March 1818, Edo Miyakoza Theatre. Feat. Onoe Kikugoro III. Lyrics by Shinoda Kinji. Music by Kiyozawa Mankichi (Kiyomoto Saibei I). Choreography by Fujima Shinzaburo, Fujima Daisuke (Kanjuro II).

登場人物　Characters

安倍保名
あべのやすな

安倍保名は平安時代の実在の陰陽師として
知られる安倍清明の父とされるが、あくまで
も芝居の上の登場人物である。恋人の榊
の前が目の前で自害し、その悲しみから心
乱れ物狂いとなって菜の花の咲き乱れる春
の野辺を彷徨い歩いてゆく。頭に巻かれた
紫縮緬の鉢巻きは病鉢巻きと呼ばれるごとく
病んでいる姿のお約束、片肌を脱ぎ恋人の
形見の小袖をまとうが、その美しさがまた哀
れを誘う。

Abe no Yasuna

Abe no Yasuna is supposedly the father of the
diviner Abe no Seimei who lived during the
Heian Period (794–1185), but Yasuna himself
is a fictional character. Having lost his mind
after witnessing his lover Sakaki commit suicide
before his very eyes, Yasuna now wanders
aimlessly in a field of rape blossoms. He wears a
purple crepe headband called a *yamai-hachimaki*
(headband of sickness), but his illness is also
manifest in his sickly appearance. Wearing his
lover's memento, a *kosode* robe, his figure is at
once beautiful and deeply pitiful.

みどころ
Highlights

1. 保名の衣裳 —— Yasuna's Costume

鴇（とき）色縮緬の、胴部分に露芝（つゆしば）柄を刺繍した着物の下に、浅葱縮緬秋草刺繍の胴着。鴇色は国鳥トキの淡い紅色を表す。紫の長袴は葛の葉柄刺繍の精好織。手には形見の朱色の小袖を抱えている。

Yasuna wears a pink crepe robe embroidered with a dewy grass pattern along the torso. The pink color, called *tokiiro* in Japanese, is that of the national bird, the crested ibis. Yasuna's undershirt is a light blue fabric with a pattern depicting autumn flora, and his *nagabakama* trousers are embroidered with an arrowroot stalk pattern. He also carries with him the *kosode* robes left to him by his now dead lover.

2. 大切な人を失ったやるせなさ —— The Despair of Loss

原作の人形浄瑠璃『芦屋道満大内鑑』には、保名が遭遇する長い物語があるが、舞踊『保名』は保名の精神のうつろいだけに焦点を当てている。若く美しい青年が絶望して正気を失い、恋人の面影を求めてただただ彷徨う哀切な姿、やるせなさが美しくクローズアップされており、それを味わうことがこの演目の見どころである。名優六世尾上菊五郎が大正時代に、近代人の嗜好を踏まえて装置や照明を印象深いものに変えている。

The original puppet theatre play, *Ashiya Doman Ouchikagami*, is a long piece depicting various encounters with Yasuna, but the kabuki buyo piece *Yasuna* focuses on his psychological state, depicting an utterly destroyed man who has lost his love. This intimate depiction of a desperate man's psyche is yet another highlight of the play. The great actor Onoe Kikugoro VI adapted the play to appeal to modern audiences in the Taisho period of Japan (1912–26).

40

3. 安倍晴明の父
—— Abe no Seimei's Father

安倍保名は阿倍野の豪族だったともいわれ、陰陽師・安倍晴明の父とも伝えられる。原作では、保名も陰陽師で、師の加藤保憲から「保」の一字を受継ぎ、保憲の後継を芦屋道満と争ったことになっている。大阪市阿倍野区には、昔「保名」と呼ばれていた地域があった。地名としては残っていないが、旧熊野街道沿いにある「阿倍野保名郵便局」の局名にその名残りを留めており、近くには晴明生誕地とされる安倍晴明神社がある。

It is said that Yasuna was from a powerful family from Abeno and that he is the father of the diviner Abe no Seimei. In this story, he is a diviner (like his son) who competed with Ashiya Doman over who would succeed their teacher Kato Yasunori (from whom Yasuna received his name). There was once a region called Yasuna in Abeno district, Osaka, and though it no longer exists, two locations still bear reference to it: Abeno Yasuna Post Office and Abe Seimei Temple, where Abe no Seimei is said to have been born.

4. 一面の菜の花
—— Rape Blossoms Far as the Eye Can See

舞台には一面に菜の花が咲き乱れている。これが『保名』第一の見どころである。しかし、悲しみにくれる保名にっては空虚な景色だ。陰一つない野原にはただ春の喜びがあふれるようだが、日本人はそこに、「春愁」という言葉が表す繊細な感情を見出す。美しい景色をよそに、うつむいてため息をつこうとする。極めて美しい清元の調べには、その春の愁いの響きがある。『保名』は「繊細な感情」を絵画にしたような舞踊だろう。

The biggest highlight of *Yasuna* is the spectacular meadow of rape blossoms which cover the entire stage. This gorgeous scene is ironically lost on the protagonist, however, who is utterly distraught at the death of his lover. This scenery may bring to mind the joy of spring to some, but to the Japanese, it has a distinct melancholy mood called "*shunshu*" in Japanese. Many in the audience are bound to divert their eyes from the scene with a languid sigh as the subtle *kiyomoto* music perfectly accentuates this melancholy mood. Yasuna thus perfectly depicts the delicate mood of springtime sorrow.

藤娘
Fujimusume

『藤娘』
2010年4月 歌舞伎座
藤の精(四代目坂田藤十郎)

Fujimusume
(Kabukiza Theatre, April 2010)
Wisteria Spirit (Sakata Tojuro IV)

あらすじ   Synopsis

絵から抜け出た可憐な娘、手には塗笠と藤の枝。
咲き誇る藤の花に囲まれ、
踊りで描く淡い恋心と近江八景の美しさ

松の大木に絡まるのは今を盛りと咲き誇る藤の花。そこに現れたのは藤の枝を担いだ娘だが、どうやらこれは大津絵に描かれた藤の精なのだろう。艶やかに踊るうち酒に酔った仕草を見せ、艶めかしさも感じさせる。そして琵琶湖の畔に夕暮れが迫る中、その娘もどこかへと姿を消してゆく。

A beautiful young woman emerges from a painting, bearing a painted *kasa* hat and wisteria branch, and begins a glorious dance depicting the *Eight Views of Omi* among stunning wisteria blossoms.

A great pine tree stands on stage, wisteria blossoms creeping and entwining about it. A young woman appears there, carrying a wisteris branch. She is the spitting image of the wisteria spirit of a great *Otsu-e* painting. She dances with a polished elegance at first, then begins to move as though tipsy in a dance that is sure to enchant audiences. As the sun sets on Lake Biwako, she finally disappears, marking the end of the performance.

暗闇の中、長唄の声が響き、鼓の音と共に舞台が一瞬にして明るくなる。

舞台中央には松の大木。その松には藤がまつわり、今や盛りと花が咲き誇っている。
その前に入るのは、黒い塗笠を被り、藤の花を肩にかけた娘。藤の花の精である。

人目せき笠
塗笠しゃんと
振りかたげたる一枝は
紫深き水道の水に
染めてうれしきゆかりの色の
いとしと書いて藤の花
エエしょんがいな
裾もほらほらしとけなく

藤の精は、近江八景にちなむ地名を読み込みながら、男の浮気心を恨む心を歌った歌詞に合わせ、踊る。

男心の憎いのは

A *nagauta* singer's voice rings through the darkness, and the lights come on with the sound of a drum.

Center stage stands a great pine tree, with creeping wisteria blossoms entwined all about it.
A young woman with a black painted *kasa* hat and a branch of wisteria blossoms appears before the tree. She is the spirit of the wisteria.

(See Japanese lyrics on left)

The enchanting spirit dances to lyrics that depict the fickle heart of man and a woman's jealousy, referring to the famous *Eight Views of Omi*.

(See Japanese lyrics on left)

藤娘

ほかの女子に神かけて
あわずと三井のかねごとも
堅い誓いの石山に
身は空蝉の　から崎や
まつ夜をよそに　比良の雪
とけて逢瀬の　あた妬ましい
ようもの瀬田にわしゃ乗せられて
文も堅田のかた便り
心矢橋の　かこちごと

　衣裳を変えた藤の精は、鄙びた曲調の藤音頭と呼ばれる
曲に合わせて踊る。
　藤は酒を与えると美しく咲くというが、藤の精も酒を飲
んでほろ酔いになる。

あらすじ

　藤の花房　色よく長く
可愛いがろとて酒買うて　呑ませたら
うちの男松に　からんでしめて　てもさても
十返りという名のにくや
かえるというは忌み言葉

花物言わぬためしでも
知らぬそぶりは奈良の京
杉に纏るも好き好き
松にまとうも好き好き
好いて好かれて離れぬ仲は
常磐木に立ちも帰らで
君とわれとか　おおうれし

　興に乗った藤の精は、明るい曲調の「手踊り」を踊る。

　松を植よなら　有馬の里へ　植えさんせ
いつまでも　変わらぬ契り　かいどり褄で
よれつもつれつ　まだ寝がたらぬ
宵寝枕のまだ寝が足らぬ
藤にまかれて　寝とござる
アア何としょうかとしょうかいな

　やがて夕暮れの鐘がなり、藤の精はいずくともなく帰っ
て行くのであった。

Changing costumes, the girl begins dancing to a rustic tune called *"fuji-ondo."*
It is said that the wisteria's blossoms are more beautiful if watered with sake, so the wisteria spirit drinks some and becomes intoxicated.

(See Japanese lyrics on left)

The wisteria girl changes her dance once again as a more colorful tune begins. She performs a *teodori* dance.

(See Japanese lyrics on left)

Finally, the bells chimes as night falls, and the spirit of the wisteria must return home.

『藤娘』　2010年4月　歌舞伎座
藤の精（四代目坂田藤十郎）

Fujimusume
(Kabukiza Theatre, April 2010)
Wisteria Spirit (Sakata Tojuro IV)

作品の概要

演目名

藤娘

作者

作詞 = 勝井源八
作曲 = 四世杵屋六三郎

概要

　人気の高い長唄舞踊。五変化舞踊『歌へす歌へす余波大津絵（かえすがえすなごりのおおつえ）』の一つとして、絵から抜け出た娘が藤枝を手に踊る趣向で初演された。関三十郎が大坂へ上るお名残狂言であった。くどきの歌詞には、男心を恨む文句に、琵琶湖南岸の景勝地・近江八景の地名をちりばめるという歌舞伎舞踊らしい遊びがある。八景とは「粟津の晴嵐」「三井の晩鐘」「石山の秋月」「唐崎の夜雨」「比良の暮雪」「瀬田の夕照」「堅田の落雁」「矢橋の帰帆」であり、「粟津」に「会わず」を掛けるなど言葉遊びを込めている。昭和12（1937）年に六世尾上菊五郎が新演出を行なった。幕開きの照明による演出や大道具などの工夫はこの時のもので、岡鬼太郎作詞による藤音頭を挿入して上演された。掲載のあらすじはこのやり方のものである。

初演

文政9（1826）年9月江戸・中村座で、二世関三十郎による。藤間大助（二世勘十郎）、四世西川扇藏振付。作詞は勝井源八、作曲は四世杵屋六三郎。藤音頭は岡鬼太郎作詞。

Overview

Title

Fujimusume

Writer

Lyrics: Katsui Genpachi
Music: Kineya Rokusaburo IV

Overview

An incredibly popular *nagauta* buyo that was first performed as part of the *Gohenge-buyo* piece *Kaesu Gaesu Nagori no Otsu-e*. It depicted the dance of a young woman who came to life from an *Otsu-e* painting and the performance was Seki Sanjuro's *nagori-kyogen* commemorating his move to Osaka. The *kudoki* ("wooing") is a playful section with lyrics depicting jealousy of a fickle man and many of the famous locations of the *Eight Views of Omi*. One of the *Eight Views* is at a location called Awazu, which allows for a play on a word meaning "not able to meet." Understanding such puns makes the lyrics to this buyo far more entertaining. *Fujimusume* has been performed with the *"fuji-ondo"* section following the *kudoki* since the 1937 revival featuring Onoe Kikugoro VI.

Premiere

September 1826, Nakamuraza Theatre. Feat. Seki Sanjuro II. Choreography by Fujima Daisuke (Kanjuro II) and Nishikawa Senzo IV. Lyrics by Katsui Genpachi. Music by Kineya Rokusaburo IV. Fuji-ondo lyrics by Oka Onitaro.

登場人物　　　　　　　　　Characters

藤の精
ふじのせい

藤の花の精が若い娘の姿になって現れ、淡い恋心や恥じらい、そして男心への嫉妬などを衣裳を替えながら可憐に踊る趣向。藤の花を大胆にあしらった衣裳を着付け、黒の塗笠に藤の枝を担いだ姿は大津絵から抜け出した藤娘の出で立ち。背景の大きな老松とそこに絡む見事な藤の花が娘の華奢な立ち姿をさらに演出する。後半の「藤音頭」では酒を呑んでほろ酔いとなり、また一味違った愛らしさを見せる。

Wisteria Spirit

The spirit of wisteria blossoms takes the form of a young woman in this buyo dance depicting the naivety and coyness of young love as well as the feelings of jealousy and resentment toward the fickleness of men. Wearing a costume beautifully decorated with wisteria blossoms and bearing a black conical *kasa* hat and wisteria branch, the dancer is meant to be the "wisteria maiden" (or *fujimusume*) come to life from an *Otsu-e* painting. The great pine tree and gorgeous wisteria blossoms of the backdrop further accentuate the dancer's opulent performance. In the latter half, a section called "fuji-ondo," the dancer performs a somewhat drunken dance that contrasts the first half of the show.

みどころ
Highlights

1. 藤の精の衣裳
— The Wisteria Spirit's Costume

朱色と梅幸茶（ばいこうちゃ）色の片身替りの振袖に、しだれ藤の柄を刺繍。片身替りは、袖と身頃の左右を違える趣向。帯やしごきにも藤柄を散らす。梅幸茶とは、初世尾上菊五郎の俳名に因む、緑がかった粋な茶色。

The wisteria spirit wears a two-tone *furisode* robe called a *katamigawari*. The robe is half vermilion and half brownish-green, and it features an embroidered wisteria branch pattern. Her *obi* and *shigoki* sashes also feature this wisteria branch pattern. The brown-green color of her costume is called *baikocha*, which subtly alludes to the famous actor Onoe Kikugoro.

2. 置き、出端、くどき、踊り地、チラシ
— The Five Parts of Kabuki Buyo

歌舞伎舞踊は、五段構成が基本。「置き」は前奏。「出端（では）」は立方の登場の場面、続いて女方ならば「くどき」、立役なら「物語」が山場の見どころとなる。後半はリズミカルな「踊り地」、エンディングの「チラシ」の五段になっている。短い『藤娘』で確かめておこう。「若紫に十返りの*」の「置き」が終わると「人目堰き笠」からが「出端」、「男心の憎いのは」からが「くどき」、「松を植よなら」からが「踊り地」になる。

＊「置き」の歌詞は上演により異同がある。

Kabuki buyo pieces traditionally consist of five parts: the *oki* prelude, the *deha* scene where the *tachikata* appears; the climactic *kudoki* (in *onnagata* buyo) or *monogatari* (when featuring a *tachiyaku*), the rhythmical *odoriji*; and the final *chirashi*. *Fujimusume*, naturally, features these five parts as well.

* Lyrics to the *oki* section differ depending on the performance.

48

3. 松が男なら、からむ藤は女
—— The Pine is Man; the Creeping Wisteria, Woman

六世菊五郎は、『藤娘』のくどきの後の部分を、岡鬼太郎が新たに書いた「藤音頭」に入れ替えた。「藤音頭」には、松の木を男に、それに絡みつく藤を女に見立てた色っぽい歌詞がある。「藤の花ぶさ色よく長く、可愛いがろうと酒買うて呑ませたら、うちの男松にからんで締めて、てもさても、と返りの…」という唄に乗せ、可憐な装いの藤の精がままならぬ男ごころのやるせなさをかき口説く。その対比が艶やかな見どころである。

Kikugoro VI used Oka Onitaro's new song *Fuji-ondo* in the *kudoki* section of *Fujimusume*. This song's lyrics liken man to a pine and woman to the creeping wisteria that tangles itself about the pine. The wisteria spirit, dressed in a charming costume, laments man's fickle heart as this melancholy song is sung.

4. 大津絵の人気キャラ
—— A Popular Character in *Otsu-e* Paintings

近江国の名物「大津絵」は、庶民のお土産物として人気の可愛い絵であった。「藤の精」は大津絵のキャラクターのひとつ。黒い塗笠を被り、藤枝をかついだ娘の絵姿は良縁を呼び寄せる効能があるといわれたそうである。大津絵にはこの他「鍾馗（しょうき）様」、「長刀弁慶」、「瓢箪鯰（ひょうたんなまず）」などがあり、みなお守りの効験があるとされた。鍾馗様は中国伝来の神で、疱瘡除けの効き目があり、端午の節句に飾られた。

Otsu-e paintings were once a popular souvenir item from the Omi Province. The wisteria spirit, Fuji-no-sei, was a popular character portrayed in these paintings as a woman wearing a black painted *kasa* hat and holding a wisteria branch. Pictures featuring her were said to bring good fortune. Of course, there were a number of other characters featured in *Otsu-e*, including Shoki-sama, Naginata Benkei, and Hyotan Namazu. Each of these characters had its own unique effect as a lucky charm. Shoki-sama, for example, was a Chinese god said to ward off pestilence. His image was often put out for the Boy's Day festivities on May fifth.

5. 昭和の新演出
—— Revived in the Showa Era

『藤娘』のもとは大津絵から抜け出る趣向で始まったが、昭和12（1937）年に六世尾上菊五郎が新演出を発表し、以来こちらがポピュラーになった。幕開きは真っ暗闇で長唄だけが聞こえ、パッと灯りが点くと、目が醒めるような大きな藤の花房が松に絡んで垂れ下がるなかに、藤の精がすっと立っている。照明で意外性を取り入れた舞台面は当時は大変斬新で、新聞に「お上りさん悶絶」と書かれたほどの評判であった。

Fujimusume was based on the idea of a woman coming to life from an *Otsu-e* painting. It didn't enjoy much popularity until Onoe Kikugoro's revival in 1937, or year 12 of the Showa Era. This new performance started with the stage in darkness as the *nagauta* song began. When the lights flashed on the audience was met with a spectacular scene—the wisteria spirit standing silently before a great pine tree entangled with the branches of a wisteria tree. This sudden lighting used to such spectacular effect was a novel idea at the time and was met with high praise from newspapers.

六歌仙容彩
Rokkasen Sugata no Irodori

03 業平

『六歌仙容彩』
2015年4月　歌舞伎座
（左から）業平（四代目中村梅玉）、
小町（二代目中村魁春）

Narihira
Rokkasen Sugata no Irodori
(Kabukiza Theatre, April 2015)
(from left) Narihira (Nakamura Baigyoku IV),
Komachi (Nakamura Kaishun II)

あらすじ　　　　　　　　　　　　　　　　Synopsis

六歌仙容彩

平安の高貴な六人の歌人、なかでも
絶世の美女・小野小町に五人の男たちは
恋を仕掛けるが、そこに見えたのは楽しい俗物ぶり

高僧の僧正遍照、歌人の文屋康秀、美男で名高い在原業平、
宮人たちが次々と小町に言い寄るもののすげなく扱われる。
粋で洒脱な僧の喜撰法師は小町の分身と見えた祇園の茶汲み女・お梶に戯れるがこれも逃げられ、
そして大伴黒主は恋の叶わぬ末、ついに謀反人の本性を現す。

──────── **Six famed poets of the Heian Period appear in this play. The five men vie for Ono no Komachi (the only female, and a peerless beauty) in a truly delightful play that shows a playful side of these high nobles.**

High priest Sojo Henjo, Bun'ya no Yasuhide, and the handsome young Ariwara no Narihira each attempt to woo and are quickly rejected by the beautiful poet Ono no Komachi. The stylish priest Kisen Hoshi, meanwhile, attempts to woo a teahouse maiden named Okaji, who, like Komachi, is a striking beauty, but he too is rejected. Finally, Otomo no Kuronushi too is rejected by Komachi, who reveals his wicked plans to seize power.

01　遍照

　幕が開くと、官女たちが宮中での歌合わせのことと小野小町の話などをしている。

　やがて重厚な竹本の曲に合わせ、僧正遍照が登場する。

　遍照はかつて良峯宗貞という公家であったが今は出家の身。しかし小町に恋い焦がれ、どんな仏の罰を受けてもいいから小町に会いたいとやってきたのである。

　遍照が小町の居間に寄ろうとすると、勅諚（天皇の命）により、歌合わせの歌を思案中であると、官女たちに引き留められる。

　と、そこに「色見えて　移ろうものは世の中の人の心の花にぞありける」と声がし、小町が現れる。

　小町は出家の身で女に迷うのは仏の道に外れると遍照を諭し、寺に帰るよう勧める。

　遍照は後を見返りながら名残惜しげに帰っていき、小町もまた奥に入る。

01　Henjo

The curtain rises on a group of court ladies discussing Ono no Komachi and a poetry contest. After a while a *Takemoto* tune begins and Sojo Henjo appears.

Henjo is the former noble Yoshimine no Munesada who has left home and entered the priesthood. He has fallen helplessly in love with Komachi, however, and vows to meet Komachi no matter what punishment the Buddha might visit upon him.

He attempts to approach Komachi but is stopped by the court ladies who say that she is in the midst of composing a poem at the emperor's behest.

Komachi appears just then and proceeds to admonish Henjo for breaking his Buddhist precepts by concerning himself with women. She insists that Henjo go back to his temple.

Henjo returns to his temple, looking back longingly as Komachi returns to the inner palace.

02 文屋

　誰もいなくなった舞台に、文屋康秀と官女たちが現れる。

　康秀も小町を慕って忍んできたのであるが、官女たちに見つかってしまった。

　清元の軽快な音楽に乗せ、康秀は、小町に恋をして、百夜にわたり小町を訪ねる約束をし、九十九夜目に倒れた深草の少将を気取ったわが身のことをおどけてみせる。また、江戸時代の吉原通いの様子などを軽妙に踊る。

　官女たちは康秀をからかい、恋尽くしの問答を仕掛ける。

　様々な恋を語りながら康秀は官女を蹴散らかし、奥を目指して走っていき、官女たちもその後を追いかける。

03 業平

　艶やかな長唄とお囃子の曲に合わせ、正面の御簾が上がると、在原業平と小町が立っている。平安の美男美女の姿である。

　色好みで知られた業平は、わが身を千鳥に譬えて小町を口説く。

　また、扇尽くしの歌に合わせ、思いのたけを訴えるが、小町はそれを振り切り奥に入ってしまう。

　残された業平はひとり寂しく帰っていく。

04 喜撰

　舞台はガラッと変わって祇園あたり。枝垂桜が満開である。

　清元と長唄囃子の連中が居並び、掛け合いで演奏される。

　喜撰法師が浮かれた様子で登場する。

　そこへ茶汲み女のお梶が出て、茶を差し出すが、お梶に見とれていた喜撰は茶をこぼしてしまう。二人が洒脱に色模様を踊るうち、お梶は喜撰を振り切って奥に入ってしまう。

　やがて大勢の所化が、喜撰を迎えにくる。雨も降らぬのに傘を持っているのは僧侶のくせに遊び呆ける喜撰への意見のためである。

　所化たちは、江戸時代に流行った住吉踊りを賑やかに踊り、喜撰も、江戸時代の願人坊主と呼ばれる大道芸人が踊ったチョボクレや、女性の振りを軽快に踊る。

　やがて喜撰はわが宿を指して帰っていく。

05 黒主

　長唄と囃子が居並ぶ舞台に、大伴黒主と小町が現れる。

　黒主は小町の和歌が古歌の盗作だと決めつける。小町が神々に祈念しながら、古歌が書かれている草紙を水で洗うと、書かれていた歌が消える。小町の歌を盗み聞いた黒主が、草紙に書き込み、それを証拠として盗作の疑いをかけたのであった。

　疑いの晴れた小町は、黒主の歌こそ天下を調伏する意図があるだろうと問い詰める。

02 Bun'ya

Bun'ya no Yasuhide and some court ladies enter the now-empty stage.

Though he hides in hopes of meeting with Komachi, the court ladies find Yasuhide.

Yasuhide dances nimbly to the *kiyomoto*-style music, his performance telling the story of Fukakusa no Shosho, who promised to visit Komachi every night for 100 nights but only made it to 99. His dance also includes scenes from Edo's Yoshiwara pleasure quarters.

The court ladies make fun of Yasuhide and begin interrogating him about love.

Yasuhide kicks the court ladies to the side while he expounds upon love, eventually running into the inner rooms of the palace. The court ladies chase after him.

03 Narihira

A bewitching *nagauta* is played as a bamboo screen is lifted to reveal Ariwara no Narihira and Komachi—a man and woman known for their peerless beauty in the Heian period.

The playboy Narihira likens himself to a plover bird as he attempts to woo Komachi.

He makes his case to a sweet *ogi-zukushi* tune, but Komachi pays him no heed, escaping to the inner rooms of the palace.

04 Kisen

The stage suddenly shifts to the Gion district of Kyoto, where the *shidare-zakura* (weeping cherry blossoms) are in full bloom.

Both a *kiyomoto* and a *nagauta* band are present, and they alternate their performances.

Kisen Hoshi makes his jovial entrance onto the stage, after which the teamaid Okaji appears to serve tea. Kisen spills his tea when he sees the beautiful Okaji. The two dance flirtatiously, but Okaji cuts their inappropriate dance short and flees to an inner room.

Just then a group of *shoke* monks arrive to pick up Kisen, knowing of his penchant for secular pleasures.

The monks perform the *sumiyoshi* dance that was popular during the Edo period. Kisen performs a street performer's dance called *chobokure* as well as a dance imitating a woman.

Finally, the disappointed Kisen returns to his home.

05 Kuronushi

A *nagauta* singer and band sit on stage as Otomo no Kuronushi and Komachi appear.

Kuronushi accuses Komachi of plagiarizing a poem from an ancient anthology, but Komachi shows that Kuronushi merely wrote her poem in the anthology to frame her. When she pours water on the page, the freshly-written poem disappears immediately, proving her innocence and showing Kuronushi to be a cheat.

Komachi proceeds to accuse Kuronushi of plotting to seize control of the country, citing lines of his own poem as proof.

実は黒主は天下を狙う大悪人であった。企みを暴かれた黒主は大勢の討手と戦うのであった。

It is thus revealed that Kuronushi is the villain, and the play ends with a great fight between Kuronushi and his pursuers.

04 喜撰

『六歌仙容彩』 2015年4月 歌舞伎座
（左から）喜撰（七代目尾上菊五郎）、お梶（七代目中村芝雀）

Kisen
Rokkasen Sugata no Irodori
(Kabukiza Theatre, April 2015)
(from left) Kisen (Onoe Kikugoro VII),
Okaji (Nakamura Shibajaku VII)

作品の概要

演目名

六歌仙容彩

作者

作詞 = 松本幸二
作曲 = 十世杵屋六左衛門（大薩摩・長唄）
　　　初世清元斎兵衛（清元）

概要

　平安時代の六歌仙（僧正遍照、文屋康秀、在原業平、喜撰法師、大伴黒主、小野小町）が登場する五変化舞踊。五人の男が皆、絶世の美女・小野小町に振られるという筋立てが面白く、現代でも全段上演が可能な変化舞踊である。遍照は年甲斐もなく小町に言い寄るが相手にされず、文屋も業平も失敗。喜撰法師は気分を変え、茶汲み女（古くはお端下女）を小町に見立てて踊る。小町と和歌の争いになる黒主は悪役で、能の『草子洗小町』を取り入れている。五人の振られ男をひとりの俳優が踊り分けるのは至難であるが、近年では勘九郎時代の十八世中村勘三郎や十世坂東三津五郎が通して踊っている。「文屋」や「喜撰」は独立した一幕としても上演され、特に「喜撰」は名人・七世坂東三津五郎以来、代々の三津五郎が踊っている。「遍照」は義太夫、「文屋」が清元、「業平」は長唄、「喜撰」は清元と長唄、「黒主」は長唄で、通し上演は豪華である。

初演

天保2（1831）年3月江戸・中村座で、二世中村芝翫（四世歌右衛門）が五歌仙、岩井粂三郎（六世半四郎）が小町・お端下女。作詞は松本幸二、作曲は大薩摩と長唄が十世杵屋六左衛門、清元が初世清元斎兵衛。振付は二世藤間勘十郎、四世西川扇蔵、中村勝五郎。

Overview

Title

Rokkasen Sugata no Irodori

Writer

Lyrics: Matsumoto Koji
Music: Kineya Rokuzaemon X
　　　　(*ozatsuma* / *nagauta*)
　　　　Kiyomoto Saibei I (*kiyomoto*)

Overview

　A *Gohenge-buyo* piece featuring all six of the Heian-period *Rokkasen* ("six sages of poetry"): Sojo Henjo, Bun'ya no Yasuhide, Ariwara no Narihira, Kisen Hoshi, Otomo no Kuronushi, and Ono no Komachi. The basic premise, that each of the five men in this group is rejected by Ono no Komachi (the sole female) is a comic and light-hearted one. Even today, the play is sometimes performed in its entirety. Henjo approaches Komachi despite their difference in age but is quickly rejected. Both Bun'ya and Narihira are unsuccessful in their wooing as well. Kisen Hoshi pretends that a tea maid (a female servant in old performances) is Komachi and attempts to woo her. Taking inspiration from the noh play *Soshi-arai Komachi*, Kuronushi is the villain who engages in a competition of verse with Komachi. It is an incredibly difficult feat for a single actor to play all five unique male roles in this piece. In recent years Nakamura Kanzaburo VIII and Bando Mitsugoro X have performed the entire play. Bun'ya and Kisen's acts are sometimes played as one-act plays. In fact, "Kisen" is often performed by the Bando Mitsugoro line of actors. Each scene is played to a different style of music—*gidayu, kiyomoto, nagauta*—making this a truly spectacular show.

Premiere

March 1831, Nakamuraza Theatre. Feat. Nakamura Shikan II (Utaemon IV) as *Gokasen* (Five Sages of Song), Iwai Kumesaburo (Hanshiro VI) as Komachi/Maid. Lyrics by Matsumoto Koji. *Ozatsuma* and *nagauta* music by Kineya Rokuzaemon, *kiyomoto* by Kiyomoto Saibei I. Choreography by Fujima Kanjuro II, Nishikawa Senzo IV and Nakamura Katsugoro.

登場人物

Characters

小野小町
おののこまち

平安時代の女流歌人。この小野小町を紅一点とし『古今和歌集』に記された代表的な六人の歌人がすなわち「六歌仙」。この演目に登場する六人がまさしくそれである。小野小町は絶世の美女の代名詞として現代にまで語り継がれる。この演目では立場の異なる五人の男性がそれぞれ小町に言い寄るが結局すべて振られてしまい、さらに大伴黒主は小町によって悪事と本性を暴かれてしまう。

Ono no Komachi

A poet of the Heian Period (794–1185), Ono no Komachi is the sole female member of the *Rokkasen*, six renowned poets whose work appears in the *Kokin Wakashu* anthology. She was known for her striking looks, and even today her name is synonymous with peerless beauty. The five men who appear in this play (each of different but very high social standing) all try and fail to woo her, and the plot finally culminates in Komachi outing the evil deeds of Otomo no Kuronushi's.

文屋康秀
ぶんやのやすひで

文屋康秀は、御所の中をバタバタと走り込んでくるなどどこか俗にくだけたところもあり、軽妙さをみせる男。御簾の中で歌を練る小町に会いにやって来たのだが、意地の悪い官女たちに阻まれ、官女たちと「恋尽くし」の間答などを繰り広げたものの、ついに小町に会うことはできずじまい。思いの叶わなかった文屋は大勢の官女を蹴倒して帰ってゆくのだった。

Bun'ya no Yasuhide

Bun'ya no Yasuhide has a somewhat uncouth side, running haphazardly around the palace. He is also somewhat of a playboy who goes in search of Ono no Komachi but is stopped by the court ladies. These cold ladies interrogate him about love for some time, and ultimately, he is unable to even meet Komachi. In the end, he kicks the cruel ladies who tormented him and leaves in a fit of anger.

喜撰法師
きせんほうし

『六歌仙』の舞踊の中で「喜撰」のところだけは御殿ではなく京の町。喜撰法師は僧侶の身ながら粋で洒脱、いかにも世俗的な風情で瓢箪を下げた桜の枝を持ち、ほろ酔い機嫌でやって来る。そこで出会ったのは小野小町ではなく、それと見紛う美しさの茶屋女・お梶。早速喜撰は口説きにかかるがまたしても振られ、迎えの坊主たちと賑やかに住吉踊り。喜撰は姉さんかぶりで女踊りを見せる。

Kisen Hoshi

Of the various interactions in *Rokkasen*, Kisen's is the only one set in town rather than in Ono no Komachi's palace. Though he is a monk, he is anything but virtuous, strutting about tipsily with a gourd attached to a cherry branch in tow. Instead of Ono no Komachi, Kisen meets the teahouse maid Okaji whom he attempts to flirt with and is soundly rejected by. The Buddhist priests who come to pick him up to begin an energetic *Sumiyoshi* dance while Kisen dances as a woman with a towel wrapped around his head.

僧正遍照
そうじょうへんじょう

桓武天皇の孫で元は良峯宗貞といい、舞踊劇『関の扉』にも登場する。仁明天皇の没後に出家して僧正となり、尊い身分の高僧かつ優れた歌人として知られる。しかしここではその立場も弁えず小町の色香に迷い緋の衣姿で小町を口説きに御殿までやって来る。官女たちに遮られながらもようやく小町に会うことが叶うが、結局小町にはすげなくされ、心を残しながら帰ってゆく。

Sojo Henjo

Emperor Kanmu's grandson formerly known as Yoshimine no Munesada, the character Sojo Henjo also appears in the *buyo* play *Seki no To*. He became a Buddhist high priest after the death of Emperor Ninmyo, and is now known for both his high social status and poetic skill. Forgetting his place as a virtuous priest, however, he brazenly attempts to woo the poet Ono no Komachi at court. Though the court ladies attempt to stop him, he eventually finds Komachi but is rejected. Utterly dejected, Henjo returns to the holy Mt. Hiei.

在原業平
ありわらのなりひら

在原業平は歴史に残る美男で稀代のプレイボーイ。平城天皇の孫にあたる。歌人としても多くの作品を残しているが、小倉百人一首に数えられる「ちはやぶる 神代も聞かず 龍田川 からくれなゐに 水くくるとは」は特によく知られている。この演目では小町と業平、まさに美男と美女の代表格同士の顔合わせとなるが、それでもあっさりと振られてしまい、業平はすごすごと帰ってしまう始末。

Ariwara no Narihira

Ariwara no Narihira is known historically as a playboy of unparalleled looks. He is Emperor Heizei's grandson and a poet most famous for poem #17 of the Ogura Hyakunin Isshu: "Even in the time of the gods / you did not hear of such a thing / as the Tatsuta River's / stunning crimson hues / dyed by the fallen leaves." Though an equal in looks to the great beauty Ono no Komachi, Narihira is rejected by her and returns home in low spirits.

お梶
おかじ

「喜撰」の場に小野小町に代わって登場するのは祇園の茶屋女のお梶。満開の桜に彩られた花見時の京の町で喜撰法師と出会う。互いにどうやらいい雰囲気を察し、二人の明るく軽妙なそしてちょっと色っぽいやり取りが続いてゆく。やがてお梶は甲斐甲斐しい世話女房の風情も見せるが、喜撰法師から熱心に口説きにかかられるとあっさりと突き放し、さっさと逃げ帰ってしまう。

Okaji

Okaji is a teahouse maid who appears instead of Ono no Komachi in Kisen's scene. She runs into Kisen Hoshi in the streets of Kyoto during cherry blossom season, and the two get along quite well at first, even flirting some. Eventually, Okaji explains that she is a dedicated wife, but Kisen makes aggressive advances which are thoroughly rejected. Finally, Kisen returns home in shame.

大伴黒主
おおとものくろぬし

六歌仙と呼ばれる名歌人の一人だが、「黒主」という名前のイメージもあって歌舞伎の中では専ら悪人・謀反人といった役柄が定着し複数の演目に登場している。ここでは小町が詠んだ歌が盗用であると訴えようとし、また小町を后にして天下を乗っ取ろうとする謀反の計略を企てている。しかしいずれも小町に見抜かれ、最後は、公家悪の本性を露呈して大きな見得で幕を切る。

Otomo no Kuronushi

Otomo no Kuronushi is one of the famous *Rokkasen* poets, but in kabuki, his name is synonymous with villainy and treason. He appears as the villain attempting to usurp power in a number of kabuki plays. In *Rokkasen*, he accuses Komachi of plagiarizing a poem as part of his plot to make her his empress and seize control of the country. His evil schemes are outed by the shrewd Komachi, however, and his robes and wig are finally upturned, revealing his true nature as the *kuge-aku* (noble villain).

みどころ
Highlights

1. お江戸の平安ごっこ
###　── Playing Heian During Edo

平安時代の名高い歌人「六歌仙」を題材に、江戸の作者が遊び心で楽しい味付けをした長編舞踊劇だ。言わば「江戸の平安ごっこ」。登場する五人の男たちはみな小野小町に振られるというのがお約束。僧正遍照はおじいさん、美男子の在原業平も形無し、文屋康秀はおどけ者になっている。喜撰はとぼけた味わい。最後に登場する黒主は悪役で、小野小町と歌で対決したという、能の「草子洗小町」の構想をはめ込んでいる。

This fun piece written in the Edo Period (1603–1868) is a made-up story about the preeminent Heian (794–1185) poets commonly known as *Rokkasen*. The five men are each rejected by the beautiful Ono no Komachi after making a fools of themselves. Henjo is an older man obsessed with the ways of love, and the beautiful Narihira shows a rather unbecoming side. Bun'ya's antics are laughable, as are the foolish Kisen's. Kuronushi, however, appears last and reveals himself to be the villain as he faces Komachi in a competition of poetry, a feature taken from the noh play *Soshiarai Komachi*.

2. 変化舞踊とは何度も美味しい
###　── Henge Buyo Don't Get Old

ひとりの踊り手がキャラクターを変えながら、複数の曲を続けて踊り抜くのが「変化舞踊（へんげぶよう）」。三変化、五変化、七変化などがあり、文化文政期に大流行した。いろいろな役柄を演じ分け、立役から女方に変わることもあった。幕間なしで通すので、衣裳を替えるのに引抜きや早替りを利用したり、大道具の仕掛も工夫する。変化舞踊は一場面だけが残ったものも多いが、『六歌仙容彩』は完成度が高く、全段が残っている。

"*Henge Buyo*" refers to a style of buyo in which a single actor performs a number of roles and musical pieces one after another. There are a number of different styles of *henge buyo*, and they were especially popular during the Bunka Bunsei Era (1804–1829). The actor must be incredibly flexible, as some changes in character are quite drastic. A change from a *tachiyaku* leading man to a gentle *onnagata* character is not out of the question with *henge buyo*. Since *henge buyo* are performed start to finish without intermission, costume changes are made via a variety of techniques, including *hikinuki* and *hayagawari*, as well as tricks using large-scale stage props. Though many *henge buyo* have not survived in their entirety, *Rokkasen* is one of the few examples of a complete *henge buyo*, making it a rare treat.

3. 小町の代わりに祇園の女
###　── A Girl from Gion in Komachi's Stead

四番目に登場する喜撰法師のパートは、ぐっと気分の変わる展開だ。実在の喜撰についてはあまりよくわかっていないからか、作者はかなり自由な創造を施している。ふらふらと喜撰が向かうのは桜の咲く祇園町で、小町ではなく茶汲み女の赤い前掛けを引っ張る趣向である。二人のやりとり、桜の枝を手にした「チョボクレ」の軽みが見どころ。喜撰は片足だけ女方の歩き方にして柔らかみを出すので、実は相当な技倆が必要なのである。

Perhaps because little is known about Kisen historically, his section of the play is quite different from the other scenes. The writer takes great liberties in this section, placing Kisen in the pleasure quarters of Gion where he pulls at the apron of a beautiful tea maid instead of trying to woo Komachi in the palace. The witty banter of the two and the "*Chobokure*" street performance are both highlights of this section. Kisen's character must be played with a subtle *onnagata* walk expressed only with one leg, making this a technically challenging role.

4. 百人一首には選ばれなかった黒主
Kuronushi—Left out of the *Hyakunin*

六歌仙は、『古今和歌集』で名高い平安時代の六人の歌人のこと。僧正遍照（出家前の名は良岑宗貞）は小倉百人一首「あまつ風雲のかよひ路吹き閉ぢよ　をとめの姿しばしとどめむ」の歌で有名だ。このほかの六歌仙の小野小町も、在原業平も、文屋康秀も、喜撰法師も百人一首に載るが、なぜか大友（伴）黒主だけが撰に漏れている。黒主は小町の才能を嫉妬したとか、天下を狙う謀反人だったとか、能でも歌舞伎でも悪人に描かれている。

The *Rokkasen* are the "six sages of song," celebrated poets of the Heian anthology *Kokin Wakashu*. Nearly all of them also have a poem included in the famous *Ogura Hyakunin Isshu* ("Ogura 100 Poems by 100 Poets"). Oddly, however, Kuronushi is the only one of the *Rokkasen* not to have this honor. Perhaps because of this, he is often depicted in noh and kabuki as a villain who covets Komachi's poetic skill and plots to seize power over the country.

『寿式三番叟』
2013年1月 新橋演舞場
(左から) 三番叟 (四代目中村梅玉)、
千歳 (二代目中村魁春)

Kotobuki Shiki Sanbaso
(Shinbashi Enbujo Theatre, January 2013)
(from left) Sanbaso (Nakamura Baigyoku IV),
Senzai (Nakamura Kaishun II)

あらすじ　　　　　　　　　　Synopsis

荘重な翁の舞で天下泰平を祈り、続く三番叟の舞では鈴を振って五穀豊穣を願う。儀式性の高い祝儀舞踊の決定版

能の『翁』に倣い面箱を携えて登場する千歳は若く澄渕とした若太夫の役目、
そして重厚で老練な翁の舞へと引き継がれ、ここで厳かに天下泰平、国土安穏が祈願される。
代わって登場した三番叟は一転して躍動的で陽気、
そして軽妙に「揉の段」から「鈴の段」へ五穀豊穣の願いを込めて舞う。

After the solemn Okina prays for peace in the realm, Sanbaso prays for a good harvest with a ceremonial bell held in his hand. This is one of the definitive pieces of ceremonial buyo in the kabuki theatre.

The character of Senzai, a youthful and vigorous character played by the *wakadayu* (successor to the theatre proprietor), sets the stage for the solemn Okina who prays for peace and tranquility in all the land. After Okina's appearance, the lively Sanbaso appears, his nimble dances meant to bring a bountiful harvest.

舞台は松羽目。長唄と囃子の連中が居並んでいる。
やがて面箱を捧げ持った千歳、三番叟を従え、翁が登場し、座に着く。

The *nagauta* vocalist and accompaniment stand on stage. Senzai (holding a mask case), Sanbaso, and finally, Okina make their entrance and take their seats.

(See Japanese lyrics on left)

　とうとうたらり　たらりら
　たらりあがり　ららりどう
　ちりやたらり　たらりら

千歳は翁の前に面箱を捧げると、進み出て舞を始める。

Senzai offers up the mask box to Okina before taking the stage and dancing.

(See Japanese lyrics on left)

　鳴るは滝の水　鳴るは滝の水
　日は照るとも　絶えずとうたり
　ありうとうとう
　君の千歳を経んことは　天津乙女の羽衣よ

千歳の舞の間に、尉の面を着けた翁は、座の櫓に一礼すると、天下泰平、国土安穏を祈る舞を厳かに舞い始める。

Okina puts on a *jomen* (old man) mask as Senzai dances, then takes the stage to perform a dance that is meant to bring peace and tranquility to the land.

およそ千年の鶴は
万歳楽と　うとうたり
また万代の池の亀は
甲に三極をいただいたり
滝の水　れいれいと落ちて
夜の月　あざやかに浮かんだり
渚の砂さくさくとして　朝の日の色を弄す

天下泰平国土安穏　今日のご祈祷なり

千秋万歳の喜びの舞なれば
一さし舞おう　万歳楽　万歳楽

めでたく舞い納めた翁は舞台を辞す。
　続いて三番叟が進み出て、地面を踏み固めるように足拍子を踏み鳴らし、「揉の段」を舞い始める。

おおさえ　おおさえ
おお喜びありや　喜びありや
我がこの処よりも
外へはやらじとぞ思う

やがて、千歳から鈴を受け取り、中啓（扇の一種）を開き、鈴を稲穂に見立て、種を蒔く振りの「鈴の段」を舞い始める。これは、五穀豊穣を祈る舞である。

四海波風静けき　君が御代は
かしこき天照神の影も曇らず
怨敵退散　五穀成就　民豊か
八百万代も　国や栄えん

やがてめでたく舞い納める。

(See Japanese lyrics on left)

After his auspicious dance, Okina exits the stage.
Sanbaso steps forward finally, firmly tapping at the ground with his feet. He begins dancing the *momi no dan* (conflict section).

(See Japanese lyrics on left)

Finally, Sanbaso receives a bell from Senzai and, opening a ceremonial folding fan, performs a dance depicting the sowing of seeds called *suzu no dan* (bell section). This dance is meant to bring a plentiful harvest.

(See Japanese lyrics on left)

This auspicious series of dances finally ends with Sanbaso's performance.

作品の概要

演目名

寿式三番叟

作者

作詞＝不詳
作曲＝十世杵屋六左衛門（長唄）
　　　豊沢団平（義太夫）

概要

　三番叟は古来の民俗芸能。能の『翁（おきな）』として形が整えられると、生命長久、五穀豊穣を祈る厳かな祝言舞となり、『式三番』とも呼ばれる。翁、千歳（せんざい）、三番叟が出る。面を付けた翁の神舞の後、三番叟が直面（ひためん）で「揉の段」、次に面をつけ「鈴の段」を舞う。歌舞伎では、江戸時代には芝居の無事や大入を願って顔見世や元日に演じられた。現在も劇場のこけら落としに演じられる。『寿式三番叟』は長唄と義太夫の曲があり、歌舞伎では両方上演されている。

　長唄曲は、十世杵屋六左衛門作曲『翁千歳三番叟』を原曲とし、昭和5（1930）年東京劇場のこけら落としで六世尾上菊五郎が演じ、舞踊曲として注目されるようになった。義太夫曲は人形浄瑠璃からの移入で明治中期に豊沢団平が改曲したもの。大らかな田植えの歌詞が加わり、二人の三番叟が競って踊る。昭和11年に二世市川猿之助が歌舞伎に移して人気となり、『二人三番叟』として猿翁十種に入れられた。

　翁・千歳を省いたり、千歳が複数出ることもある。掲載のあらすじは長唄曲による上演のものである。

昭和初期の上演

長唄曲　昭和5（1930）年4月東京劇場こけら落としで、翁に六世尾上梅幸、千歳に十五世市村羽左衛門、三番叟が六世尾上菊五郎。
義太夫曲　昭和11（1936）年4月東京劇場で、翁に二世實川延若、千歳に市川八百蔵、三番叟に二世市川猿之助（初世猿翁）と、三世市川段四郎。振付は二世花柳寿輔。

Overview

Title

Kotobuki Shiki Sanbaso

Writer

Lyrics: Unknown
Music: Kineya Rokuzaemon X (*nagauta*)
　　　　Toyozawa Danpei (*gidayu*)

Overview

　"*Sanbaso*" refers to an ancient form of folk entertainment. In the noh theatre, it was taken and made into a celebratory dance entitled *Okina* which was meant to bring long life and good crops. It is also called *Shikisanban*. After the masked Okina dances, Sanbaso appears and dances the "*momi no dan*," after which he dawns a mask and dances the "*suzu no dan*". It was performed in the kabuki theatre during the Edo period at annual events such as *kaomise* and the new year as a ritual for the success of the theatre. It is still performed today to open theatres. The *nagauta* song is based on Kineya Rokuzaemon X's *Okina-senzai-sanbaso* and was performed for the opening ceremony of Tokyo Theatre in 1930. Kikugoro VI featured in that performance, and the piece came to be associated with buyo thereafter. The *gidayu* version was adapted from the puppet theatre by Toyozawa Danpei in the mid-Meiji period. In this version, the lyrics make reference to rice-planting, and the performance features two competing Sanbaso characters. Ichikawa Ennosuke II adapted the play to the kabuki theatre in 1936, after which it became quite popular. It became known as one of the 10 exceptional plays selected by Ennosuke II (*en'o jusshu*) under the title *Ninin Sanbaso*. Depending on the performance, the characters of Okina and Senzai are sometimes omitted, and some performances feature multiple Senzai characters.

Premiere (Early Showa Era)

Nagauta-kyoku: Opening ceremony of Tokyo Theatre, April 1930. Feat. Onoe Baiko IV as Okina, Ichimura Uzaemon XV as Senzai, and Onoe Kikugoro VI as Sanbaso.
Gidayu-kyoku: Tokyo Theatre, April 1936. Feat. Jitsukawa Enjaku II as Okina, Ichikawa Yaozo as Senzai, Ichikawa Ennosuke II (En'o I) / Ichikawa Danshiro III as Sanbaso. Choreography by Hanayagi Jusuke II.

登場人物 / Characters

三番叟
さんばそう

三番叟というのは三番目の老人といった意味で、千歳、翁に続いて三番目に登場する。この演目は能の『翁』から歌舞伎に移されたもので、能の主役が荘厳な翁であるのに対し、歌舞伎では三番叟の躍動感や軽妙さに重点が置かれて主役が入れ替わるが、そこが歌舞伎らしさともいえる。三番叟は前半「揉の段」では力強く足拍子を踏み、後半「鈴の段」では鈴を用いて種蒔きの様子を描き五穀豊穣を願う。

Sanbaso

"Sanbaso" literally means "the third old man," and as such he is the third character to appear, after Senzai and Okina. This play is based on the noh play *Okina*, but instead of the lead role being the solemn Okina, this honor is given to the light-hearted and active Sanbaso in the kabuki adaptation. You might say that this is in line with the spirit of kabuki, which is generally more light-hearted than noh theatre. Sanbaso is seen dancing vigorously in the first half of the play, while he prays for a bountiful crop in the latter half, his dance evoking images of sowing seeds while holding a bell.

千歳
せんざい

翁と対照的に若さの象徴として登場する。翁を太夫元が演じて来たのに対し、この千歳は太夫元の後継者である若太夫が勤めるのが江戸の芝居町の決まりであった。千歳は開幕と同時に翁の面を持って登場し、翁と共に神への畏敬の念を表す。やがて「鳴るは滝の水」と謡って舞台中央に進み、千歳の若々しく颯爽とした舞が繰り広げられるが、続く翁の格調高い舞への導入の役割も果たしている。

Senzai

Senzai represents youth, in contrast to the old man Okina. While the *tayumoto* played Okina, it was common for the *wakadayu* (successor to the *tayumoto*) to play the role of Senzai. He appears at the raising of the curtains holding the mask of Okina, and proceeds to express reverence toward the *kami* with Okina. Invoking the words *"naru wa taki no mizu,"* Senzai steps into the center of the stage and performs a youthful, invigorating dance which also serves as a lead-in to the dignified and solemn dance of Okina.

翁
おきな

翁とは老人を指し、あるいは老人の敬称として用いられるが、この登場人物も高い神格を持った老人で厳かに神事を司る。「とうとうたらり」という呪文を唱えて天下泰平、国土安穏（こくどあんのん）を祈り、天地人の舞から千穐万歳（せんしゅうばんぜい）を祝って静かに立ち去ってゆく。能の『翁』では主役であるシテ方がこの役を勤めるが、江戸の芝居町では芝居小屋の経営者にあたる太夫元（たゆうもと）がこの翁を勤めるのを決まりとしていた。

Okina

"Okina" means "old man," a term of reverence befitting this character, who solemnly does the work of the gods. He speaks the holy words *"toto-tarari"* while praying for peace and tranquillity throughout the realm, while his dance is meant to bring long life. Though he is played by the leading actor in the noh play *Okina*, during the Edo Period it was common practice for the playhouse proprietor, called *tayumoto*, to play this role.

みどころ
Highlights

1. 三番叟の叟は、おじいさんの意味
—— Sanba-So—An Old Man

『三番叟』は古来からの日本の芸能である。「叟」はおじいさんの意味で、三番目に踊るからとも、三人踊るからともいわれる。五穀豊穣を祈る神聖曲として扱われる能の『翁』では、翁の荘重な舞の後、狂言師が三番叟を演じ、種蒔きを模した所作や躍動的な所作が展開される。歌舞伎では、昔は顔見世や元日などに非公開で関係者が踊る儀式舞踊でもあった。今でも劇場のこけら落とし(開場式)に踊られる。

"Sanbaso" refers to an ancient performance art in Japan, while the "so" of *sanbaso* means "old man." Thus the word can be interpreted as implying both the "third dancer" and by extension that there are three dancers in the performance. The noh version of this piece, *Okina*, is meant as a ceremony to pray for a plentiful harvest. In this rendition, the solemn dance of Okina is followed by the more playful Sanbaso who performs a dance depicting, among other lively activities, the sowing of seeds. In the kabuki tradition, this piece was often performed at *kaomise* festivities and the new year in private performances not open to the public. Today it is performed at the openings of theatres.

2. とうとうたらりたらりら
—— "To-to Tarari"—a Chant of Unknown Origin

『三番叟』の冒頭に「とうとうたらり たらりら たらりあがり ららりどう」という歌詞がある。意味は伝えられていない。古い時代の祝言の呪文のようなものであろうか。賑やかな歌舞伎の舞台でも、これを聞くと神妙な心持ちにとらわれる。一説によれば、チベットの古い祝儀の曲に同様の歌詞があるとも。三番地（さんばじ）と呼ばれる独特のリズムも懐かしい響きで、はるか昔から伝えられてきた音の様式を伝えているのだろう。

Sanbaso begins with the lyrics "to-to tarari-tarari ra, tarari agari, rararido." The meaning of these words is unknown, though they may be some ancient incantation spoken at certain celebratory ceremonies in the past. Despite the lively trappings of the kabuki theatre, those who hear these opening lines are bound to feel a certain quiet awe. One theory states that these same words can be found in a Tibetan song of celebration. There is also something nostalgic about the ancient "sanbaji" rhythm that makes you feel it must have been used for some ancient ceremony.

3. 義太夫の『二人三番叟』は踊りを競う
—— Two Competing Sanbaso's

現在歌舞伎で『寿式三番叟』として上演される義太夫曲は、もとは人形浄瑠璃で演じられてきた内容を歌舞伎に移したもの。翁と千歳の厳かな舞の後に、三番叟が儀式的だが軽妙な振り事を見せる。人形同様に三番叟を二人出すこともあり、どちらかがヘトヘトになるまで踊りくるう、という趣向が実に楽しい。演者が親子や兄弟などで、顔や容姿がそっくりだとさらに面白い。翁と千歳をカットして三番叟のみが上演されることもある。

The kabuki version of Sanbaso is in the gidayu style and was adapted from the puppet theatre version. After the more solemn dances of Okina and Senzai, Sanbaso performs a ceremonial but relatively lively dance. Like in the puppet theatre, some performances feature two Sanbaso characters who dance until one of the two becomes too exhausted to dance. This playful version becomes all the more entertaining when the actors playing the two Sanbaso's are related and have a certain familial resemblance—it's really as if there are two Sanbaso's on stage! Some performances even cut out the previous two dancers, making it a Sanbaso solo show.

4. 三番叟のいろいろ
—— The Many Forms of Sanbaso

歌舞伎の『三番叟』は儀式から離れ、次第にエンターテインメント化して様々なヴァージョンができた。舞踊志賀山流に伝わる『舌出三番叟』は、足の使い方に古い形を残し、途中で口を開け赤く塗った舌を出す独特の所作がある。『操三番叟』は、人形の三番叟が後見に操られる趣向で人形振りで踊り、途中に糸が絡まりそれを直すあいだ動きが止まる演出がある。ほかに『種蒔三番叟』、『廓三番叟』、清元の『四季三番叟』など。

Kabuki's Sanbaso has been adapted into many different forms for entertainment since the art was separated from its ceremonial roots. Shitadashi Sanbaso in the Shigayama tradition of buyo has kept a traditional style of footwork and has a unique highlight involving the performer opening his mouth to reveal his tongue, which is painted a bright red. Ayatsuri Sanbaso is performed as though the actor playing Sanbaso were a puppet being manipulated by strings. In the middle of the performance, his strings become tangled and he is temporarily immobilized while they are being untangled. There are a number of other Sanbaso's as well, including Tanemaki Sanbaso, Kuruwa Sanbaso, and Shiki Sanbaso (in the kiyomoto style).

『連獅子』 2012年1月 新橋演舞場
(左から) 狂言師左近・仔獅子の精 (初代中村廣之資)、
狂言師右近・親獅子の精 (二代目中村吉右衛門)

Renjishi (Shinbashi Enbujo Theatre, January 2012)
(from left) Kyogenshi Sakon / Spirit of Shishi Cub
(Nakamura Takanosuke I), Kyogenshi Ukon / Spirit of
Parent Shishi (Nakamura Kichiemon II)

あらすじ　　　　　　　　　　　　　　　Synopsis

白い毛の親獅子と、赤い毛の仔獅子が豪快に 長い毛を振る、歌舞伎舞踊の中でも人気の高い作品

前半は狂言師が霊地・清涼山にある石橋や、獅子の子落としの様子を踊る。
獅子の勇ましいさまや、子を案じる親獅子の姿などが描かれ、演者それぞれの持ち味や表現が見どころ。
宗派の違う二人の僧の滑稽なやりとり「宗論」を挟み、白い毛の親獅子と、
赤い毛の仔獅子が豪快に長い毛を振る見せ場となる。

——— The white-haired parent and red-haired cub wave their manes about in a spectacular show that is one of the most popular buyo plays in kabuki.

In the first half, two *kyogenshi* tell the story of *shishi* lions pushing their cubs into the ravine of the sacred mountain Seiryo. Their dance expresses the courageous spirit of the *shishi* and the loving concern of a parent for its cub. After a comic interlude involving two monks arguing over their differing beliefs, the lion cub and parent are reunited and give a magnificent show of shaking their long manes about the stage.

舞台は松羽目。長唄と囃子が居並んでいる。
やがて手獅子を携え、二人の狂言師が登場する。

文殊菩薩が住むという霊地・清涼山には、石橋（しゃっきょう）と呼ばれる、自然と出来た石の橋がある。その石橋の謂れをはじめ、文殊菩薩の使わしめである霊獣・獅子の住む清涼山の風景を踊りで見せる。

是ぞ文珠の在します　其の名も高き清涼山
峰を仰げば千丈の　漲る瀧は　雲より落ち
谷を望めば　千尋の底　流れよ響く松の風
見渡す橋は夕陽の　雨後に映ずる虹に似て
虚空を渡るが如くなり

続いて狂言師たちは、獅子がわが子を谷に突き落とし、切り立つ崖を駆け登れた子だけを育てるという伝承を踊りで見せる。

かかる嶮岨の巌頭より　強臆ためす親獅子の
恵みも深き谷間へ　蹴落とす仔獅子は
ころころころ　落つると見えしが

A nagauta accompaniment sits on a *matsubame* stage. Two *kyogenshi* enter carrying small *shishi* lion props.

There is a naturally formed stone bridge on the sacred Mt. Seiryo, where the bodhisattva Manjushri is said to live. As the legends of this sacred place are sung, the two *kyogenshi* begin to dance, depicting Mt. Seiryo, the habitat of the sacred *shishi* lions who are said to serve Manjushri.

(See Japanese lyrics on left)

The *kyogenshi* continue to depict an ancient practice by which lions would push their cubs from the cliff to test their strength, only raising the ones that were able to make it back up from the ravine.

(See Japanese lyrics on left)

身を翻し爪を蹴立てて　駈け登るを
また突き落とし　突き落とされ
爪をたてとも嵐ふく　木陰にしばしやすらいぬ

　なかなか上がってこない仔獅子を親獅子はいても立って
もいられぬ様子で案じ、谷を覗き込む。

登り得ざるは臆せしか
あら育てつる甲斐なやと
望む谷間は雲霧に
それともわかぬ八十瀬川

　谷底の川の流れに映った親獅子の姿をみた仔獅子は、勢
いを得て谷を一気に駈け上がる。

水に映れる面影を
見るより仔獅子は勇み立ち
翼なければ　飛びあがり
数丈の岩を難なくも
駈け上がりたる勢いは
目覚ましくもまた勇ましし

　こうして、親子の獅子の様子を舞い描いた狂言師たちは、
再び手獅子を持つと、飛んで来た胡蝶に誘われるように去っ
て行く。

　二人の狂言師が去ると、二人の僧が登場し、間狂言の「宗
論」が始まる。
　文殊菩薩の御姿を拝もうと、浄土の僧の遍念と法華の僧
の蓮念が清涼山にやって来た。互いの姿を見つけた二人は、
旅の道連れが出来たと喜び合う。しかし、言葉を交わす内、
互いの属する宗派が異なると知ると、その優劣を巡って諍
いを始める。そこへ一陣の風が吹き寄せ、獅子が出現する
のであろうと恐れ戦いた二人は、その場から逃げ去って行く。

　長唄と囃子の曲調は勇壮かつ荘重なものになり、やが
て、白色の毛の親獅子の精、赤色の毛の仔獅子の精が出現し、
牡丹の花に戯れ遊ぶさまを見せる。

獅子団乱旋の舞楽のみきん
牡丹の花房匂い満ち満ち
大巾利巾の獅子頭
打てや囃せや　牡丹芳　牡丹芳
黄金のずい　あらわれて
花に戯れ　枝に伏し転び
実にも上なき　獅子王の勢い

　そして、勇ましく毛を振り、獅子の狂いを見せた後、めで
たく舞い納め、幕となる。

The parent *shishi*, worried that the cub has still not returned, looks down into the ravine.

(See Japanese lyrics on left)

The cub sees the parent reflected in the river's surface and is struck by a surge of energy. He suddenly rushes up the ravine to the parent.

(See Japanese lyrics on left)

A butterfly appears before the *kyogenshi* and leads them from the stage.

Once they are gone, two monks appear on stage, and the *"Shuron"* ("Religious Debate") interlude begins.

Jodo practitioner Hennen and Hokke practitioner Rennen have come to Mt. Seiryo to worship Manjushri. They run into each other on the road and rejoice to have a fellow traveler for company. When they realize that they practice different sects of Buddhism, however, they begin to argue over whose sect is better. When a *shishi* lion suddenly appears with a gust of wind, the two monks flee in fear.

The *nagauta* takes on a majestic mode as the white-haired parent lion and red-haired cub appear, frolicking among the peonies.

(See Japanese lyrics on left)

Finally, the two *shishi* wave their long manes about in a wild, magnificent show.

作品の概要

演目名

連獅子

作者

作詞 = 河竹黙阿弥
作曲 = 三世杵屋正治郎

概要

　歌舞伎舞踊の中でも人気の高い作品。能『石橋（しゃっきょう）』を歌舞伎舞踊化した作品は「石橋物」と呼ばれ、本作もその一つ。曲は長唄である。能『石橋』の、紅白の獅子が舞う小書（特殊演出）「連獅子」に想を得、さらに親獅子が仔獅子を谷に落とす場面を加えた。

　現在上演される『連獅子』の成立過程は複雑である。まず文久元（1861）年5月、舞踊家・初世花柳寿輔、二世花柳芳次郎の親子の素踊りの舞踊として上演された。河竹黙阿弥作詞、作曲は二世杵屋勝三郎。ついで明治5（1872）年7月東京・村山座で、五世坂東彦三郎、二世澤村訥升（六世澤村宗十郎）により、劇中劇の趣向で取り上げられる。振付は初世花柳寿輔で、これが歌舞伎での初演である。その際黙阿弥により歌詞が増補され、三世杵屋正治郎が新たに作曲を行なった。また、明治34（1901）年2月東京座において二世市川段四郎（初世市川猿翁）と四世市川染五郎（七世松本幸四郎）が杵屋勝三郎の曲を使用して上演。この時、竹柴晋吉作の「宗論」が間狂言に加えられ、舞台が松羽目になるなど、全体の構成や扮装などが整えられた。現在は、この時の演出をもとに、杵屋正治郎作曲の長唄を用いて上演される。

初演

明治5（1872）年7月、東京・村山座で、五世坂東彦三郎、二世澤村訥升（六世宗十郎）による。

Overview

Title

Renjishi

Writer

Lyrics: Kawatake Mokuami
Music: Kineya Shojiro III

Overview

　One of the most popular kabuki buyo pieces, *Renjishi* is a *nagauta* kabuki buyo adaptation of the noh play *Shakkyo* which is part of a sub-genre called *shakkyomono*. This play takes the "Renjishi" section of *Shakkyo*, which features a cub and parent lion, and alters it to show the parent pushing cub into the ravine.

　Renjishi's history is a complicated one. Initially, it was performed as a *suodori* (a dance where actors wear robes bearing their family crest rather than costumes) in 1861 by Hanayagi Jusuke I and his son Hanayagi Yoshijiro II. The lyrics were written by Kawatake Mokuami and the music was by Kineya Katsusaburo II. It was next performed as a play within a play at the Murayamaza Theatre in 1872 (starring Bando Hikosaburo V and Sawamura Tossho II). Mokuami added lyrics and Kineya Shojiro III wrote new music for this version. In 1901, Ichikawa Danshiro II (Ichikawa En'o I) and Ichikawa Somegoro IV (Matsumoto Koshiro VII) performed *Renjishi* with Kineya Katsusaburo's music, adding Takeshiba Shinkichi's "*Shuron*" ("Religious Debate") as a comic interlude and featuring a *matsubame* stage set and proper costume designs. The current version of *Renjishi* is based on this 1901 production and uses Kineya Shojiro's *nagauta* music.

Premiere

July 1872, Murayamaza Theatre. Feat. Bando Hikosaburo V and Sawamura Tossho II (Sojuro VI).

登場人物　Characters

狂言師右近 後に 親獅子の精
きょうげんしうこん のちに おやじしのせい

狂言師右近は、もう一人の狂言師・左近と共に清涼山の獅子の伝説を舞に乗せて語り描く。霊獣の獅子はわが子を深い谷底に落とし、元気に這い上がってきた子だけを育てるという言い伝えがあり、右近は白い獅子頭を持って親獅子を演じてゆく。最後は牡丹の花に戯れる勇壮な獅子の姿となり、白い毛を激しく振って狂いの様子をみせる。

Kyogenshi Ukon / Spirit of the Parent Shishi

Ukon is a *kyogenshi*, or a kabuki actor who performs at the homes of great daimyo lords. He dances with Sakon to tell the legend of the *shishi* lions of Mt. Seiryo. These sacred beasts are said to have pushed their cubs down into a deep ravine to test their strength, only raising those strong enough to climb back up. Ukon takes up the *shishigashira* mask and performs the part of the father lion. The show ends with Ukon playing among the peonies, throwing his mane about in a wild manner.

狂言師左近 後に 仔獅子の精
きょうげんしさこん のちに こじしのせい

右近と共に登場した左近は年若い狂言師で、赤い獅子頭を手に仔獅子を演じる。谷底に突き落とされた仔獅子は爪を立てて登ってゆくが再び落とされ、やがて眠りについてしまう。登ってこない子を思う親獅子が谷を覗き込むと、水面に互いの姿が映り仔獅子は勇んで親獅子のもとへ駆け上がり歓喜の舞を見せる。そして獅子の精となり、赤い毛の仔獅子は親獅子と競うように激しく毛を振る。

Kyogenshi Sakon / Spirit of the Shishi Cub

Sakon is a *kyogenshi* like Ukon, though he is younger. He takes the red *shishigashira* mask and plays the part of the young *shishi* cub. Pushed down into a dangerous ravine, he claws his way back up only to be pushed down again. Eventually he falls asleep in his exhaustion, and his parent peeks down into the valley, worried about him. The cub sees his parent's reflection in a pond, which encourages him to climb back up again. Finally, Sakon is overcome by the spirit of the *shishi*, and he and the parent *Shishi* perform a wild dance, shaking their magnificent manes about in a spectacular show.

法華の僧蓮念
ほっけのそうれんねん

清涼山を目指してやって来た旅の僧。途中で同じく旅僧の遍念と出会い、仲良く同道を始めるが、自らは法華の僧、相手は何と宗旨の違う浄土の僧であった。旅は道連れといいながら何かと反発し合い、二人とも互いに譲らぬ始末。蓮念が団扇太鼓を叩いて「南無妙法蓮華経」と唱えれば、遍念は負けじと鉦を取り出す。やがて空の雲行きが怪しくなり、激しい風音におののいて逃げてゆくのだった。

Hokke Monk Rennen

A traveling monk on his way to Mt. Seiryu. He meets Hennen on his journey and asks if he would like to travel together. Hennen, however, belongs to a different sect of Buddhism, and the two get into a dispute. Rennen takes out an *uchiwa-daiko* (a type of drum) and begins exalting the Lotus Sutra, but Hennen, not wanting to lose, takes out a handbell. Stormclouds begin to gather, and Rennen finally runs away as the winds pick up.

浄土の僧遍念
じょうどのそうへんねん

清涼山への途中で蓮念と出会い共に旅を続けるが、次第に相手の様子がわかってみれば宗旨の違う浄土の僧と法華の僧。蓮念が「南無妙法蓮華経」と唱えれば、遍念は「南無阿弥陀仏」と言い返す。互いに仏の道と念仏のありがたさを主張し合う宗論となるが、「ナモダ」「レンゲキョウ」「ナモダ」「レンゲキョウ」と競って唱え合ううち、ついには互いの念仏を取り違えて二人共に苦笑する。

Jodo Monk Hennen

Hennen meets Rennen on his way to Mt. Seiryo but soon finds that they belong to different sects of Buddhism. Rennen extols the Lotus Sutra, but Hennen responds with praise of Amitabha (the Buddha of the western paradise). The two engage in a back-and-forth recitation of sacred texts until they become confused and make a mistake, finally breaking down and laughing together.

みどころ
Highlights

1. 獅子には牡丹が似合う
—— Lions and Peonies—a Perfect Match

「獅子に牡丹」は豪奢な図柄の代表で、歌舞伎座東階段に掲げられた日本画の大作『青獅子』（川端龍子作）にも白牡丹が獅子に添えられている。獅子は百獣の王であり、牡丹は百花王（ひゃっかおう）と呼ばれる。美しい無敵の取り合わせであり、獅子は牡丹の露を好むとの伝説もある。舞台に設えられる二畳台には必ず紅白の牡丹が添えられ、牡丹の枝を手にした獅子の狂いは能の「石橋」と同様だが、歌舞伎ならではの華々しさがある。

The depiction of *Shishi* lions with peonies has deep meaning in Japan and can even be seen in Kawabata Ryushi's grand *Aojishi* painting located along Kabukiza Theatre's eastern staircase. In Japan, the *Shishi* is considered "King of the Myriad Beasts" while peonies are similarly referred to as "King of the Myriad Flowers." Their combination, therefore, is a fitting one, and there is even a legend that states that lions are fond of the dew of peonies. The basic stage setting of *Renjishi* is similar to the noh play *Shakkyo*, with a *nijodai* stand decorated with red and white peonies and a *Shishi* lion carrying a peony branch. Despite this, *Renjishi* has its own unique charm that you can only see in kabuki.

2. 日本の獅子は二本足
—— Lions on Two Legs

獅子とは百獣の王ライオンを元に、東アジアでイメージされる霊獣だ。仏教では文殊菩薩の乗物とされ、霊山・清涼山にかかる石橋に棲むという。橋は幅一尺足らず、苔ですべり、下の谷の深さは千尋に及ぶ。橋の先は文殊菩薩の浄土だ。能の獅子物『石橋（しゃっきょう）』では、霊場を訪ねる僧が石橋にたどり着くがとても渡れず、待っていると獅子が現れる。能や歌舞伎の獅子は二本足。鹿（しし）踊りなどの芸能とも通じる点であろうか。

Shishi are sacred beasts in east Asian countries modeled after the lion, king of the beasts. The bodhisattva Manjushri is said to have ridden on a *Shishi*, which were believed to live on the stone bridge of the sacred mountain Seiryo-zan. This narrow bridge, covered in slippery moss, extends over a bottomless ravine beyond which lies manjushri's paradise. In the noh play *Shakkyo*, a Buddhist monk arrives at the stone bridge but cannot get across when a *shishi* appears before him. The *shishi* of noh and kabuki notably walk on two legs, and there are some similarities between this depiction and the tradition of *shishi-odori* in Japan.

3. 花道は千尋の谷底
—— The *Hanamichi*, a Fathomless Ravine

前半の狂言師は柔らかな色合いの着物に袴を着け、獅子頭を手に品格高い舞を見せる。獅子が子を千尋の谷へ突き落として厳しく育てるありさまを表現するのだが、せりふは一切ない。蹴落とされた仔獅子は舞台から花道へと転がり落ちる。このとき舞台と花道は千尋の高低差があることになる。花道で子が蹲ると、舞台の親は遥か高いところから心配して下を覗く様を見せる。花道を谷底に見立てた、巧みな表現である。

The *kyogenshi* performs an elegant dance with the *shishigashira* in hand, his subdued kimono with *hakama* trousers only adding to his dignified air. The dance depicts the custom of *Shishi* throwing their children down the ravine as a test of strength, but there are absolutely no spoken lines here. The *Shishi* cub rolls down the *hanamichi* to express his fall into the ravine, the main stage and *hanamichi* representing the stone bridge and the ravine bottom, respectively. When the cub reaches the *hanamichi*, we see the parent *Shishi* looking downward, worried about his young cub. This clever depiction of such a steep vertical height is one of the unique highlights of the show.

4. 見事な揃いの毛振り
—— The Awesome *Keburi*

後半は勇壮な親獅子と仔獅子の連れ舞が大きな見どころ。狂言師とは打って変わった隈取も荒々しい獅子の舞は、歌舞伎を代表する見せ場である。赤毛を被った仔獅子が花道から先に出て、続いて白毛の親獅子が威厳を持って現れる。技巧を凝らした毛振りには、その形から「髪洗い」「巴」「菖蒲打」などの名が付いている。息を合わせた舞姿には親子の情愛や、親から子への厳しい芸道修業の姿も重なって見え、観客の心を大きく打つ。

The awesome *tsuremai* (two-man dance) in the latter half of the play is one of the biggest highlights. The sudden change of the actors' *kumadori* makeup is one of the trademarks of kabuki that is bound to impress. First, the red-haired cub enters from the *hanamichi*, followed by the majestic father *shishi*. What follows is a breathtaking dance called *keburi*, in which the lions whip their long manes about the stage. This *keburi* dance goes by many names, including *kamiarai*, *tomoe*, and *shobu-uchi*. Watching the father and cub dance perfectly in sync, audiences are sure to be moved not only by the spectacular expression of the love between a parent and cub, but also by the sense of tradition passed down between generations.

春興鏡獅子
Shunkyo Kagamijishi

『春興鏡獅子』
2009年1月　歌舞伎座
弥生・獅子の精（十八世中村勘三郎）

Shunkyo Kagamijishi
(Kabukiza Theatre, January 2009)
Yayoi / Shishi Spirit (Nakamura Kanzaburo XVIII)

あらすじ　　　　　　　　　Synopsis

近代を象徴する歌舞伎舞踊。「獅子物」の代表曲。
女小姓の舞から勇壮な獅子の舞へ、
見事な変身の妙が展開される

江戸城大奥は正月行事の鏡曳で賑わっている。
そこへ手を引かれて出てきた女小姓の弥生が恥じらいながら可憐な踊りを見せるが、
供えてある獅子頭を手にするとその激しい力に引かれて姿をくらます。
代わって現れたのは白く長い毛を引いた獅子、戯れる蝶と共に勇壮な狂いの様子を見せる。

―――――― A representative *shishi-mono* piece, a genre synonymous with modern kabuki buyo. The deft transformation from elegant woman to brave *shishi* lion is a must-see.

Edo Castle is alive with the *kagami-biki* new year celebrations. The shy chambermaid Yayoi is made to perform a charming dance, but she eventually pulls back after touching the ceremonial *shishigashira* mask, awakening the lion spirit. In her place appears a white *shishi* lion who frolics wildly about the stage, playing with butterflies on stage.

　幕が開くと舞台は江戸城の大広間。今日は初春の行事である「鏡曳」の日である。
　将軍の所望で女小姓の弥生が踊りを披露することになり、そのために、家老と用人、大奥の老女と局が、将軍秘蔵の獅子頭もその場に飾られていることなどを話す。

　それぞれが去ると、長唄囃子連中の唄に合わせ、女小姓の弥生が老女と局に手を引かれて現れる。

　茶を点てているところを無理に引き出された弥生は、恥ずかしがって逃げ出してしまう。しかし再び引き出され、将軍の前であることに気がつくと観念して踊り始める。

　弥生は手踊りに始まり、川崎音頭を取り入れた踊りを踊る。
　川崎音頭は伊勢国の廓で歌い始められた曲で、伊勢音頭ともいう。鬟や髱、櫛、元結、平打（かんざし）など髪に縁のある言葉で、御殿女中の恋の難しさを唄いこんだ歌詞に合わせ、茶の湯で使う袱紗捌きも見せながら踊る。

　続いて、扇を手にした弥生は、春から、初夏の田植えの頃までの季節の移り変わり、早乙女たちの田植えの様子、

The curtain opens revealing the great hall of Edo Castle. It is *kagamibiki*, an important new year celebration.
　Kosho Yayoi is to dance at the shogun's request, and the various retainers, stewards, and other ladies-in-waiting discuss the *shishigashira* mask installed as a decoration for the festivities.

　As the others make their exit, Yayoi is led out onto the stage by the other ladies-in-waiting as a *nagauta* tune begins.

　Yayoi, who had been serving tea beforehand, runs away in embarrassment but is soon drawn back onto the stage where she begins to dance, realizing it is the shogun himself she is to dance for.

　Yayoi begins with a *te-odori* and then moves on to a *kawasaki ondo*-inspired dance.
　Kawasaki-ondo is a tune originating in the pleasure quarters of Ise Province, and it is sometimes called *Ise-ondo*. The song lyrics depict the hardships of love for ladies-in-waiting at the shogun's palace and are filled with words pertaining to hair. Yayoi's dance makes use of her tea cloth that she had previously been using in her tea-serving duties.

　Yayoi proceeds to perform a dance depicting the planting of rice by young girls in the spring and early summer. This

春興鏡獅子

朧月夜に時鳥（ほととぎす）が鳴き渡るさまなどを踊る。

そして咲き乱れる牡丹の花の様子や、花を見て憂さを忘れる姿を見せる。

さらに、仕舞で使う扇を二本持ち、これを巧みに用い、牡丹の花の様子を様々に表すなど艶やかに舞った後、文殊菩薩の霊地・清涼山にあるという石橋の有様を踊る。

やがて祭壇に祀られた獅子頭を手にし、獅子の踊りを披露しようとする。この獅子頭は文殊菩薩の霊夢によってできたもので、弥生が踊るうちに魂が入り、蝶を追って自然と動き出し始める。その様子に驚く弥生だったが、獅子頭に引かれるようにして、いずこかに去ってしまう。

続いて舞台には、台に乗って胡蝶が押し出され、羯鼓（かっこ）や振鼓（ふりつづみ）を打ち鳴らし、可憐に踊る。

やがて舞台に牡丹の枝も持ち出され、厳かに獅子の精が現れる。獅子は清涼山に住む、文殊菩薩の使わしめの霊獣である。

獅子の精は、豪快に毛を振る、獅子の狂いを見せ、めでたく舞納めるとその座に直るのだった。

あらすじ

dance calls for folding fans as well and depicts the romantic image of cuckoos chirping on a moonlit night.

Finally, we see Yayoi forget the sadness of the world at the sight of peonies in full bloom.

Last, Yayoi deftly manipulates her two folding fans to depicts the blossoming peonies and, finally, the stone bridge on Mt. Seiryo , a sacred ground where the bodhisattva Manjushri lives.

Finally, Yayoi takes hold of the *shishigashira* mask to perform the *shishi* lion dance. This mask is said to be made from the sacred dreams of Manjushri, and as such it soon takes on a life of its own, chasing after a butterfly as Yayoi dances. Yayoi is startled and soon disappears from the stage as though taken away by the power of the *shishigashira*.

Soon Kocho appears on the stage, offering a charming dance accompanied by a variety of drums.

Finally, the *shishi* lion appears on stage. *Shishi* lions are said to be sacred beasts which serve bodhisattva Manjushri himself.

The *shishi* spirit dances wildly, flinging stray strands of hair about the stage.

『春興鏡獅子』
2009 年 1 月　歌舞伎座
弥生・獅子の精（十八世中村勘三郎）

Shunkyo Kagamijishi
(Kabukiza Theatre, January 2009)
Yayoi / Shishi Spirit (Nakamura Kanzaburo XVIII)

作品の概要 / Overview

演目名

春興鏡獅子

Title

Shunkyo Kagamijishi

作者

作詞 = 福地桜痴
作曲 = 三世杵屋正治郎

Writer

Lyrics: Fukuchi Ochi
Music: Kineya Shojiro III

概要

　新歌舞伎十八番の代表的な長唄舞踊の大曲。ひとりの俳優が前半に可憐な女小姓の舞を、後半は姿を変じて荒々しい獅子の狂いを見せるコントラスト豊かな構成である。歌舞伎の特徴である華麗な女方舞踊と、勇壮な隈取をした獅子の舞が一度に観られるので、観客には大変喜ばれる。舞台は千代田城（江戸城）。正月六日、鏡餅を曳き遊ぶ「鏡曳」の行事の余興に、女小姓弥生が舞を所望される。弥生はお茶の御用をしていたため手にしていた袱紗や、二枚の扇を使って舞い始める。だが祀られた獅子頭を手にして舞い始めると、獅子の精が乗り移ってしまうという緊迫の展開になる。獅子頭に引かれて弥生が消え去ると、長唄の雛壇の奥から可愛らしい胡蝶ふたりが登場する。羯鼓などを使った胡蝶の舞の後、獅子の登場となる。歌舞伎にはもともと女方が舞う『枕獅子』という傾城の獅子物舞踊の伝統があったが、明治になり品格高い新曲が求められて作られた。江戸城大奥を舞台にすることは江戸時代には考えられないことであった。

Overview

　One of the representative examples of *nagauta buyo*. The contrast between the gentle woman of the first half and the wild beast of the second half is the biggest highlight of the show. Viewers from overseas are especially fond of this play that shows both an elegant onnagata buyo and the *kumadori* makeup of the *shishi* dance. Set in Chiyoda Castle (Edo Castle) on the 6th day of the new year, the day of the annual tradition of *kagamibiki* (named after the decorative *kagamimochi* rice cakes). While serving tea, the lady-in-waiting Kosho is asked to dance and so begins an elegant dance using a tea cloth and two folding fans. While dancing, she accidentally touches the ceremonial *shishigashira* mask and is possessed by the *shishi* lion's spirit. Yayoi disappears as an enchanting butterfly appears on stage. The butterfly dances with a *kakko* drum for some time before the *shishi* lion appears. There had been a traditional piece called *Makura-jishi*, performed by an *onnagata* actor, but this piece featured a courtesan and did not take place in Edo Castle. Such a setting would have been inconceivable in Edo Era, but with the Meiji Era came a demand for a *shishi-mono* of a higher class than those of old.

初演

明治26（1893）年3月歌舞伎座で、九世市川團十郎による。作詞は福地桜痴。作曲は三世杵屋正治郎。振付は九世市川團十郎、二世藤間勘右衛門。

Premiere

March 1893, Kabukiza Theatre. Feat. Ichikawa Danjuro IX. Lyrics by Fukuchi Ochi. Music by Kineya Shojiro III. Choreography by Ichikawa Danjuro IX and Fujima Kan'emon II.

登場人物 Characters

小姓弥生 後に 獅子の精
こしょうやよい のちに ししのせい

江戸城の大奥で仕える女小姓。正月のお
鏡曳の日に将軍の前で踊ることを所望され、
お茶のお点前の最中に無理やり手を引かれ
てくる。逃げることも叶わずようやく恥じらい
ながら踊り始めるが、座敷に供えてある獅
子頭を手に持って踊るうち、宿っていた獅
子の魂が息づいたかのように強く引かれて
ゆく。やがて勇壮な獅子が現れ、牡丹の花
と胡蝶に戯れながら激しい狂いの様子を見
せる。

Kosho Yayoi / Shishi Spirit

Kosho is a lady-in-waiting serving in Edo castle.
The Shogun demands that she dance on the day
of *kagamibiki*, grabbing her hand forcefully as
she attempts to serve tea. With no recourse but
to comply, she begins dancing but soon awakens
the lion spirit after touching a ceremonial mask
called *shishigashira*. A great *shishi* lion finally
appears and performs a wild dance, frolicking
among peonies and butterflies.

胡蝶の精
こちょうのせい

美しく愛らしい蝶の精で、牡丹の花に戯れ
るように飛んできて舞い遊ぶ。伝説上の霊
獣である獅子は動物の王だが、牡丹は花
の王。そして獅子を癒してくれる唯一のもの
もまた牡丹の花。それゆえ獅子のある所に
は必ず牡丹の花と蝶が登場する。小姓弥
生が姿を消すとどこからともなく胡蝶の精が
現れて舞い始めるが、獅子の精が登場する
と、互いに激しさと愛らしさの対照を見せな
がら舞い続ける。

Kocho Spirit

The beautiful butterfly spirit Kocho performs a
whimsical dance reminiscent of a frolic among
peonies. Though the *shishi* lion is king of the
animals, the peony is king of flowers and the
only thing capable of calming the wild *shishi*.
Because of this, wherever a lion appears, so do
peonies and butterflies. As soon as Kosho Yayoi
disappears, Kocho appears and begins to dance,
and soon after so does Shishi. The contrast
between the enchanting butterfly and the wild
lion dancing together is truly a sight to behold.

みどころ
Highlights

1. 大奥のお正月行事〜鏡曳
Kagamibiki—a New Years Festivity in the Palace Women's Quarters

国立国会図書館所蔵　楊州周延「千代田の大奥 鏡餅曳」
From the National Diet Library collection: Yoshu Chikanobu, "Chiyoda no Ooku: Kagamimochibiki"

江戸城では、正月七日に諸侯大名から贈られたたくさんの鏡餅を大橇に乗せて、男たちが曳いて歩く「鏡餅曳」の行事があった。行事は午の刻（昼）から深夜に及び、余興も催され、大奥にも入った。この日ばかりは大奥の女中たちも透き見などして大いに楽しみ、窮屈な暮らしの息抜きにしたという。元大奥勤めの老女の聞書などをまとめた三田村鳶魚の『御殿女中』（1930年刊）などで、奥勤めの女性たちの生活を知ることができる。

There is a New Year tradition in Japan which involves the cutting of *kagamimochi* rice cakes, called *kagamibiraki*. It is said that the maids of Edo castle had their own tradition of offering these ritual rice cakes, called *kagamibiki*. The celebration represented a full day during which the maids could relax and not worry about standing on ceremony. We know so much about these women's lives because of Mitamura Engyo's 1930 compilation of recollections and writings of ladies who once worked in the palace. Because palace ladies were forbidden from speaking to others about what occurred in the palace, such topic matter was irresistible to the common folk, and it has since become the focal point of many dramatic works.

2. 作者は、歌舞伎座を建てた福地桜痴
—— Written by Fukuchi Ochi, Who Erected the Kabukiza Theatre

作者・福地桜痴は天保12（1841）年に長崎で生まれた。学業優秀で江戸に出て幕府の英語通訳を務め、幕末に二度洋行し、彼の地の舞台芸術に触れている。維新後は政府の役人、新聞記者・議員などを務め、明治22（1889）年に歌舞伎座を建て、九世市川團十郎の活歴物の作者として長く活躍した。時代の変化を間近に見てきた目が、従来の「獅子物」の伝統とは全く異なる、「御殿女中から獅子へ」という斬新な舞踊を書かせたといえるだろう。

The writer Fukuchi Ochi was born in Nagasaki in 1841 and enjoyed an incredibly illustrious career. He was a brilliant student who went on to work as an English interpreter for the Shogun. He traveled abroad twice in the late days of the Tokugawa Shogunate, where he was introduced to western forms of drama. He served as a government official after the Meiji Restoration, as well as chief editor of a newspaper firm. In 1889, Fukuchi erected the Kabukiza Theatre and was the writer of many of Ichikawa Danjuro IX's *katsurekimono* plays. It is easy to see how someone like Fukuchi, who saw the times change with his own eyes, could come up with such an original concept as the plot of this play, which combines such radical elements—palace ladies and wild *shishi* lions.

3. 前半はたおやかな女方
—— The Graceful *onnagata* of the First Half

前半は振袖姿で髪を高島田に結い上げた弥生の舞。九世市川團十郎の初演以来、代々の歌舞伎俳優が磨き上げてきた華麗な振り事が続いていく。宮仕えの娘心を忍ばせた慎ましやかな舞い始めから、端正な舞が続く。二枚扇の振りには、京舞の影響があるといわれる。牡丹を愛でる仕草も美しい。獅子頭を手にしてからはテンポが速まり、獅子頭に引きずられて花道を入る姿は圧巻だ。

The first half of this play shows a graceful *onnagata* performance, the lady Yayoi donning a *furisode* robe and sporting a *shimada* hairstyle. There are many highlights in this performance, including the solemn opening dance, the *kawasaki*-style *teodori*, and gestures depicting a person looking up to the magnificent Mt. Fuji. The portion of the dance that uses two folding fans is said to have been influenced by the *kyomai* style of buyo. The charming depiction of a maiden admiring peonies is yet another highlight. When Yayoi touches the *shishigashira* mask, the tempo finally speeds up as she is pulled off stage in a magnificent exit.

4. 後半は獅子の精に大変身
—— The Wild *Shishi* Lion of the Second Half

前半の女方の舞と、後半の勇壮な踊りのコントラストが見どころである。牡丹に戯れる胡蝶の精の可愛らしい舞の合間に、美しい女方を演じていた俳優が衣裳を替え、隈取を施し、長い毛の頭を被って獅子の精となって再び現れる。初めての観客にはとても信じがたい変身であろう。牡丹咲き乱れる二畳台に座した姿は王の佇まい。台を上り下りする仕草は威圧感がある。大迫力の毛振りは劇場全体を圧倒し尽くす。

One of the biggest highlights of this show is the startling contrast between the first and second half. During the interlude when Kocho the butterfly spirit plays among the peonies, the actor who had been performing Yayoi's graceful *onnagata* changes off-stage, reappearing with the long mane of the fearsome *Shishi* lion. The transformation is so startling that first-time viewers may have trouble believing it's really the same actor. The actor, now possessed by the *Shishi* spirit, sits in a kingly posture among the peonies on a small platform. His movements off of and back onto the platform are said to mimic the aggressive movements of a bear. His great *keburi* (a flinging motion of his great mane) is an absolutely overwhelming feat that you can't miss.

船弁慶
Funa Benkei

『船弁慶』
2009年8月　歌舞伎座
(左から) 平知盛の霊 (十八世中村勘三郎)、武蔵坊弁慶 (三代目中村橋之助)

Funa Benkei
(Kabukiza Theatre, August 2009)
(from left) Taira no Tomomori
(Nakamura Kanzaburo XVIII),
Musashibo Benkei (Nakamura
Hashinosuke III)

あらすじ　　　　　　　　Synopsis

旅立つ義経としばしの別れとなる静御前。
そして海上に現れた平知盛の霊、
二役を能仕立てで魅せるその鮮やかさ

都を落ちてゆく義経は愛妾の静御前に別れを告げるが、
悲しみを胸に秘めた静は優雅な舞で一行を見送る。やがて大物浦から船で旅立つ義経主従、
しかし海は俄かに荒波と化し、現れたのは壇ノ浦の海に沈んだ平知盛。
凄まじい形相で襲い掛かる知盛の霊を鎮めたのは、弁慶の祈りの法力だった。

────────── **The lady Shizuka Gozen as she parts from her lover Yoshitsune and the eerie ghost of Taira no Tomomori who appears at sea. These two roles performed by a single actor are truly a sight to behold.**

Yoshitsune flees the capital with his concubine Shizuka Gozen, but they must part ways now. Shizuka sees her lover and his retinue off with a graceful dance. As Yoshitsune and his men depart from Daimotsu Bay, the spirit of Taira no Tomomori, who died at the Battle of Dannoura, rises up from the sea. The enraged spirit attacks Yoshitsune's party, but Benkei expels him by praying in earnest to the Buddha.

　幕が開くと舞台は松羽目。正面雛壇には、長唄と囃子の連中が居並んでいる。

　武蔵坊弁慶が登場し、源義経が兄・頼朝と不仲になり、都を逃れ九州に向かうことになった次第を語る。ここは摂津国・大物浦で、弁慶は一足先にやってきているのである。
　やがて義経一行が現れる。出迎えた弁慶は、義経に、ここまで同道してきた愛妾・静御前を都に帰すよう進言し、義経は承諾する。
　義経と静御前は盃を交わして別れを惜しむ。弁慶は静に舞を舞って門出を祝うよう勧め、烏帽子を渡す。静は、義経の所望により、その昔堀川御所で歌い舞った、都の名所を歌い込んだ今様を舞う。

　　春の曙　しろじろと
　　雪と御室や地主初瀬
　　花の色香にひかされて

The curtain opens to reveal a *matsubame* stage. On a tiered stage sit the *nagauta* accompaniment.

　Musashibo Benkei appears, explaining that his master Yoshitsune, fleeing from his older brother Yoritomo, is on his way to Kyushu. Benkei has come ahead of his master to Daimotsu Bay in Settsu Province.
　As Yoshitsune and the rest of his men arrive, Benkei speaks with Yoshitsune. His master's concubine Shizuka Gozen has been accompanying them, but Benkei recommends having her return to the capital, which Yoshitsune agrees to.
　Yoshitsune shares a farewell drink with his lover, and Benkei suggests she see them off with a dance, handing her an *eboshi* hat as a memento. At Yoshitsune's request, Shizuka performs a modern dance depicting various places in the capital.

　(See Japanese lyrics on left)

船弁慶

盛りを惜しむ諸人が
散るをばいとや嵐山
花も青葉の夏木立
茂り鞍馬の山越えて
泣いて北野の時鳥

ここへ船出の支度が整ったとの知らせ。静は名残を惜しみつつ都に帰り、義経一行は船へ乗り込む。
舟長（ふなおさ）と舟子たちは、舟歌を賑やかに歌い踊る。

やんら目出度や天照す
神の御国は榊葉の
栄えさかゆく秋津洲の
八隅にかがやく　御かがみの
曇らぬ御代の時津風

漕ぎ進むうち、俄かに黒雲が広がり、風が変わり波が高くなってきた。舟長たちは必死に舟を漕ぐが一向に進まない。
その時、弁慶が海上を見ると、源氏に敗れ、壇ノ浦で滅びた平家の一門の亡霊たちの姿が続々と浮かび上がってくる。なかでも、大将であった新中納言平知盛の霊が、義経を共に海に沈めようと長刀を持って襲いかかる。

そもそもこれは
桓武天皇九代の後胤
平知盛幽霊なり
あら珍しや　いかに義経
思いもよらぬ　浦波の

義経一行も少しも臆せず、太刀を抜いて応戦。そのさなか、弁慶が数珠を揉んで一心に祈り始める。
なおも襲いかかる知盛の亡霊だったが、とうとう祈り伏せられ、引く潮と共に波間深くに消えていくのだった。

あらすじ

The boat master informs them that their boat is ready for them. Shizuka returns to the capital with a heavy heart and Yoshitsune boards the boat with his men.

(See Japanese lyrics on left)

As they set out from the bay, black clouds suddenly spread across the sky and the wind picks up. The boatmen struggle to row against the violent waves.
Benkei looks out to sea where he sees the ghosts of the Taira warriors who were killed there at the Battle of Dannoura. Among those ghosts is the enraged spirit of general Taira no Tomomori who strikes out at Yoshitsune with a pole weapon.

(See Japanese lyrics on left)

Yoshitsune unflinchingly draws his sword, ready to fight. Benkei meanwhile pulls out his prayer beads and begins to pray in earnest.
Tomomori is soon expelled by Benkei's prayers, disappearing as the waves calm down.

『船弁慶』
2012年12月　京都南座
源義経（四代目坂田藤十郎）

Funa Benkei
(Kyoto Minamiza Theatre, December 2012)
Minamoto no Yoshitsune (Sakata Tojuro IV)

作品の概要

演目名

船弁慶

作者

作詞＝河竹黙阿弥
作曲＝三世杵屋正治郎

概要

　松羽目物の長唄舞踊の大曲で、新歌舞伎十八番の一つ。本作以前に謡曲『船弁慶』を歌舞伎化する試みとして、幕末に四世中村芝翫が常磐津で、また明治に入って二世杵屋勝三郎が作曲した『勝三郎船辨慶』が作られ、その後、明治18（1885）年に本作が誕生した。原作の能『船弁慶』は、前シテが女性、後シテが武将の怨霊という、まったく異なる人物を演じ分けるところに特徴がある。歌舞伎でもこれを踏襲しているので、前シテ・静御前は、能の女性の装束である唐織（からおり）を着て、化粧も能面に似せ表情を抑えて演じる。後シテ・知盛の化粧は、能面を象った藍隈（あいぐま）で怨霊の凄まじさを表現する。初演には能と同様の船を象徴する作り物（小道具）を用いていたが、やがて使われなくなり、簡潔な身振りとせりふ、迫力ある長唄で船上の争いが描き出されるようになった。花道に出現する知盛の怨霊は荒波の上にいるわけなので、客席は渦巻く瀬戸内の海ということになる。

初演

明治18（1885）年11月東京・新富座で、静と知盛に九世市川團十郎、弁慶に初世市川左團次、義経に八世市川海老蔵、船子三保太夫に四世中村芝翫。作詞は河竹黙阿弥、作曲は三世杵屋正治郎。振付は初世花柳寿輔。

Overview

Title

Funa Benkei

Writer

Lyrics: Kawatake Mokuami
Music: Kineya Shojiro III

Overview

　Funa Benkei is one of *matsubamemono* in the *nagauta* style. A buyo piece in the *tokiwazu* style based on the noh song *Funa Benkei*, this dramatic dance was written by Nakamura Shikan IV at the end of the Edo Period. Another piece entitled *Katsusaburo Funa Benkei* was written by Kineya Katsusaburo II in the Meiji Period. The modern version of *Funa Benkei* was written in 1885. The original noh piece features completely contrasting lead roles (played by the same actor) in the former and latter half, a defining characteristic that the kabuki version keeps. Shizuka Gozen, wearing elegant *karaori* robes, is the lead in the first half, while the enraged ghost of Taira no Tomomori wears ghastly indigo *kumadori* makeup as the lead role of the second half. As in the original noh piece, a *tsukurimono* prop was used at the kabuki debut to represent Yoshitsune's boat, but this tradition soon died out. The dialogue was also shortened over time, and the play came to focus mostly on the battle at sea between Tomomori's ghost and Yoshitsune's party. Tomomori enters through the *hanamichi*, meaning that the audience themselves are the stormy seas upon which Yoshitsune is traveling.

Premiere

November 1885, Shintomiza Theatre. Feat. Ichikawa Danjuro IX as Shizuka and Tomomori, Ichikawa Sadanji I as Benkei, Ichikawa Ebizo XIII as Yoshitsune, and Nakamura Shikan IV as Miho Dayu. Lyrics by Kawatake Mokuami. Music by Kineya Shojiro III. Choreography by Hanayagi Jusuke I.

登場人物 — Characters

静御前
しずかごぜん

源義経の愛妾で、元は都の白拍子なので美しい舞を舞う。義経は兄・頼朝との不仲により京の都を離れ西国へ落ち延びてゆくこととなるが、静も大物浦まで義経に伴ってやって来たものの、これより先に同行はならぬと告げられ義経の所望で別れの舞を舞う。特に京の四季の景色と数々の名所を織り込んだ「都名所」で義経と過ごした楽しい日々を回顧し、形見に烏帽子を賜って去ってゆく。

Shizuka Gozen

Minamoto no Yoshitsune's concubine, Shizuka Gozen is a talented dancer due to her previous experience as a *shirabyoshi* dancer in the capital. Though she accompanies Yoshitsune as far as Daimotsu Bay as he flees the capital and his older brother Yoritomo, he tells her that he must make the rest of his journey into exile alone. At Yoshitsune's request, she performs a farewell dance depicting famous locations about the capital that remind the two of their time together there. She receives an *eboshi* hat to remember her lover by before leaving him to journey on alone.

源義経
みなもとのよしつね

歴史的にもまた歌舞伎のヒーローとしてもとりわけ人気の高い源氏の武将。平家との合戦で功を立てながらも兄の頼朝から疎まれ、都を落ちて旅を続ける悲劇の姿が人々の心に焼き付いている。愛妾の静御前と別れ九州方面を目指して船出するが、海上に現れた平知盛の霊に襲われ、しかし「そのとき義経すこしも騒がず」と太刀を抜き毅然と立ち向かう。その窮地を武蔵坊弁慶が救う。

Minamoto no Yoshitsune

A hero both in history and in the kabuki tradition, Minamoto general Yoshitsune is an incredibly popular character. Though he was pivotal in the war against the Taira clan, he falls out of favor with his older brother Yoritomo after the war and is forced to flee the capital. In this play, Yoshitsune travels west from the capital with his concubine Shizuka Gozen, but is attacked by the spirit of Taira no Tomomori as he boards a ferry headed for Kyushu. The brave Yoshitsune draws his sword without flinching and is saved by his faithful servant Benkei.

亀井六郎・片岡八郎・伊勢三郎・駿河次郎
かめいのろくろう・かたおかはちろう・いせのさぶろう・するがのじろう

源義経が登場する数々の芝居、その場面に必ず従っている家臣たちで、芝居の上では四人が決まりとされ「四天王」と呼ばれる。実在の家臣の名から取られているが、人物像等は必ずしも史実通りではなく、各役もさほど個性的には描かれていない。

Kamei no Rokuro / Kataoka Hachiro / Ise no Saburo / Suruga no Jiro

Yoshitsune's four faithful retainers appear in many plays featuring the famous hero. They are known as *shitenno* ("four heavenly kings"), and though their names were taken from Yoshitsune's historical retainers, their personalities are not given much individuality in the play.

平知盛の霊
たいらのとももりのれい

平知盛は平清盛の四男で平家の中でもとりわけ優れた武将だが、壇ノ浦の合戦で義経の軍勢に敗れ入水している。ここでは船出した義経主従に亡霊となって襲い掛かり一行を苦しめるが、武蔵坊弁慶の懸命な祈りにより退散を余儀なくされる。その際、薙刀（なぎなた）を担ぎ渦巻のようにぐるぐると回転しながらの花道の引っ込みが圧巻。この役は静御前と同じ俳優が二役で勤めるのが決まりである。

Ghost of Taira no Tomomori

The fourth son of Taira no Kiyomori, Tomomori was a particularly accomplished warrior in his time. He drowned together with Emperor Antoku after losing to Yoshitsune's men at the Battle of Dannoura. His ghost attacks the boat that Yoshitsune and his servant are taking into exile but is expelled by Musashibo Benkei's earnest prayers. Tomomori's exit along the *hanamichi* is a spectacular moment in the show. He spins round and round with a great halberd in hand before disappearing beyond the *hanamichi*.

武蔵坊弁慶
むさしぼうべんけい

源義経の家臣の中でもひときわ武勇優れた豪傑として知られるが、ここでは大物浦からの船出に静御前を連れてゆこうとする義経を諌め、静を都へ帰すように諭す。そして船の用意をさせ天候をうかがいながら船出をするが、海上には思いもよらぬ知盛の亡霊の出現。船上の一行に激しく襲い掛かる霊に向かい、弁慶は数珠を懸命に揉み上げて仏の法力によって見事これを退散させた。

Musashibo Benkei

Benkei is known among Yoshitsune's retainers for his unparalleled loyalty and military prowess. In this play, he advises Yoshitsune against taking his concubine Shizuka Gozen along with him on his dangerous journey, leading his master to part with her at Daimotsu Bay. He proceeds to procure a boat to take them to Kyushu, but they are attacked by the spirit of Taira no Tomomori as they depart. Benkei uses his prayer beads to invoke the power of Buddha, expelling the spirit in spectacular fashion.

三保太夫
みほだゆう

大物浦の舟長（ふなおさ）で、弁慶とは旧知。義経一行のため快く船を手配し、天候をうかがいながら船出の時を計る。そしていよいよ船出をと義経一行を促す。

Miho Dayu

The boatman of Daimotsu Bay and an old friend of Benkei's, Miho Dayu happily prepares a boat for Yoshitsune and his men to ride in, making sure to watch the weather before seeing them off from the bay.

みどころ
Highlights

1. 能の『船弁慶』
── The Noh Version of Funa Benkei

原作の能『船弁慶』はほぼ同じ構成で、前シテの静御前と、後シテの知盛の怨霊を一人の俳優が演じる。前半は優美な唐織装束の静御前、後には凄まじい知盛の怨霊で、静と動の落差を見どころにするところを歌舞伎はそのまま受け継いでいる。能では、弁慶はワキ方が勤め、船頭は狂言方が勤める。大きな違いは、能では義経を高貴な存在として子方が勤めること。歌舞伎では子役としないので、静御前との別れの悲しみが印象深い。

The kabuki version of *Funa Benkei* is structured similarly to the noh version. The first half features Shizuka Gozen as the lead, while the latter half features the ghost of Tomomori as the lead. The drastic contrast between the elegant dance and costume of Shizuka and the ghastly Tomomori is one of the biggest highlights of the show, both in the noh and kabuki theatres. In noh, Benkei is played by a *wakikata* actor while the boatman is played by a *kyogenkata* actor. One of the biggest differences that can be seen in the noh version is that Yoshitsune is played by a *kokata* (child) actor. In the kabuki version, he is not portrayed as a child, making the sadness of his parting from Shizuka much more endearing.

2. 悲しみの舞の艶やかさ
── A Melancholy Yet Captivating Dance

前半の見どころは、静御前の優美さ。能装束由来の唐織の衣裳で、能面を意識した化粧で感情を殺した表現になっている。時代物の『義経千本桜』にも都落ちする義経と静御前の別れの場面があるが、『千本桜』の静が別れがたい気持ちをストレートに表現するのに較べると、『船弁慶』の静はとても大人しく、悲しみの表情も控えめだ。しかし別れに際し、二人の思い出深い都名所を綴る静の舞には、胸が切なくなるような華やぎがある。

Shizuka's elegant performance is the highlight of the first half. Her *karaori* robes are patterned after noh costumes and her makeup, meant to show a stoic expression void of sentiment, is also meant to resemble a noh mask. The historical play *Yoshitsune and the Thousand Cherry Trees* also shows the parting of Shizuka and Yoshitsune, but their depictions of Shizuka are very different. In *The Thousand Cherry Trees*, Shizuka wears her emotions on her sleeves, while in *Funa Benkei* she shows restraint, refusing to let her emotions show in her expression. Regardless of this, her farewell dance, which depicts the many places in the capital where the two went together, is sure to pull at the audience's heartstrings.

3. 海に浮かび上がる怨霊
── A Ghost Out of the Sea

能では白い輪のような作物(つくりもの＝小道具)の船を象徴的に出し、それに一行が乗る。歌舞伎でも最初は同様にしていたが、現在では船を表す道具は使われない。船出は動きで表現し、賑やかな船子たちの踊りが、前半の静と後半の動の合間をつなぐ。荒れる海は大薩摩と囃子が表現。知盛の怨霊が、薙刀を両肩に担いでくるくる回る幕外の引っ込みが見どころ。渦巻く海の波に浮かぶ怨霊の恐ろしさがリアルに伝わってくる。

In the noh version, a white wheel-shaped *tsukurimono* is used to represent the boat that Yoshitsune and his men board. In the kabuki theatre a similar stage prop was used, but modern productions no longer use a prop to depict the boat. Instead, the actors' movements show that they are on a boat in a portion of the dance that connects the former and latter halves of the play. Meanwhile, the *hayashi* orchestra and *ozatsuma* music are meant to represent the rough seas. One of the biggest highlights of this dance is the ghost of Tomomori's grand exit, spinning back through the curtain with a pole weapon resting on either shoulder.

4. 藍隈(あいぐま)の怨霊
—— The Indigo *Kumadori* of a Ghost

知盛の怨霊には、義経に滅ぼされた平家一門の恨みが凝縮されている。怨霊は黒々とした髪を乱し、隈取は藍隈で、能の知盛の面(おもて)を写してさらに凄みを際立たせている。弁慶たちの必死の祈りに次第に遠ざけられ、怨霊が花道をくるくると回りながら退いていく様には、歌舞伎らしい華やかさもある。だが怨霊を退散させても、義経一行に安堵は訪れないことを、観客は知りつつ見ている。義経の皮肉で哀しい生涯への愛惜の念が「判官びいき」である。

Tomomori's ghost is filled with the Taira clan's rage toward Yoshitsune. The disheveled hair and indigo *kumadori* makeup are meant to resemble the mask of Tomomori used in noh, a truly ghastly image. Though the prayers or Benkei and Yoshitsune's other retainers eventually drive the ghost away, neither Yoshitsune nor his men show any real sense of relief. The irony of being saved yet still doomed to exile is a deeply moving one that is sure to touch viewers of this play.

紅葉狩
Momijigari

『紅葉狩』
2015年9月　歌舞伎座
更科姫実は戸隠山鬼女（七代目市川染五郎）

Momijigari
(Kabukiza Theatre, September 2015)
Princess Sarashina / Female Demon of Mt. Togakushi (Ichikawa Somegoro VII)

あらすじ　　　　　　　　　　　　Synopsis

目にも鮮やかな戸隠山の紅葉。
平維茂は美しい更科姫の宴に招かれるが、
目覚めてみれば眼前には恐ろしい鬼女の姿

平維茂は従者を従えて戸隠山での紅葉狩り。
そこで出逢ったのは更科姫と侍女たちの華やかな一行、維茂は誘われるままに宴を共にする。
睡魔に襲われた維茂が寝入ると、姫は声を荒らげ形相を変えて姿を消す。
その本性は人々から恐れられている戸隠山の鬼女。維茂は名剣・小烏丸を抜いて挑む。

———— The dazzling autumn foliage of Mt. Togakushi. Taira no Koremochi is invited to a party by the beautiful Princess Sarashina, but when he wakes from a drunken slumber, he finds her transformed into an evil demon.

Taira no Koremochi leads his men to Mt. Togakushi to view the autumn foliage, where he meets the beautiful Princess Sarashina, who is accompanied by a number of maids. They are invited to a party, where Koremochi falls into a drunken sleep only to find the princess gone when he awakens. She has transformed into the fearsome demon of Mt. Togakushi, who Koremochi must now face with his famed sword Kogarasumaru.

幕が開くと、正面に大きな松の古木があり、背景は紅葉の山々。秋たけなわの信州戸隠山の体である。そこに長唄、常磐津、竹本が居並び、掛け合いで上演される。

余吾将軍平維茂が、従者の右源太、左源太を率い登場する。
木陰に幔幕を張り巡らせ、紅葉を愛でる一行を見かけ、その姓名を尋ねるが、お忍びの外出なので名を明かすことはできないという答え。これを聞いた維茂は、一行は高位の方々であろうと推量、邪魔をしないように立ち去ろうとする。
その時、幔幕の内から維茂を呼び止める声。声を掛けたのは局や侍女を数多連れた高貴な女性、更科姫であった。姫は、維茂に共に紅葉狩りを楽しもうと誘う。
維茂は女性ばかりの一行でもあり遠慮するが、侍女たちのさらなる勧めに従い、酒宴が始まる。

やがて、侍女の野菊が舞を披露する。主君と共に杯を重ねていた右源太と左源太も、返礼代わりにそれぞれおかしみあ

The curtains open to reveal a great pine tree in the center of the stage, with autumn mountains in the background—a scene depicting Shinshu's Mt. Togakushi in the glory of mid-autumn. *Nagauta*, *tokiwazu*, and *takemoto* accompaniments sit side by side, playing in turns throughout the performance.

Taira no Koremochi appears with his men Ugenta and Sagenta following behind.
They spot a group who are enjoying the view of autumn foliage, but when Koremochi asks their names, they reply that they are traveling in secret and must not reveal themselves. Koremochi leaves them be, believing they must be of high status to be on such a secret journey.
After this, a voice calls to Koremochi from the other side of a curtain. The voice is that of Princess Sarashina, who is accompanied by her maids. The princess invites Koremochi to enjoy the autumn leaves with her.
Seeing that there are only women present, Koremochi politely declines at first, but Princess Sarashina eventually convinces him to drink with them.
One of the ladies named Nogiku begins to dance. As

紅葉狩

ふれる踊りを披露する。

　さらに、姫も、皆の勧めに応じ恥らいながら舞を始め、さらに、二枚の舞扇を手に、艶やかに踊ってみせる。

　舞を楽しむ維茂一行であったが、酔いもあり、いつしか寝入ってしまう。その様子を見た更科姫は、怪しい雰囲気を漂わせ侍女たちを引き連れ足早に立ち去ってしまう。

　さてそこへ現れたのは戸隠山の山神。八幡大神の命により、姫が実は戸隠山の奥に隠れ住む鬼であることを維茂たちに知らせに来たのである。山神は、寝入る維茂たちを起こそうと足拍子を踏み鳴らし踊るが、一行は目を覚まさないため、ついに姿を消してしまう。

　吹き下ろす夜風に目を覚ました維茂は、山神の告げにより姫の正体を知り、後を追って行き、右源太、左源太は恐れおののき一目散に逃げていく。

　やがて維茂が持つ、名剣・小烏丸の威徳により、鬼女の本性を現した更科姫は、維茂に襲いかかる。互いに激しく戦うが、最後は維茂に討たれるのだった。

あらすじ

thanks for their hospitality, Ugenta and Sagenta perform a charming dance of their own.

Finally, the princess gives in to the crowd who insist she dance too. She performs a dazzling dance with two folding fans in hand.

Koremochi and his men become drunk and fall asleep. As soon as Princess Sarashina sees this, she takes on a sinister demeanor and suddenly whisks her attendants away.

Sanjin, the god of Mt. Togakushi then appears to tell Koremochi that the princess is actually the evil demon who lives on the mountain. Sanjin attempts to wake Koremochi by stomping on the ground but gives up when both he and his men refuse to stir.

Finally, a breeze from the mountain wakes Koremochi, who makes the realization that Sarashina is a demon thanks to Sanjin's words to him while he was sleeping. He immediately follows after the demon, but Ugenta and Sagenta flee in fear as soon as they catch sight of her.

Koremochi's mystical sword Kogarasumaru reveals Princess Sarashina's true form, and the demon attacks him. After a fierce battle, Koremochi finally cuts her down once and for all.

『紅葉狩』
2015年9月　歌舞伎座
(左から) 局田毎 (十一代目市川高麗蔵)、更科姫実は戸隠山鬼女 (七代目市川染五郎)

Momijigari
(Kabukiza Theatre, September 2015)
(from left) Tsubone Tagoto (Ichikawa Komazo XI), Princess Sarashina / Female Demon of Mt. Togakushi (Ichikawa Somegoro VII)

作品の概要

演目名

紅葉狩

作者

作詞 = 河竹黙阿弥
作曲 = 鶴沢安太郎（義太夫）
　　　六世岸沢式佐（常磐津）
　　　三世杵屋正治郎（長唄）

概要

　信濃国戸隠山で、若き武将が美しい姫に化けた鬼女に遭遇するロマンチックな舞踊。新歌舞伎十八番の一つ。義太夫、常磐津、長唄の豪華な三方掛け合いは、海外からの観客も見据えた趣向であったといわれ、明治外交の社交場の役割も担った新富で初演された。戸隠鬼女伝説を元にした能の『紅葉狩』を原作とするが松羽目物ではない。紅葉の山々を背景に描き、大道具の松の大樹が置かれた舞台である。時代考証を大切にする活歴物と呼ばれた歴史劇を次々に発表した九世市川團十郎の志向がよくわかる作品で、平維茂の典雅な衣裳などにその考証が顕著である。間狂言となる「山神」は初演は老体であったが、後に少年になった。平成19（2007）年3月には、パリ・オペラ座で更科姫に市川海老蔵、維茂に十二世市川團十郎、山神に二代目市川亀治郎（四代目猿之助）で上演され喝采を浴びた。鬼が姫姿のまま本性を現して凄む場面が西洋の観客を驚かせた。

初演

明治20（1887）年10月東京・新富座で、更科姫が九世市川團十郎、維茂が初世市川左團次、山神が四世中村芝翫。作詞は河竹黙阿弥、作曲は義太夫が鶴沢安太郎、常磐津が六世岸沢式佐、長唄三世杵屋正治郎。振付は九世團十郎。

Overview

Title

Momijigari

Writer

Lyrics: Kawatake Mokuami
Music: Tsruzawa Yasutaro (*gidayu*)
　　　　Kishizawa Shikisa VI (*tokiwazu*)
　　　　Kineya Shojiro III (*nagauta*)

Overview

A romantic buyo play set on Mt. Togashi in Shinano Province, where a young warrior meets with the evil female demon of the mountain disguised as a beautiful princess. *Momijigari* mixes three styles of music (*gidayu*, *tokiwazu*, and *nagauta*), a feature that is said to have made it an appealing play to foreign visitors. It was first performed at the Shintomiza Theatre, a theatre used to entertain foreign diplomats during the Meiji Period (1868–1912). Though based on the noh piece *Momijigari*, the kabuki version is not a *matsubamemono*. A great pine tree stands center-stage, with a mountainous backdrop vivid with autumn foliage. The piece is one that shows off the unique style of Ichikawa Danjuro IX, who wrote many historical *katsurekimono* plays. The elegant robes of Koremochi particularly show Danjuro's attention to historical detail. Sanjin, who appears in the comic interlude (*aikyogen*), was originally performed as an old man, but in recent years this role is performed as a boy. Ichikawa Ebizo, Ichikawa Danjuro XII, and Ichikawa Kamejiro (Ichikawa Ennosuke IV) played Princess Sarashina, Koremochi, and Sanjin in March 2007 to thunderous applause at the Paris Opera House. The audience was enthralled by the unique depiction of the demon in the robes of a princess.

Premiere

October 1887, Shintomiza Theatre. Feat. Ichikawa Danjuro IX as Princess Sarashina, Ichikawa Sadanji I as Koremochi, and Nakamura Shikan IV as Sanjin. Lyrics by Kawatake Mokuami. Music by Tsuruzawa Yasutaro (*gidayu*), Kishizawa Shikisa VI (*tokiwazu*), and Kineya Shojiro III (*nagauta*). Choreography by Danjuro IX.

登場人物 / Characters

更科姫 実は 戸隠山鬼女
さらしなひめ じつは とがくしやまのきじょ

紅葉の鮮やかな信州戸隠山にやって来たのは更科姫、大勢の侍女たちを従え紅葉を愛でながら賑やかに酒宴を催そうとしている。しかし戸隠山には恐ろしい鬼女が棲んでいて夜な夜な人を食うというが、実はこの更科姫こそ、その鬼女である。更科姫は山中で出会った平維茂に声をかけ一緒に宴を楽しむが、維茂が酔って寝入ったすきに正体を現す。しかし維茂の持つ名刀の前に屈するのだった。

Princess Sarashina / Female Demon of Mt. Togakushi

Princess Sarashina mingles with the other maids who have come to enjoy the beautiful autumn leaves on Mt. Togakushi in Shinshu Province. Everyone is oblivious to the fact that she is, in fact, the evil demon that haunts the mountain night after night. Sarashina talks with Taira no Koremochi and the two enjoy the party together for a time. As soon as Koremochi falls into a drunken sleep, however, she transforms into her demon form and attacks Koremochi. In the end, the demon is no match for Koremochi's celebrated sword.

平維茂
たいらのこれもち

平維茂は武勇の誉れ高い平家の武将。美しい紅葉を見物しようと従者を連れて戸隠山へやってくるが、ちょうど出会ったのは艶やかな更科姫の一行。席を共にと誘われるままに宴を楽しみ、酒と余興を満喫する。すっかり酩酊して眠りについた維茂だが、気づいてみれば目の前に現れた恐ろしき形相の鬼女。さては世に聞こえたる戸隠山の鬼女かと立ち向かい、名刀の小烏丸（こがらすまる）で見事これを退治する。

Taira no Koremochi

Taira no Koremochi was an illustrious military leader of the Taira clan. He brings his men with him to Mt. Togakushi to view the autumn foliage. He meets with the gorgeous Princess Sarashina on the way, who invites him to a party on the mountain where they drink and enjoy the entertainment. Koremochi eventually falls into a drunken sleep, but he soon wakes to see a ghastly female demon instead of Sarashina. He faces and defeats the demon of Mt. Togakushi with his celebrated sword, called Kogarasumaru.

山神
さんじん

戸隠山を守護する神である。鬼女に酒を呑まされすっかり寝入ってしまった維茂を救おうと、懸命に足拍子を踏んで起こしにかかるが、なんとしても目を覚まさず、ついに諦めて帰ってしまう。初演時には老練の俳優がこの役を演じていたが、再演時に年若い尾上丑之助（後の六世尾上菊五郎）が演じ、以来今日においても若手俳優によって演じられることが多い役である。

Sanjin

Sanjin is the god who protects Mt. Togakushi. He attempts to wake the drunken Koremochi after he is tricked by the demon, but no matter how much he stomps on the ground, Koremochi will not wake up. He eventually gives up and returns to the mountain. Originally played by an experienced veteran actor, the young Onoe Ushinosuke (later known as Onoe Kikugoro VI) performed at a revival, establishing a new tradition of young actors playing this role.

みどころ
Highlights

1. 長唄、常磐津、義太夫の豪華掛け合い
── *Nagauta, Tokiwazu,* and *Gidayu* ─ a Splendid Medley

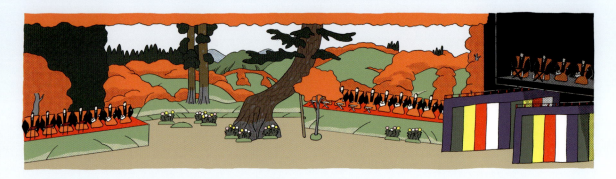

長唄と常磐津、義太夫と地方（じかた）が三方掛け合いで豪華に演奏される。正面に長唄、下手に常磐津、上手に義太夫が居並び、それぞれにパートを分けて演奏する画期的で大変に派手なスタイルである。『紅葉狩』初演は明治20（1887）年東京・新富座。当時ぞくぞくと日本を訪れていた海外からの観客も意識した企画だったといわれている。新富座にはガス灯による照明が導入され、洋装の観客が靴のまま座れるように、椅子席も用意されていた。

This piece features three different styles of music: *nagauta, tokiwazu,* and *gidayu*. The *nagauta* band sits at center stage, while the *tokiwazu* and *gidayu* accompaniments sit to the left and the right, respectively. They each take turns in performing at different parts of the play in a truly extravagant show. It debuted at the Shintomiza Theatre in 1887 and is said to have been written with foreign visitors in mind—a play where one could see the full range of Japanese buyo music. The theatre adopted gas lighting and table seats where guests from abroad could sit without removing their shoes.

2. 美女が鬼になる
── A Beauty Becomes a Demon

『紅葉狩』は西洋のバレエなどにもなりそうなロマンチックな舞踊劇。しかし、美しい姫が実は鬼であった！などというバレエはちょっと思い浮かばない。これがもし女優だったらどうか。魔女ならばともかく、女優が鬼女を演じると、どうにも楽しめないのではなかろうか。にやりと笑って本性を現し、大股で去って行く鬼。凄まじい隈取を施してからの鬼の大きさ凄まじさは、やはり歌舞伎の女方でなくては成立しそうもない。

Momijigari is a romantic piece that one could imagine becoming a ballet piece if it weren't for the twist—a beautiful princess becoming a demon! A woman performing as a fearsome demon might be somewhat difficult, especially in depicting the impressive gait of the demon as she exits the stage. Kabuki *onnagata* actors, however, are quite well-suited to the savage makeup and dreadful presence required for such a performance.

3. 信濃戸隠山の鬼女伝説
—— The Legend of the Female Demon of Mt. Togakushi

戸隠山の鬼女伝説には諸説ある。『紅葉狩』初演前年の明治19（1886）年に、正説を収集したとする実録風の『戸隠山鬼女紅葉退治之伝』が出版されている。それによると奇術を使う美貌の娘・紅葉は、かつて都で源経基の寵愛を受けたが、罪を得て戸隠に押し込められた。戸隠で紅葉は男子を産み、やがて将門の残党をも従え賊徒の首領となったが、33歳で亡ぼされたとか。創作の部分も多いと思われるが、諸説の一つとして読んでみるのも面白い。

There are many versions of the legend of Mt. Togakushi's female demon. In 1886, the year before *Momijigari* debuted, a definitive version of the legend was published, entitled *Togakushiyama Kijo Momiji Taiji no Den*. According to this legend, there was once a beautiful young woman with strange powers who was loved by Minamoto no Tsunemoto but was later imprisoned in Mt. Togakushi for certain crimes. There, she gave birth to a son and later went on to become the leader of bandits who were surviving supporters of Taira no Masakado. She passed away at the age of thirty-three. It is believed that most accounts include fabrications but reading and comparing these stories is in itself quite interesting.

4. 明治32年に映像化
—— At the Time of the Debut

日本最古の映画は明治32（1899）年の『紅葉狩』の舞台を撮影したもので、尺（上映時間）は約6分。歌舞伎座裏の屋外に仮設舞台を作り陽光の下で撮影されている。発明されて日の浅い映画というものを日本に広めるために製作されたが、結果として明治の名優の動く舞台姿を残してくれることとなった。九世市川團十郎の鬼女、五世尾上菊五郎の維茂、丑之助時代の六世菊五郎の山神の配役で、もちろんサイレント。重要文化財に指定されている。

The oldest Japanese film was a 6-minute reel captured in 1889 that showed a portion of *Momijigari*. It was shot at a temporary stage erected outside of the Kabukiza theatre in order to capture the performance in sunlight. Though this film was shot to spread the technology of film around Japan, it ended up becoming an important record of three famous Meiji-period actor's performances. This silent film features Ichikawa Danjuro IX as the demon, Onoe Kikugoro V as Koremochi, and Kikugoro VI (Ushinosuke at the time) as Sanjin. It has been designated as an Important Cultural Property.

『身替座禅』
2014年3月 歌舞伎座
(左から)太郎冠者(三代目中村又五郎)、
玉の井(二代目中村吉右衛門)

Migawari Zazen
(Kabukiza Theatre, March 2014)
(from left) Taro Kaja (Nakamura Matagoro III), Tamanoi (Nakamura Kichiemon II)

あらすじ	# Synopsis

すぐにも逢いたい恋しい花子。
山の神を欺いて出かけたものの、ついには運の尽き。
古今東西・万国共通の恐妻物語

山蔭右京には恋しい花子がいるが、しかし奥方の玉の井は片時もそばを離れようとしない。
そこで仏に詣でるため旅に出たいと計略を案じるが、ようやく一夜限りの座禅が許される。
太郎冠者を身替りにまんまと出かけた右京だが、ほろ酔いで戻ってみれば身替りの身替りは奥方、
その形相は世にも恐ろしい。

━━━━ A husband's less-than-subtle infidelity and his wife's jealous reaction—this universal comedy is sure to delight audiences around the world.

Yamakage Ukyo is enamored by Hanago, but his doting wife can't stand to be away from him.

When he claims he wishes to go on a religious pilgrimage, his wife is reluctant, only allowing him to spend a night alone in Zen meditation. Ukyo decides to have his servant Taro Kaja sit in meditation in his place while he sneaks off to see Hanago. When stumbles home drunk, he is shocked to find his livid wife in Taro's place.

幕が開くと舞台は松羽目。上手に常磐津連中が居並び、前半は常磐津を交え進行する。

ここは都の外れにある山蔭右京の屋敷。

右京は先頃東国に下る途中、美濃国に泊まり、花子という女と深い仲になった。その花子がこの度都に上り、北白川の宿から右京に会いたいと何度も手紙を寄越した。しかし右京には奥方・玉の井があり、片時もそばを離れない。何とかして花子に会いたいと願う右京は一計を案じ、玉の井を呼び寄せる。

玉の井が侍女の千枝と小枝を伴い現れると、右京はこのところ夢見が悪いので仏詣に出かけたいと伝える。しかし、その仏詣が何年もかかると聞き、玉の井が嘆き悲しむので、侍女たちは家の中で行をするように勧める。そこで右京は屋敷の持仏堂に七日七夜籠もっての座禅を申し出るが、玉の井はそれも頑なに拒む。見かねた侍女たちも口を添え、ようやく一晩限りの座禅が許されることとなった。

坐禅堂を覗いてはならぬ、と言う右京に対し、はいと答えながらも、座禅は一夜限りと何度も念を押す玉の井であった。

玉の井と別れると、右京は召使いの太郎冠者を呼び出す。

The curtain opens onto a *matsubame* stage setting. On the right side of the stage sits a *tokiwazu* accompaniment, featured in the first half of the show.

The setting is Yamakage Ukyo's residence, located on the outskirts of the capital.

On his journey to the eastern provinces recently, Ukyo met and had an affair with a girl named Hanago. He has now received several letters from her stating that she is in the area and wishes to meet, but Ukyo has a wife, Tamanoi, who hates to be away from him. Ukyo comes up with a plan to sneak away and meet Hanago and calls Tamanoi to him.

Tamanoi appears with her maids Chieda and Saeda, and Ukyo explains that he wishes to go on a Buddhist pilgrimage to help with nightmares he's been having. Tamanoi is distraught to hear that this pilgrimage will take several years, and her maids suggest that he instead pray from inside their home so that he needn't go away for so long. Ukyo then suggests that he be left alone for seven days to practice meditation at the Buddhist altar in their home, but Tamanoi rejects this idea as well. The maids echo her sentiments and finally, Ukyo is allowed one night alone to meditate.

Ukyo warns Tamanoi not to enter the altar room while he is meditating, but Tamanoi reminds him that it is only for

もし玉の井が持仏堂を覗いた時のために、自らの身替りに座禅をさせようというのである。

玉の井の怒りを恐れ承知をしない太郎冠者だったが、ついに座禅衾を頭から被り、身替りを勤めることにする。右京は、決して衾を取ってはならぬと言いおき、急いで花子の元へ向かう。

一方夫の様子を案じる玉の井は、坐禅堂を覗き、さらに見舞いと称し侍女たちを引き連れやってくる。驚いた太郎冠者は無言で応対するが、せめて顔だけでも見せてくれと、衾を剥ぎ取られてしまう。玉の井から問い詰められた太郎冠者は右京の企てを白状。謀られたと知った玉の井は怒り、右京を懲らしめるため太郎冠者の代わりに衾をかぶり、右京の帰りを待つことにする。

ここから長唄と囃子が加わり、後半の舞台が展開する。

明け方も近くなる頃、花子と過ごした右京が、花子の小袖を羽織りほろ酔い加減で持仏堂に帰ってくる。衾の中にいるのが太郎冠者だと思い込んでいる右京は、玉の井の前で花子との逢瀬の様子を語り始める。

花子と過ごした甘い一夜の一部始終を語り終え、さらに玉の井の顔の様子までこき下ろし、満足した右京が無理に衾を剥ぎ取ると、そこにいたのは恐ろしい形相の玉の井。

口からでまかせを言って取り繕い、その場を逃げ出そうとする右京を、玉の井が追いかけて行くうちに幕が閉まる。

one night.

When Tamanoi leaves him, Ukyo calls his servant Taro Kaja and asks him to sit in meditation in his place, just in case his wife comes snooping.

Taro Kaja is hesitant at first, fearing Tamanoi's wrath, but eventually, he is convinced to wear a meditation mat over his head so that his face can't be seen. Warning Taro not to remove the mat while he is away, Ukyo leaves to see Hanago.

Tamanoi becomes anxious and decides to check in on her husband, taking her maids with her. Shocked, Taro remains completely silent, but Tamanoi insists on seeing her husband's face, removing the meditation mat. Interrogated by Tamanoi, Taro fesses up to Ukyo's schemes. Tamanoi is livid to hear that her husband has gone to such lengths to deceive her and decides to take up Taro's place and wait for him to return.

The second half of the show continues with a *nagauta* accompaniment.

Ukyo returns in the early morning, somewhat tipsy. Believing it is Taro under the meditation mat, he talks all about his night with Hanako.

Ukyo caps his story by bad-mouthing his poor wife, then removes the meditation mat to find his wife who is absolutely livid.

Ukyo scrambles to make up some excuse and run away, but Tamanoi chases after him and the show ends.

作品の概要

演目名

身替座禅

作者

作詞＝岡村柿紅
作曲＝七世岸沢式佐（常磐津）
　　　五世杵屋巳太郎（長唄）

概要

　浮気男が妻に懲らしめられるという喜劇舞踊。狂言の大曲『花子（はなご）』を原作とする常磐津・長唄掛合いの松羽目物で、陽気な喜劇だが品格があり、新古演劇十種の一つに選ばれている。恐妻家の夫・山蔭右京だが、旅先の美濃で花子という女性と良い仲となり、花子がはるばる都の近くまで訪ねてきて度々右京に恋文を寄越す。なんとも風雅な設定である。右京は無理に召使を座禅の身替りにし、一夜花子の元へ。浮かれて朝帰りする右京は、座禅衾を被った妻を召使だと思い込み、あれこれ惚気話をしてしまう。狂言『花子』は、惚気話を小歌仕立てで聞かせるせりふに大変な技巧を要するが、歌舞伎では話の中の右京と花子の踊り分けが眼目になる。『身替座禅』が初演された明治43（1910）年は、1月には新富座が松竹傘下に入ったものの5月まで歌舞伎興行は実現せず、歌舞伎座は2、3月とも休場中。市村座3月の若手の菊五郎、吉右衛門の舞台に注目が集まったことだろう。

初演

明治43（1910）年3月東京・市村座で、山蔭右京に六世尾上菊五郎、奥方に七世坂東三津五郎、太郎冠者に初世中村吉右衛門。作詞は岡村柿紅、作曲は常磐津が七世岸沢式佐（六世岸沢古式部）、長唄が五世杵屋巳太郎。

Overview

Title

Migawari Zazen

Writer

Lyrics: Okamura Shiko
Music: Kishizawa Shikisa VII (*tokiwazu*)
　　　Kineya Mitaro V (*nagauta*)

Overview

　This comic buyo is about an unfaithful man punished by his wife. *Migawari Zazen* is a *matsubame-mono* based on the *kyogen* play *Hanago*. Though a comedy, there is something elegant to the story of Yamakage Ukyo, a married man who receives a love letter from his lover, Hanago. Ukyo decides to have his servant to meditate in his place as he sneaks off to see Hanago. When he returns in the early morning, he finds his wife in Taro's place, but only realizes this after he has drunkenly recounted his night's adventures. The original *kyogen* play *Hanago* requires great finesse in the delivery of the lyrics, while the kabuki version focuses more on Ukyo and Hanago's dance. In 1910, the year *Migawari Zazen* debuted, Shintomiza Theatre had just come under Shochiku's ownership but did not begin showing kabuki plays until May, while Kabukiza was temporarily closed for February and March of that year. The highly anticipated play was therefore perfomed at Ichimuraza Theatre and featured the young Kikugoro and Kichiemon.

Premiere

March 1910, Ichimuraza Theatre. Feat. Onoe Kikugoro VI as Yamakage Ukyo, Bando Mitsugoro VII as Tamanoi, and Nakamura Kichiemon I as Taro Kaja. Lyrics by Okamura Shiko. Music by Kishizawa Shikisa VII (*tokiwazu*) and Kineya Mitaro V (*nagauta*).

登場人物   Characters

山蔭右京
やまかげうきょう

京の都あたりのお屋敷に住む大名。かねてより懇意にしている遊女の花子（はなご）から手紙をもらい、今すぐにでも駆け付けたいが問題なのは人一倍情の深い奥方。ようやく太郎冠者を身替りにして花子のもとへ。ほろ酔い機嫌で帰り、楽しかったひと夜の顛末そして奥方の悪口を散々言った挙句、被り物を取ればそこにいたのは奥方。まさしく万国共通、いつでもどこでも人気の衰えない癒しの主人公。

Yamakage Ukyo

A daimyo lord living in a mansion close to the capital, Ukyo receives a love letter from his courtesan lover Hanago one day. Though he would like to leave immediately to see her, his touchy wife would surely be suspicious. Ukyo decides to dress his servant Taro Kaja in his robes so he can slip away without his wife's knowing. He returns late at night feeling rather tipsy and begins to tell Taro all about his night, including how he bad-mouthed his wife to Hanago. When he looks under Taro's disguise, however, he finds his wife! Ukyo is an archetypical role whose antics are sure to raise laughs from audiences around the world.

玉の井
たまのい

山蔭右京の奥方で「山の神」と呼ばれる。山蔭右京が恐妻家、この奥方・玉の井はいかにも恐ろしい鬼嫁……と思われがちだが、とりわけ情が深く片時も離れていられないという一途な女性であろう。しかし嘘をつかれて騙され、さらに自らの悪口を散々言われた悔しさが怒りとなって表れ、最後は恐ろしい形相となる。この役は立役が演じることが多いが、最初から怖い女性ではないはず。

Tamanoi

Ukyo's wife, also knowns as "*yama no kami*" or "god of the mountain," Tamanoi may be seen as a fiercely jealous wife who has her husband under her thumb. In reality, however, she is a deeply loving and faithful wife who cannot stand to be away from her husband. Despite herself, she is driven to jealousy and anger when her husband makes a fool of her and runs off to see another woman. This role is often played by a *tachiyaku* leading man, and she is not meant to be portrayed simply as an angry woman from the very beginning.

太郎冠者
たろうかじゃ

冠者というのは本来成人した男子を指すが、主に武士などに仕える従者で、太郎という名から使用人の筆頭格という場合が多い（次席は次郎冠者）。この演目でも主人の言いつけには逆らえぬ従順な下僕として描かれ、命令通り被り物をするが、奥方との間に挟まれていよいよ立場なし。一方、太郎冠者にも紅梅という馴染みの女性がいるというので、このあたりはほのぼのと風が通る。

Taro Kaja

The word "*kaja*" refers to a young man who has come of age, specifically one who serves a samurai. "*Taro*," meanwhile, often expresses rank (the next title being "*jiro*"). He is depicted as a faithful servant who simply does as he is commanded, wearing his master's headdress to fool Ukyo's wife. The drama between husband and wife takes center stage, however, making him a very minor role. His connection to a geisha named Kobai, however, adds a little bit of color to him.

千枝 小枝
ちえだ さえだ

奥方玉の井に仕える、いずれも忠実な侍女たち。きびきびとし毅然とした動きは、人間味と個性あふれる人たちの中で一服の清涼剤ともなる登場人物。

Chieda, Saeda

Tamanoi's faithful maids, Chieda and Saeda both move with a refreshing combination of energy, purpose, and individuality.

みどころ
Highlights

1. 山蔭右京の衣裳 —— Yamakage Ukyo's Costume

狂言由来の、白地紅葉柄の厚板（あついた）に、浅葱色龍紋に薬玉柄の長素袍（ながすおう）。素袍は略式正装。右京は戻りには、花子から贈られた黒地に枝垂桜を華やかに刺繍した小袖を片身に重ね着し有頂天で帰ってくる。

Ukyo's wears a white *atsuita* robe with an autumn foliage pattern over a light-blue *nagasuo* with a decorative *kusadama* pattern (a *suo* is a relatively informal outfit). He returns from his night out wearing a black *kosode* with an embroidered *shidarezakura* pattern he received from his lover Hanago.

2. きのどくな召使、太郎冠者 —— Taro Kaja—the Pitiful Servant

一番可哀想なのは、ご主人様の身替りに座禅をさせられる太郎冠者である。ご主人様からは刃を向けられて身替りを承諾させられている。ご主人様のお供をした折に、自身も花子の召使いの紅梅といい仲になったいきさつもあるので、つい片棒を担いでしまう。しかし怒りくるった奥様に責め立てられると、ご主人の行く先を白状してしまう。召使い物のコメディーに定番の、賢い悪巧みなどはできない、実に気の毒な太郎冠者なのだ。

The most sympathetic character of this play is Taro Kaja, the servant who is forced to sit in meditation in place of his master, a ploy to fool his wife. He truly has no choice but to obey his master, especially considering his relationship with Kobai, Hanago's servant whom he met while accompanying Ukyo on one of his journeys to the pleasure quarters. When Ukyo's wife finds him, however, she flies into a rage that leaves him no choice but to rat out his master. He is the archetypical comical servant, a truly pitiful character who is not clever enough to cover up for his master.

3. 恐妻家コメディー
—— The Comedy of a Henpecked Husband

怖い妻の言いなりになっている気の弱い夫が、妻の目を盗んで浮気して見つかるというストーリーは、万国共通のコメディーのタネだ。結婚した経験があるならば、どの国の人間でも字幕がなくとも、『身替座禅』は理解できる。見終わって、どうしてこんなにも男はずるく、女は容赦がないのかとため息が出るかというと、そうでもない。人は何度懲りても、なかなか性根が直らない生き物なのだと、どの国の人間でもご存じのはずである。

The story of the pushover husband who cheats on his overbearing wife is one used in comedies around the world. Anyone who's been married before is sure to understand *Migawari Zazen* even without subtitles. At first, one might be inclined to wonder how men could be so dishonest, or how women could be so unforgiving, but the ultimate takeaway is the universal truth that humans are incapable of going against their nature.

4. 原作の狂言『花子』には煙草はない
—— No Tobacco in the Noh Version

原作は狂言の『花子（はなご）』で、とても難しい大曲とされる。ストーリーは同じだが、狂言のシテ（夫）のほうが少しずるい性格。歌舞伎では山蔭右京という名前がつき、よりおっとりした人物に造型される。帰りの浮かれた舞や、うっかり奥方に聞かせる惚気にもお人好し感が漂う。ちなみに右京の話では、花子は吸付け煙草を渡してくれたそうだが、これは原作狂言にはない。室町時代には、まだ煙草は日本に渡来していないからだ。

The noh version of this story, *Hanago*, is a rather difficult piece to perform. Though the story is essentially the same, the husband character is shown in a more cunning and dishonest. The name Yamakage Ukyo, as well as the general performance, lends a softer image to the husband in the kabuki version. His lighthearted return home and his fond retelling of the night spent with Hanago show him to be a gentle-hearted man despite his infidelity. He receives tobacco from Hanago in *Migawari Zazen*, which is not part of the original *kyogen* piece. This is because tobacco hadn't come to Japan in the Muromachi Era when it was written.

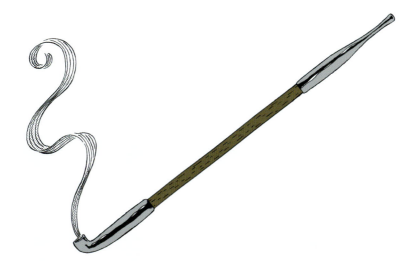

土蜘
Tsuchigumo

『土蜘』
2013年6月 歌舞伎座
僧智籌実は土蜘の精(七代目尾上菊五郎)

Tsuchigumo
(Kabukiza Theatre, June 2013)
Chichu / Tsuchigumo Spirit (Onoe Kikugoro VII)

あらすじ   Synopsis

源頼光の館を訪れた怪しい僧の名は智籌。
映りしその影は人間のものにあらず、
なんと正体は千筋の糸を吐く土蜘

武勇に優れ妖怪退治の誉れ高い源頼光だが、思わぬ病に臥せっている。
そこへ現れたのは智籌と名乗る僧、しかし何やら様子が怪しげ。
そして頼光に近づく智籌の影は人ではなくまさしく土蜘、頼光は名剣・膝丸で斬りつけるが
糸を吐いて姿を消す。能の『土蜘蛛』に材を得た明治期の名作舞踊劇。

———— A suspicious monk named Chichu visits Minamoto no Yorimitsu's residence. His shadow shows him not to be human, but rather Tsuchigumo, the evil spider spirit that weaves a vast web out of a thousand threads.

The great warrior Minamoto no Yorimitsu, known especially for his prowess against monsters, is now sick in bed. The monk Chichu comes to pray over him, but his true identity is made known by his shadow, which does not take a human form. Yorimitsu, sensing danger, immediately draws his blade Hizamaru and strikes at the evil spirit Tsuchigumo, but the spider spews his web and disappears. This celebrated piece of buyo is a Meiji-period work of kabuki based on the noh play *Tsuchigumo*.

舞台は松羽目、正面雛壇には長唄と囃子の連中が居並んでいる。場面は源頼光の館である。

頼光の家臣・平井保昌が登場し、頼光が病で館に引き籠っていることを語る。やがて頼光が登場。保昌は頼光の病が落ち着いているのを見て安堵して控えに戻っていく。

そこに侍女の胡蝶が宮中の典薬頭から賜った薬を持参する。頼光の尋ねに応じ、胡蝶は都の秋の景色とその様子を語りながら舞を舞う。

その名高尾の山紅葉
暮るるもしらで　日暮らしの
滝の名しのぶ　愛宕山
峯は夕日にまばゆきも
麓はくらき小倉山
梢をいとう嵐山
散りて流れて流れて散りて

Stage setting in the *matsubame* style. On a tiered platform sit the *nagauta* singer and accompaniment.
The scene is Minamoto no Yorimitsu's residence.

Hirai Yasumasa, Yorimitsu's retainer, enters and says of his master's bedridden state. Yorimitsu makes his entrance, and Yasumasa, relieved to see that he is feeling better, exits.
The maid Kocho arrives, bearing medicine from the palace. At Yorimitsu's bidding, she performs a dance depicting the beauty of autumn in the capital.

(See Japanese lyrics on left)

『土蜘』
2013年6月　歌舞伎座
（左から）平井保昌（十世坂東三津五郎）、
源頼光（二代目中村吉右衛門）

Tsuchigumo
(Kabukiza Theatre, June 2013)
(from left) Hirai Yasumasa (Bando Mitsugoro X), Minamoto no Yorimitsu (Nakamura Kichiemon II)

土蜘

錦織るちょう　大井川
飽かぬながめの景色かな

やがて夜が更け再び発熱した頼光が床に臥せると、枕元に一人の僧が忽然と現れる。僧は比叡山の僧・智籌と名乗り、頼光の病気平癒の祈禱に来たと語る。そしてこれまでの難行苦行の様子を語り始める。

　　身は雲水の定めなく
　　樹下石上に墨染の
　　衣つゆけき旅の空
　　昨日は法のみちの奥
　　千松島に杖を引き
　　今日は行方も不知火の
　　心筑紫に足を留め
　　降り積む雪に薪水の
　　行を我が身にたくらべて
　　道なき山に分け登り
　　または舟なき川を渡り
　　風に吹かれ　雨に打たれ
　　難行苦行の功積みて

　信頼した頼光が祈禱を依頼し、智籌が傍らに進み出ると、頼光の太刀持ちの音若が、灯影に映る智籌の姿を怪しむ。すると、風も吹かぬのに灯が消えてしまう。その様子から智籌を化生と察した頼光は、名刀の膝丸で斬りつける。智籌は千筋の糸を繰り出し、いずこかへ姿を消してしまう。
　物音を聞きつけた保昌が詰所から駆けつけ、智籌の正体を土蜘の精であろうと推量する。頼光は保昌に退治を命じる。保昌は、智籌の残した血汐を辿りながら、その場を立ち去っていく。

　頼光らが奥へ入ると、間狂言となる。
　館の広庭では、土蜘退治のための供触れがなされた。皆、物の怪を恐れて仮病を使う中、番卒の太郎と次郎は、土蜘退治が成就するよう石神の像に祈ることにする。巫女榊が舞を舞うが、石神の像は実は小姓四郎吾が化けていたものであった。

　やがて舞台には、能の作り物を模した塚が運ばれてくる。東寺近くの、土蜘の精の棲む古塚である。
　保昌はじめ、頼光の四天王たちが登場。軍兵たちが塚を壊すと、中から葛城山で年を経た土蜘の精が現れる。
　土蜘の精は、日本を魔界に変えようとしたが果たせず、大立廻りの末、保昌はじめ四天王に退治されてしまう。

As the night wears on, Yorimitsu returns to bed with a fever. At his bedside there suddenly appears a mysterious monk who claims to be Chichu from Mt. Hiei. He claims to be there to pray for Yorimitsu's recovery and proceeds to tell of his difficult journey.

(See Japanese lyrics on left)

Yorimitsu asks the monk to pray for him, but as Chichu moves toward him, Yorimitsu's sword-bearer Otowaka notices that his shadow has taken a strange form. Just ask Otowaka sees this, the lantern is suddenly put out, though there is no wind. Yorimitsu, guessing that Chichu is hiding his true form, strikes at him with the sword Hizamaru. Chichu then spits out a thousand threads and vanishes suddenly.

Yasumasa rushes in after hearing the commotion and he surmises that Chichu is actually the spider spirit Tsuchigumo. Yorimitsu commands him to go after and kill Tsuchigumo. Yasumasa exits, following a trail of blood left by Tsuchigumo.

Yorimitsu and the others exit, and a comic interlude begins.

An announcement is made in the courtyard about the extermination of Tsuchigumo. As the various servants each feign sickness out of fear of the evil apparition, two sentries named Taro and Jiro pray to a statue of Ishigami (stone god). The shrine maiden Sakaki also offers up a dance to Ishigami, but it is revealed that the statue is, in fact, Kosho Shirogo in disguise.

Finally, a great mound modeled after *tsukurimono* of the noh theatre is brought to the stage. This mound is, in fact, Tsuchigumo's lair.

Yasumasa, following by the *Shitenno*, enter the stage. The warriors destroy the mound, forcing Tsuchigumo to come out.

The evil spirit Tsuchigumo plans to make the entire country into his own personal underworld, but Yasumasa and the *Shitenno* defeat him.

作品の概要

演目名

土蜘

作者

作詞 = 河竹黙阿弥
作曲 = 三世杵屋正治郎

概要

能の『土蜘蛛』が原作の長唄舞踊の大曲。妖しい土蜘退治の物語は、平安時代の源頼光と四天王の世界の伝説として芸能の題材となり、歌舞伎にも複数伝わっている。三世尾上菊五郎三十三回忌追善として五世尾上菊五郎が初演し、新古演劇十種の一つとなっている。前半では病に苦しむ源頼光の寝所に謎の僧が近づくが、影から正体を知られる。後半は四天王が土蜘を退治する。前半では侍女胡蝶の舞、蜘蛛の素性を隠した僧の物語、恐ろしい畜生口の見得などが歌舞伎らしい味わいを見せる。小さな巫女と番卒たちのユーモラスな間狂言も楽しい。一番の見どころは後半の、土蜘と四天王との立ち廻りである。繰り出される千筋の蜘蛛の糸が観客の視界を遮るばかりに広がり、凄まじい印象を残す。蜘蛛の糸については、「千筋之伝」を伝える能楽師から直接指導を受けている。

初演

明治14（1881）年6月東京・新富座で、五世尾上菊五郎の土蜘、初世坂東家橘の頼光、九世市川團十郎の番卒軍内、初世市川左團次の平井保昌、二世尾上菊之助の胡蝶。作詞は河竹黙阿弥、作曲は三世杵屋正治郎。振付は花柳寿輔。

Overview

Title

Tsuchigumo

Writer

Lyrics: Kawatake Mokuami
Music: Kineya Shojiro III

Overview

A *nagauta* buyo piece based on the noh play *Tsuchigumo* (which uses different kanji than the buyo version). The Heian Period legend of Minamoto no Yorimitsu and Four Brave Retainers (*Shitenno*) who defeat the evil spider spirit Tsuchigumo was one that has been adapted to various performance arts, including multiple works in the kabuki theatre. Onoe Kikugoro V played as part of the 33rd Buddhist memorial service of Kikugoro III. In the first half of the play, a mysterious monk approaches the sickbed of Minamoto no Yorimitsu, but his true identity is revealed by his shadow, which shows him to be the spider Tsuchigumo. In the latter half, the *Shitenno* (Four Brave Retainers) chase after and kill Tsuchigumo. The maid Kocho dances in the first half of the play, and the comic interlude between the shrine maiden and the sentries adds some flavor to this otherwise serious show. The *tachimawari* fight between Tsuchigumo and the *Shitenno* is the greatest highlight of *Tsuchigumo*. The vast threads of Tsuchigumo's spider web are sure to hold the audience in awe. The threads of the spider's web are made using a technique called *chisuji-no-den* (secret of the thousand threads), taught by a qualified instructor of noh.

Premiere

June 1881, Shintomiza Theatre. Feat. Onoe Kikugoro V as Tsuchigumo, Bando Kakitsu I as Yorimitsu, Ichikawa Danjuro IX as the sentry, Ichikawa Sadanji I as Hirai Yasumasa, and Onoe Kikunosuke II as Kocho. Lyrics by Kawatake Mokuami. Music by Kineya Shojiro III. Choreography by Hanayagi Jusuke III.

登場人物 / Characters

叡山の僧智籌 実は 土蜘の精
えいざんのそうちちゅう じつは つちぐものせい

比叡山の僧と名乗って源頼光の館にやってくるが、実は土蜘の精。日本全土を我が支配の魔界にせんと企て、頼光を病気にして討とうとしている。夜も更けた頃、頼光の館を訪ね病気平癒の祈禱をするが、太刀持ちの音若に影が怪しいと告げられ正体を見破られる。頼光の名刀膝丸（ひざまる）で斬りつけられ、その血汐の跡から古塚を見つけられて平井保昌や四天王に退治される。智籌の名は別読みの蜘蛛（ちちゅう）に由来する。

Chichu, the Priest from Eizan / Spirit of Tsuchigumo (Earth Spider)

Tsuchigumo comes to Minamoto no Yorimitsu's home claiming to be a priest as part of his schemes to turn all of Japan into his own personal underworld. He attempts to slay the sick Yorimitsu but the sword-bearer Otowaka sees through Tsuchigumo's disguise. With the famed sword Hizamaru, Yorimitsu cuts Tsuchigumo down but fails to stop him from escaping. Hirai Saemonnojo Yasumasa and four warriors known as the *Shitenno*, follow Tsuchigumo's trail of blood to an old tomb where they finally kill him. Notably, the name Chichu derives from a homophone in Japanese that means spider.

源頼光朝臣
みなもとのよりみつあそん

平安時代の武将で父は源満仲（みなもとのみつなか）。大江山酒吞童子（おおえやましゅてんどうじ）など鬼退治の説話にしばしば登場し、頼光を「らいこう」と音読することも多い。ここでは重い病にかかった頼光を様々な人が訪ねてくるが、夜半に見慣れぬ僧が現れて病気を治す祈禱をするという。しかし明かりに映った影は人間のものではなくどうやら物の怪（もののけ）、糸を投げつけるその姿こそまさしく土蜘。すかさず頼光は名刀の膝丸を振りかざす。

Minamoto no Yorimitsu Ason

A military commander of the Heian Period, Minamoto no Yorimitsu's father was Minamoto no Mitsunaka. He appears in the legend of Mt. Oeyama, defeating the evil demon Shuten-doji. His name is sometimes read as "Raiko" instead of Yorimitsu. In this play, Yorimitsu is visited by a number of people concerned about his grave condition, one of whom is a mysterious monk who says he wants to pray for Yorimitsu's recovery. However, the shadow the monk casts is not that of a human but a ghost, revealing his true identity as the evil spirit Tsuchigumo. When Yorimitsu sees this, he hastens to draw his famed sword Hizamaru.

平井左衛門尉保昌
ひらいさえもんのじょうやすまさ

史実をたどれば平安貴族の藤原保昌だが、住んだ土地に因み平井保昌とも呼ばれる。源頼光の武勇伝などにしばしば家臣として登場し、四人の家臣＝四天王とは別の、もう一人の強い武者＝ひとり武者として大江山酒吞童子の鬼退治などにその名を残している。この演目では冒頭に頼光を見舞うが、物音を聞いて駆け付け血汐をたどって土蜘の後を追い、四天王と共に勇敢に戦った末ついに成敗する。

Hirai Saemonnojo Yasumasa

Actually, based on the historical Fujiwara no Yasumasa, this character is also referred to as Hirai Yasumasa, a reference to the region where he lived. He often appears as a retainer in stories of Minamoto no Yorimitsu's military exploits. He is famed as an exceedingly strong warrior on par with the Four Brave Retainers (*Shitenno*). He visits the sick Yorimitsu at the beginning of this play, and later follows Tsuchigumo's trail of blood, eventually defeating the evil spirit with the help of the *Shitenno*.

侍女胡蝶
じじょこちょう

侍女とは貴人に仕える女性。胡蝶は宮廷医療の長官職である典薬頭（てんやくのかみ）からの薬を届けに頼光のもとへとやってくる。そして頼光に所望されて都の紅葉の名所の様子や、高尾、愛宕、小倉、嵐山と名だたる名山名所の美しい景色や風情などを、艶やかな舞に乗せて語り描いてゆく。気落ちしている頼光も自ずと目の前に広がる光景にしばし癒される。やがて胡蝶は薬の用意をと奥へ入ってゆく。

Jijo Kocho

A *jijo* is a maid who serves the nobility. In this play, Kocho arrives to deliver medicine from the court physician to the sick Yorimitsu. While there, Yorimitsu asks her to dance, so she performs a beautiful dance depicting various scenic views including the autumn leaves in the capital and famous mountains such as Takao and Arashiyama. The previously dispirited Yorimitsu is comforted by this spectacle, and Kocho eventually retreats to prepare his medicine.

太刀持音若
たちもちおとわか

頼光の名刀「膝丸」を捧げ持ち、常に側に仕える少年。頼光に近づこうとする智籌の灯に映る影が怪しいと見破り、すかさず注意を促す。その素早い行動は誠にお手柄。

Tachimochi Otowaka

Otowaka is Yorimitsu's young sword-bearer, always at his side with the famed blade Hizamaru. He is the one who sees that the monk Chichu's shadow is that of a specter, and he wastes no time in warning his master. His quick action is a truly remarkable feat that ends up saving Yorimitsu.

四天王
してんのう

渡辺源次綱・坂田主馬之丞公時・碓井靭負之丞貞光・卜部勘解由季武の四人はいずれも武勇優れた頼光の家臣で、仏教の守護神になぞらえ「四天王」と称される。ここでは四人揃って活躍するが、渡辺綱は『戻橋（もどりばし）』『茨木（いばらき）』といった演目で主役の座にあり、坂田公時は幼名時の名が金太郎、足柄山でおとぎ話の主人公にもなっている。碓井貞光は信濃の碓氷峠の出身、公時を見出した人物ともいわれる。卜部季武は頼光の父満仲の家臣・卜部季国の子、渡辺綱により頼光の家臣となる。

Shitenno

These four capable warriors are referred to as *Shitenno* (Four Brave Retainers) after the famed Buddhist guardian deities. In this play, the four appear together, but Watanabe no Genji Tsuna notably appears as the protagonist of *Modoribashi* and *Ibaraki*. Likewise, Sakata no Kintoki's childhood name was Kintaro, making him the protagonist of the famous fairytale of Mt. Ashigarayama. Usui Sadamitsu is said to be from Usui Pass in Shinano Province, where he discovered Kintoki. Lastly, Urabe Suetake was a retainer of Yorimitsu's father Mitsunaka who came to serve Yorimitsu through Watanabe no Tsuna.

登場人物 Characters

番卒（太郎・次郎・藤内）
ばんそつ（たろう・じろう・とうない）

番卒とは見張り番のこと。能の「間狂言（あいきょうげん）」にあたる繋ぎの部分に登場し、コミカルで軽妙な演技でしばし観客を和ませる。

Bansotsu (Taro, Jiro, Tonai)

The word *bansotsu* means "lookout." This character appears in the comic interlude (called "*aikyogen*" in the noh theatre), offering comic relief to the audience with his deft performance.

石神 実は 小姓四郎吾
いしがみ じつは こしょうしろうご

運ばれてきた石神がにわかに踊り出すので番卒たちはびっくり。実は小姓の四郎吾のいたずら。極めて小さい子役が演ずるので、ここは客席もひときわ和む。

Ishigami / Kosho Shirogo

Bansotsu and his retinue are shocked when Ishigami (a stone god that was brought to them) suddenly begins to dance before their very eyes. It is revealed that this is a prank put on by Kosho Shirogo. The role, which is performed by a very small child actor, brings a comic touch to the play to relieve some of the pent-up tension of the plot.

巫女榊
みこさかき

番卒たちと共に、土蜘蛛退治が成就するよう石神の踊りを奉納しようとやってくる。

Miko Sakaki

Miko Sakaki, together with Bansotsu, offers a dance to the stone god Ishigami, praying that Tsuchigumo is defeated.

みどころ
Highlights

1. 土蜘蛛がたとえたもの — A Figurative Term

はるか昔の日本では、大和朝廷に従わない部族を土蜘蛛と呼んだという。地下に巣穴を掘って潜むツチグモにたとえるほどに不気味で恐れられる存在でもあったのだろうか。その伝承が、能や歌舞伎など芸能に今でも残されているのは驚くべきことだ。歌舞伎には本作のほかにも、『蜘蛛の拍子舞』や『関八州繋馬』など蜘蛛が登場する舞踊劇がある。いずれも蜘蛛の精が変化(へんげ)となって、さまざまに害をなし最後は退治される物語だ。

In old Japan, clans who didn't express fealty to the Imperial Court of Yamato were called "Tsuchigumo," or "ground spiders." Thus, such people were likened to spiders who drew their webs on the ground—filthy creatures that were nonetheless to be feared. It is quite surprising that such a term has survived in noh and kabuki. In kabuki alone there are a number of other buyo plays featuring the character Tsuchigumo, including *Kumo no Hyoshimai* and *Kanhasshu Tsunagiuma*. In all these plays, Tsuchigumo goes through a transformation and brings misfortune on other characters but is finally defeated.

2. まき散らされる蜘蛛の糸 — The Sprawling Web of Tsuchigumo

能の場合、繰り出された蜘蛛の糸は舞台からこぼれ落ち橋がかりにも絡まり、凄まじい印象を残す。蜘蛛の糸は昔はもっと太いものだったそうだが、金剛流の金剛唯一が安政2(1855)年に「千筋之伝」の小書(演出)で、現在のような細い糸の工夫をしたという。初演の五世尾上菊五郎は金剛唯一の能を見物する機会を得て、糸の秘伝も直接伝授されて現在の歌舞伎『土蜘』を創造した。『土蜘』と二字表記は宝生流の表記に倣う。

The great spider's web extends from the stage, spilling out over the *hashigakari* in a truly spectacular show. A much thicker thread was used originally, but since Kongo Tadaichi's 1855 production, a finer thread has been used for the "*chisuji no den*" ("tradition of the thousand threads") performance. Onoe Kikugoro V, who starred in the first performance, studied the traditions of Tadaichi's noh to create the kabuki version of *Tsuchigumo*. The two Chinese characters used in the title are based on the *Hosho* school of noh.

3. ツチグモを退治した名刀 — The Celebrated Sword

源頼光(よりみつ)は藤原道長の側近として活躍した人物で、大江山の酒呑童子退治など数々の武勲で名高い。頼光とその家来たちは、江戸時代の芝居や絵本の人気キャラクターとして親しまれた。その頼光が所持する名刀「膝丸(ひざまる)」は「友切」と並ぶ源氏の重宝。罪人を切った折に膝まで切り下げることができたから「膝丸」の名が付けられたと伝わる。ツチグモを退治したので、後に「蜘蛛切(くもきり)」の別名がついたという。

The historical Yorimitsu served at Fujiwara Michinaga's right hand, and he appears in the legend of Mt. Oeyama wherein he defeats the evil demon Shuten-dogi. He and his retainers (knows as the *Shitenno*, "four heavenly kings") are popular characters featured in Heian period dramas and storybooks. Sakata no Kintoki, one of the four retainers, was known as Kintaro (a famous character from a Japanese fairytale) when he was young. The celebrated sword Hizamaru, used to cut Tsuchigumo, was later called "Kumokiri" ("spider cutter").

4. 気配もなく現れる蜘蛛 —— A Spider from the Shadows

蜘蛛の字を音読みするとチチュウだ。頼光の寝所へ近づく僧の名「智籌（ちちゅう）」と通じる。智籌が花道に登場するときには、揚幕を音をさせずに開け、照明も暗いまま。演者は気配を消して出るので、観客が気づいたときにはすでに花道の上に立っていることになる。家の中に蜘蛛を見つけると人間はぞっとする。そんな感じを受ける演出になっている。智籌には、数珠を口に当てて広げる、畜生口と呼ばれる見得がある。

The Chinese characters for *kumo* (spider) can also be read as Chichu, which is the same pronunciation as the mysterious monk's name. When he first enters on the *hanamichi*, the lights are dimmed and the actor makes absolutely no noise when coming through the curtain. When the audience finally sees him there, it is with a sense of disgusted shock, as when one finds a spider in a dark corner of one's house. Chichu touches his prayer beads to his lips in a *mie* pose called *Chikushoguchi*.

棒しばり
Bo Shibari

『棒しばり』
2013年8月 歌舞伎座
次郎冠者（十世坂東三津五郎）

Bo Shibari
(Kabukiza Theatre, August 2013)
Jiro Kaja (Bando Mitsugoro X)

あらすじ　　　　　Synopsis

主人の留守に酒を盗み呑む太郎冠者と次郎冠者。手を縛られるがそれでも巧妙に酒を呑む、その踊りの楽しさは無類

曽根松兵衛は自分の留守中にいつも太郎冠者と次郎冠者が酒を盗み呑むので、この度は次郎冠者の手を棒に縛り、太郎冠者も縛り上げて出かける。しかし懲りぬ二人はまんまと酒を呑み、帰ってきた主人と大立廻り。自由を奪われながらも見事に踊って観客を沸かせる、舞踊の巧みさが見どころとなる演目。

────── **Taro Kaja and Jiro Kaja never miss the opportunity to get drunk in their master's absence, even when their hands are literally tied...**

Sone no Matsubei decides to tie his servants' hands before leaving his residence, knowing of their penchant for drink. Taro and Jiro nonetheless find a way to get their hands on drink, engaging in a drunken *o-tachimawari* brawl when their master returns. Their nimble movements despite their shackles are sure to rouse audiences.

舞台は松羽目。場面は大名曽根松兵衛の館である。

松兵衛が登場し、所用のため外出をするのだが、留守の間、家来の太郎冠者と次郎冠者が酒蔵の酒を盗み呑むのが心配だと語る。

一計を案じた松兵衛は、太郎冠者を呼び出し、次郎冠者を懲らしめる案はないかと尋ねる。これに対し、太郎冠者は、次郎冠者が近頃棒術の稽古をしているので、技を遣って見せる隙に棒に縛り付けてしまおうと答える。これを聞いた松兵衛は、次郎冠者を呼び出し、棒術を見せるように言うが、次郎冠者は見せたがらない。

しかし松兵衛から、自分も舞を見せるのでとまで言われ、次郎冠者は棒の手を見せることを承諾する。

ここで、最初の松羽目がとび、後ろの正面雛壇の長唄囃子連中が姿を現わす。

松兵衛の舞の後、次郎冠者が棒を遣っている隙を窺い棒に縛り付け、さらに太郎冠者も後ろ手に縛り上げると、松兵衛は安堵した様子で出かけていく。

The stage is set in the *matsubame* style. The setting is Daimyo Sone no Matsubei's residence.

Matsubei enters and states that he must go out for business, but is worried that his servants Taro Kaja and Jiro Kaja will drink his *sake* while he is away.

Matsubei calls Taro out and asks him if there is any way that he might punish Jiro. Taro tells him that Jiro has been practicing a pole-based self-defense technique. Matsubei might ask for a demonstration from Jiro then tie his hands to the pole while he is distracted. Matsubei calls for Jiro, but Jiro refuses to show him his pole technique.
Matsubei finally convinces Jiro by offering to dance for him if he cooperates.

The *matsubame* setting flies away and a *nagauta* band appears on a tiered platform on stage.

After Matsubei dances, Jiro begins his demonstration and soon finds his hands tied. While he's at it, Matsubei grabs Taro and likewise ties his hands. He leaves the house now, sure that his servants won't get into any trouble.

Taro and Jiro realize that their master means to keep them from drinking while he is away. The two, however, tied

棒しばり

自分たちが縛られたのは酒を盗まれまいためと悟った二人は、縛られたまま酒蔵に忍び込み、力を合わせて酒を呑み始める。

酔った二人は、酒の肴に互いに舞うことにし、まず、太郎冠者が小舞を舞う。

　御簾のおもかげ　物越しに
　見染め聞きそめ　うかうかと
　いのと思えど後ろ髪
　ほれや恋には身も細り
　二重の帯が　ホヤレホヤレ　三重まわる

ついで、次郎冠者が棒に縛られたまま踊り始める。

　十七八は棹に干した細布
　とるよりゃいとし
　たぐるよりゃいとし
　糸より細い　腰にしむれば
　たんとなおいとし

あらすじ

さらに、太郎冠者の所望に応じ、棒を巧みに操りながら舞を舞う。

　東からげの塩衣
　汲めば月をも袖に持つ
　汐の汀にかえる浪
　夜の翁と見えつるは
　汐曇りにかきまぎれて
　後をもみえずなりにけり

興に乗った二人は連れ舞を始める。

　酒のさの字はよい酒
　よいさの字　様に焦がれて
　ちょっと思いざし　さってもせい
　手まずさえぎる　この盃を指そうか
　押さよか　さってもせい
　今日の肴はなんなんなんの
　鯛や鰹はそりゃよその事
　小唄小舞でさってもせい　さってもせい

二人が上機嫌のところに松兵衛が帰館。怒って二人を追い回すが、これを躱し、詫び言を言いながらその場から逃げ去るうちに幕となる。

up as they are, work together to get to the wine cellar and begin drinking.

Now drunk, the two decide to dance for entertainment. First Taro performs a dance called *komai*.

(See Japanese lyrics on left)

Jiro also begins dancing, though he is still tied to the pole.

(See Japanese lyrics on left)

At Taro's request, Jiro dances using the pole as a prop.

(See Japanese lyrics on left)

Next, the two begin a two-man dance (*tsuremai*).

(See Japanese lyrics on left)

At the height of their festivities, Matsubei suddenly returns. Enraged, he chases after them but has trouble catching them. Taro and Jiro apologize as they run off stage, signaling the end of the show.

『棒しばり』 2015年1月 大阪松竹座 太郎冠者（初代中村壱太郎）
Bo Shibari (Osaka Shochikuza Theatre, January 2015) Taro Kaja (Nakamura Kazutaro I)

作品の概要

演目名

棒しばり

作者

作詞 = 岡村柿紅
作曲 = 五世杵屋巳太郎

概要

　大変わかりやすく楽しい狂言舞踊である。歌舞伎に馴染みのない観客でも十分楽しめる内容となっている。狂言を原作とし、大正年間に松羽目物として初演された、シンプルな作品。留守にすると酒を盗み呑みする召使たちに手を焼いた主（あるじ）が一計を案じる。日頃棒術の鍛錬を自慢しているのに目を付け、次郎冠者に「夜の棒」という暗闇の護身術を見てみたいとおだてる。そして次郎冠者が両手で棒を水平に担ぐ技を見せたところで、その手を棒に縛ってしまい、ついでに太郎冠者も背後から後ろ手に縛る。主は安心して出かけるが、召使たちは工夫してうまい手を思いつき、やはり酒を呑んでしまう。歌舞伎でもほぼストーリーは同じだが、棒術自慢はややあっさり。酒に酔った二人が足で軽快に拍子を取って踊り出すところを膨らませて見せ場にする。棒を汐桶の棒に見立てて『汐汲』の踊りを見せたり、くるくる回って打ち寄せる波を描いたり、リズミカルな踊りに目が奪われる。

初演

大正5（1916）年1月東京・市村座で、次郎冠者は六世尾上菊五郎、太郎冠者は七世坂東三津五郎、大名が初世中村吉右衛門。作詞は岡村柿紅、作曲は五世杵屋巳太郎。

Overview

Title

Bo Shibari

Writer

Lyrics: Okamura Shiko
Music: Kineya Mitaro V

Overview

　A simple, easy-to-understand *kyogen-buyo* piece that even viewers from abroad with little knowledge of kabuki can enjoy, *Bo Shibari* was first performed in the Taisho Era (1912–1926) as a *matsubamemono* based on the original *kyogen* piece. Fed up with his servants' habit of drinking while he is away, Master Matsubei comes up with a plan. He asks Jiro Kaja to perform a self-defense technique called *"yoru no bo,"* knowing that Jiro has been practicing. As Jiro brings out a great pole needed for the technique, however, Matsubei ties his hands to it. He then ties Taro Kaja's hands as well. Matsubei leaves the house without a worry, but while he is gone his ingenious servants find a way to get drunk anyway. The kabuki version is essentially the same as the original *kyogen*, with the two servants jumping nimbly around the stage in their drunken euphoria. Audiences are sure to be captivated by the rhythmical dance of Taro and Jiro, who perform choreography from the play *Shiokumi*.

Premiere

January 1916, Ichimuraza Theatre. Feat. Onoe Kikugoro VI as Jiro Kaja, Bando Mitsugoro VII as Taro Kaja, and Nakamura Kichiemon I as Daimyo Sone no Matsubei. Lyrics by Okamura Shiko. Music by Kineya Mitaro V.

登場人物　　　　　　　　Characters

次郎冠者
じろうかじゃ

主人に仕える従者・召使といった役柄で、通常は先輩格である太郎冠者の次に位置するが、この演目では次郎冠者の方に演技・踊りの仕どころが多いので、こちらが主人公的な立場になる。主人から棒術の「夜の棒」の使い方を所望されるが、隙を突かれて両手を棒に縛られてしまう。それでも酒を呑みたいので、太郎冠者と協力し合って奇想天外な方法で鮮やかに酒を呑み、戻った主人にも酔った勢いで歯向かう。

Jiro Kaja

One of Sone no Matsubei's servants, Jiro Kaja's rank is technically below Taro's, but his performance is the main attraction, making him somewhat like the protagonist of this piece. His master requests that he perform a pole technique called "yoru no bo," but as he reaches for the pole Matsubei ties his hands to the pole to keep him from drinking. Jiro and Taro, however, will not be kept from their drink. The duo put their heads together and come up with a brilliant yet rather bizarre plan to get drunk despite not having free use of their hands. When Matsubei returns, the two, having thwarted their master, drunkenly mock him.

太郎冠者
たろうかじゃ

狂言舞踊における典型的な従者の役で、相方の次郎冠者と共に軽妙な舞台で笑いを誘う。二人は主人の留守にいつも酒を盗み呑むのでついに主人から諫められ、次郎冠者は両手を棒に、太郎冠者は後ろ手に縛られてしまう。それでも工夫を凝らして酒蔵の鍵を開け、次郎冠者と交互に酒を呑んでみせる。やがて興に乗って踊り出し、酔いつぶれた頃に主人が戻ってくるが、主人は呆れるやら怒るやら……。

Taro Kaja

A typical jusha (servant/follower) role in kyogen-buyo, the antics of Taro and his partner Jiro never fail to bring a smile to audiences. Taro and Jiro have a habit of drinking when their master is away, but this time he decides to tie his servants' hands to a pole to keep them from getting drunk. Despite this, the duo masterfully find ways around their handicap to open the wine cellar and get drunk anyway. As Taro and Jiro revel in their drunkenness, their master returns but it is difficult to say whether he is more dumbfounded or angry at the state he finds them in…

曽根松兵衛
そねのまつべえ

いずれかの領地を所有する主人。自分が所用で出掛けるたびに太郎冠者と次郎冠者が蔵の酒を盗み呑んでしまうので、一計を案じ二人の手を縛り上げて出掛ける。しかし帰ってみると二人とも酒を呑み酔いつぶれている。曽根松兵衛という役名は菅原道真の手植えとされる「曽根の松」に由来するが、播磨の国の曽根天満宮にあり、この役を初演した初世中村吉右衛門の屋号・播磨屋に因んだと思われる。

Sone no Matsubei

An eminent land-owner whom Taro and Jiro serve. He is aware of his servants' tendency to drink when he is away, so he ties their hands to a pole before leaving one day. He is surprised to find when he returns that they have found a way to get drunk anyway. It is said that the role of Sone no Matsubei is derived from the pine (matsu) tree that Sugawara no Michizane planted at Sone Tenmangu in Harima Province. The stage name of Nakamura Kichiemon I—Harimaya—is said to have influenced the character's name due to its affinity to Harima Province.

みどころ
Highlights

1. 縛られたまま、後ろ向きに回る妙技
—— Tied up and Backward-facing

原作の狂言『棒縛』は歌舞伎とほぼ同様の内容。次郎冠者と太郎冠者が不自由な身体の手先と口先を器用に使って蔵を開け、扇を杯（さかずき）として酒を呑むのも狂言の着想だ。しかし酔った二人が浮かれて調子よく扇を投げてふざける場面などは、歌舞伎ならではの楽しさがあふれる。次郎冠者が棒に縛られたまま後ろ向きでくるくると回るところなどはとても技倆が必要で、見どころである。

Both the *kyogen* and kabuki versions depict the same basic plot. Jiro and Taro are tied up but cunningly find their way to the wine cellar and use folding fans as cups to get drunk. It is only in the kabuki version, however, that you see the drunken duo romp about the stage, throwing their fans about. Jiro's role, particularly his drunken, backward-facing walk along the *hanamichi*, demands an especially skilled dancer.

2. 踊りのうまい演者の手を縛る
—— Tying the Hands of a Skilled Dancer

初演した六世尾上菊五郎と七世坂東三津五郎は、踊りの名手として伝説的な俳優である。初演の大正5（1916）年1月は六世が30才、七世が33歳で、若手としてまさに張り切っていた頃だ。その二人の手を縛り上げ、動きを封じたらどうなるかが見どころだったのだ。昭和から平成にかけて『棒しばり』を八回も演じた十八世中村勘三郎と十世坂東三津五郎は、それぞれ六世菊五郎の孫、七世三津五郎の曽孫である。

Both Onoe Kikugoro VI and Bando Mitsugoro VII were famous for their superb dancing when they appeared in the debut performance of *Bo Shibari*. Thirty and thirty-three years old at the time (January 1916), both were at their prime and everyone was looking forward to what would happen when the theatres best dancers were tied up. Nakamura Kanzaburo XVIII (Kikugoro VI's grandson) and Bando Mitsugoro X (VII's great-grandson) famously performed *Bo Shibari* a total of eight times from the Showa through the Heisei eras of Japan.

3. 冠者は、もと冠を被った青年のこと
—— Kaja—A Young Man

狂言には身勝手な主人と、小ずるい召使が知恵比べする作品が多い。『棒縛』と同様に、留守番する太郎冠者たちが主人の砂糖を食べてしまう狂言に『附子（ぶす）』がある。主人が酒を猛毒の附子と偽ったので、死のうと思って呑んだと言い訳する。『附子』は教科書にも掲載されたので、「冠者」という言葉を覚えている方も多いのではないだろうか。元服した青年を指す言葉の冠者（かんじゃ）が訛って「かじゃ」。それが若い召使を指す言葉となった。

Many *kyogen* plays depict the relationship between a selfish master and a clever servant. The *kyogen* play *Busu* shows Taro Kaja eating the sugar while his master is away. When he must explain himself, he cleverly claims that he thought it was *busu* poison and that he had meant to kill himself. This play is in Japanese textbooks, so Japanese viewers may be familiar with the term "*kaja*"—a colloquial version of *kanja*, or a young man who has gone through his coming-of-age ceremony. The word eventually came simply to refer to a young man.

扇は日本の発明
—— Folding Fans—A Japanese Invention

団扇（うちわ）は中国伝来の品物だが、扇（おうぎ）は日本の発明なのをご存じだろうか。古代に文字を書いた木簡（もっかん）の片端を綴じて扇形に広げ、風を送ったのが始まりと言われる。平安朝の女性が手にしていた檜扇（ひおうぎ）が古い形を残している。竹と紙で作り、畳めるようにした扇は実にコンパクトな日本の発明品。狂言や舞踊、落語などで扇は杯のほか、お銚子、箸や煙管（キセル）などをさまざまに表す欠かせない小道具である。

Uchiwa fans are from China, but *ogi* folding fans are a Japanese invention. It is said to have been created by tying ancient *mokkan* (strips of wood used for record-keeping) together and fanning them out. Fans used by Heian-period court ladies, called *hiogi*, have survived to the present day. These unique fans made of bamboo or paper are capable of folding into a very compact form—what an ingenious Japanese invention!

二人椀久
Ninin Wankyu

『二人椀久』
2013年12月　京都南座
椀久（六代目片岡愛之助）

Ninin Wankyu
(Kyoto Minamiza Theatre, December 2013)
Wankyu (Kataoka Ainosuke VI)

あらすじ　　　　　　　　　Synopsis

椀屋久兵衛すなわち「椀久」。
恋しい松山に逢えたのは夢か幻か……
やがて消えゆくその姿、残るのは儚さのみ

豪商の椀屋久兵衛は大坂新町の遊女・松山に入れ上げ、放蕩の末に閉じ込められる。
しかしいつしか抜け出した椀久が彷徨い歩くうち、遭遇したのは恋焦がれる松山。
懐かしい桜の花の下で過ぎし日の楽しい思い出と共に舞うが、次第に姿は消えてゆく。
残された椀久は打ちひしがれるばかり。

Wanya Kyubei, otherwise known as Wankyu. Was it a dream or an illusion that he saw... The visage of his dear Matsuyama who left behind only emptiness.

Wanya Kyubei, the son of a wealthy merchant, has fallen in love with a geisha in Osaka's Shinmachi. His parents attempted to keep him shut away in punishment for his vulgar ways. Now escaped, Wankyu wanders aimlessly and happens upon his beloved Matsuyama. The two dance together, remembering their memories together under the cherry blossoms, but Matsuyama mysteriously disappears, leaving a grief-stricken Wankyu behind.

幕が開くと舞台には大きな松があり、さざ波の音がしている。

　たどり行く
　　今は心も乱れ候
　　末の松山　思いの種よ

しっとりとした長唄の後、椀久が登場する。
　椀久は椀屋久兵衛といい、大坂新町の豪商。新町の傾城・松山太夫と馴染んで豪遊を重ねたため、親から勘当されてしまう。髪を切られて座敷牢に閉じ込められたが、松山恋しさのあまりに心乱れ、牢を抜け出して彷徨い歩いている。

　干さぬ涙にしっぽりと
　　身にしみじみと可愛ゆさの
　　それが嵩じた物狂い
　　とても濡れたる　身なりゃこそ
　　親の意見もわざくれと

A huge pine tree comes into view as the curtain rises. The sound of the waves can be heard.

(See Japanese lyrics on left)

Wankyu enters after a long *nagauta* intro.
Wankyu is the nickname of the wealthy merchant Wanya Kyubei, who has been disinherited by his parents after he fell in love with the beautiful geisha Matsuyama Dayu and squandered his money. He was previously put on house arrest and his hair shorn, but his longing for Matsuyama was unbearable and he eventually escaped his prison. Now he wanders the streets aimlessly.

(See Japanese lyrics on left)

兎角耳には入相の
鐘に合図の
廊へ行こやれ　行こやれ
さつさ行こやれ　昨日は今日の昔なり

本舞台に彷徨い来た久兵衛は、松の前でまどろむ。すると、松山の幻が現れる。松山もまた、廊で椀久を慕っていたのである。

全盛を誇る松山といえど、いわば籠の鳥。椀久の紋のついた羽織を椀久と思い身に着けているのだという。

Kyubei, who has now wandered into the main stage, dozes off in front of the great pine tree. Suddenly, the spectre of Matsuyama appears. She, too, has been pining for her dear Wankyu.

Though a beauty beyond measure, Matsuyama is but a caged bird. She wears a *haori* jacket bearing Wankyu's crest out of her love for him.

(See Japanese lyrics on left)

誓文ほんに全盛も
我は廊を放し鳥　籠は恨めし
心くどくとあくせくと
恋しき人を松山は
やれ末かけてかいどりしゃんと
しゃんしゃんともしおらしく
君が定紋　伊達羽織
男なりけり　また　女子なり
片袖主と眺めやる

やがて二人は昔日の華やかな逢瀬や、能の『井筒』に取り入れられた『伊勢物語』の幼い恋をしっとりと踊る。

The two recall the lurid trysts of their former days and perform a dance reminiscent of a story of young love from *The Tales of Ise*.

(See Japanese lyrics on left)

思いざしなら武蔵野でなりと
何んじゃ織部の薄盃を
よいさ　しやうがえ

筒井筒井筒にかけし
まろがたけ
老いにけらしな
いも見ざる間に

さらに、「按摩けんぴき」という歌に合わせ、華やかな連れ舞となる。

Next a two-man dance begins to the song "Anma-kenpiki."

(See Japanese lyrics on left)

自体　それがしは東の生まれ
お江戸町中見物様の
馴染み情けの御贔屓つよく
按摩けんぴき

廊での騒ぎを踊るうちに、松山の幻は消え失せ、あとに残された椀久は一人泣き沈む。

As Matsuyama performs a dance depicting the bustle of the pleasure quarters, she eventually vanishes. Wankyu, seeing that she was but an illusion, cries alone on the stage, marking the end of the play.

『二人椀久』
2013年12月 京都南座
松山（初代片岡孝太郎）

Ninin Wankyu
(Kyoto Minamiza Theatre, December 2013)
Matsuyama (Kataoka Takataro I)

作品の概要

演目名

二人椀久

作者

作詞 = 不明
作曲 = 錦屋金藏

概要

　官能的でテンポの速い連れ舞が見どころの長唄舞踊。彷徨い歩く椀久が恋人・松山太夫の幻に巡り会い、束の間逢瀬を楽しむ夢物語だ。「二人〜」とは椀久が二人現れるのではなく、幻の松山が椀久の着物を身につけ、二人が並ぶさまから来ている。歌舞伎や人形には椀久物と呼ばれる系統がある。江戸初期の大坂堺筋に実在した豪商・椀屋久右衛門が、新町の傾城・松山太夫に入れ上げて財産を使い果たし、座敷牢に入れられてしまったという実話に基づいて作られた作品群である。歌舞伎では貞享元（1684）年に椀久の七周忌にちなんで演じられた舞台が最初といわれる。椀久の遊びは桁外れだったらしく、その有様は井原西鶴が書いた『椀久一世の物語』などに詳しい。一部欠損があるが、昭和初期に活字化されたものが国会図書館のデジタルデータで読める。心を狂わせた男が女の幻を追いかけるというテーマは舞踊に適した題材で、他にも多数の作品が伝わっている。一中節『椀久道行』、長唄『二人椀久』『一人椀久』、常磐津『三面椀久』、清元『幻椀久』など。

初演

安永3（1774）年5月東京・市村座で、椀久が九世市村羽左衛門、松山が瀬川富三郎。作詞者は不明。作曲は錦屋金藏。

Overview

Title

Ninin Wankyu

Writer

Lyrics: Unknown
Music: Nishikiya Kinzo

Overview

　This sensual, fast-paced buyo in the *nagauta* style tells the story of the wealthy merchant Wankyu, who meets once more with his love Matsuyama only to find that it was all a dream. *"Ninin"* means "two people," but this doesn't refer to two Wankyu's. Rather, it is a reference to the fact that Matsuyama wears Wankyu's robes, so that when the two stand on stage together it is as though there are two Wankyu's. There is also a sub-genre of works called *wankyu-mono* which feature the wealthy merchant Wanya Kyuemon, an actual person from the early Edo period who is famous for squandering his fortune on the beautiful couresan Matsuyama and getting himself locked away for his debauched ways. The first performance of the Wankyu story in the kabuki theatre was in 1684, the seventh anniversary of Wankyu Kyubei's death. Wankyu's exploits in the pleasure quarters were legendary, and are especially well chronicled in Ihara Saikaku's *Wanya Issei no Monogatari*. The text as printed in the early Showa Period (1926–89) is available in digital format on the National Diet Library website, although there were some textual corruptions in the source document. Something about the story of a man seeing crazed visions of the woman he loves was seen as especially fitting to the buyo format, resulting in a number of dances with this exact plot. Some examples include *Wankyu Michiyuki* (in the *icchu-bushi* style), *Ninin Wankyu* (*nagauta*), *Mitsumen Wankyu* (*tokiwazu*), and *Maboroshi Wankyu* (*kiyomoto*).

Premiere

May 1774, Ichimuraza Theatre. Feat. Ichimura Uzaemon IX as Wankyu and Segawa Tomisaburo as Matsuyama. Lyricist unknown. Music by Nishikiya Kinzo.

登場人物 Characters

椀屋久兵衛
わんやきゅうべえ

大坂の陶器商・椀屋久右衛門という実在した人物がモデルとなっている。新町の遊女・松山と深く馴染み、しかしあまりの豪遊のため座敷牢に幽閉され物狂いとなるが、家を抜け出して町を彷徨う。月明かりの夜道で恋しい松山の姿を見つけ、かつての楽しかった想い出に浸りながら楽しく二人で舞うが……それは幻想、やがて松山の姿は消え、一人残された椀久は寂しさの中で打ちひしがれてゆく。

Wanya Kyubei

Based on an Osaka ceramics merchant named Wanya Kyuemon, Wanya Kyubei is hopelessly in love with the courtesan Matsuyama. He is put in a detention home for spending far too much time and money in the pleasure quarters, but eventually escapes and wanders the town aimlessly. When he comes upon his lover Matsuyama in the street, the two rejoice, dancing as they remember their precious memories together. Matsuyama eventually vanishes, however, revealing that their reunion was but an illusion. Left alone, Wankyu is overcome by profound loneliness.

松山太夫
まつやまだゆう

大坂新町の丹波屋抱えの遊女。本作のほか紀海音（きのかいおん）の『椀久末松山（わんきゅうすえのまつやま）』、井原西鶴の『椀久一世の物語』など複数の作品に登場する。ここでは松山が椀久の羽織を身にまとって舞い、椀久が二人いるかのように見えるところから『二人椀久』という題名になっている。松の大木が月明かりに浮かぶほの暗い海辺近く、どこからともなく現れた松山はやさしく美しく幻想的に舞うが、それはまさしく幻であった。

Matsuyama Dayu

A courtesan in Osaka Shinmachi, the character of Matsuyama appears in a number of other works, including Kino Kaion's *Wankyu Sue no Matsuyama* and Ihara Saikaku's *Wankyu Issei no Monogatari*. In this piece, Matsuyama appears wearing Wankyu's haori coat, making it seem as though there are two Wankyu's dancing on the stage, a feature hinted at in the title. The beautiful Matsuyama appears from nowhere and dances on a beach bathed in soft, mysterious moonlight. Dancing in such a dreamlike setting, it comes as no surprise that her appearance is nothing but an illusion.

みどころ
Highlights

1. 狂おしい恋の心
—— The Crazed Heart of a Man in Love

会えないはずの恋人がときどき目の前に見える。椀屋の主人・久兵衛はそう思っている。人はそれを狂乱とみる。歌舞伎舞踊には、狂乱をテーマに据えた作品群がある。椀久物は、なかでも優美でドラマチックな色合いで知られる。平凡な人生を大事に生きれば、狂乱することもなく恋の悲しみも忘れていくものだ。しかし、恋慕の気持ちを全身で表出する椀久の舞姿を観たら、観る側も、忘れていたはずの狂おしい心を呼び覚ましてしまうかもしれない。

At times, Wankyu sees visions of his dead lover, though viewers are sure to see that he has been driven mad by his loss. Among the sub-genre of kabuki buyo centering around such madness, those featuring Wankyu ("wankyu-mono") are some of the most refined and dramatic. Most of us live rather average lives, taking each day as it comes in a way that allows us to stay sane and eventually forget the tribulations of our past loves. *Ninin Wankyu*, however, is sure to bring such feelings bubbling up to the surface.

2. 名残の十徳
—— The Lingering Attachment of a *Juttoku* Robe

椀久が羽織っているのは十徳と呼ばれる薄手の上着。夢に現れた松山太夫が、その十徳をやさしく拾いあげる。その仕草は男の未練な願いが形になった幻想だ。女が恋人の衣服を着るというなまめかしい趣向は、能の『井筒』にも通じる見どころだ。舞台には昔に変わらぬ廓の華やかな雰囲気があふれてくる。豪奢な裲襠（うちかけ）を手にした踊りの楽しいこと。しかし夢醒めると、残された十徳が抜け殻のようで、空しさが際立つ。

Wankyu wears a thin robe called a *juttoku*, which Matsuyama Dayu picks up in a dreamlike scene representing the lingering attachment Wankyu feels toward her, his dead lover. The act of a woman wearing her lover's robes is a charming one that can also be seen in the noh play *Izutsu*. For a moment, the stage is filled with the glamorous atmosphere of the pleasure quarters as Matsuyama dances with a splendid *uchikake* robe in her hands. But this only serves to amplify Wankyu's deep sorrow when she disappears, leaving only the robe behind like a cast-off skin.

3. 夢中になって、ふたりで狂う
—— Two Dancers Lost in a Mad Reverie

最大の見どころは、ふたりの連れ舞。まるで双子の男女でもあるかのように、椀久と松山の息がぴったり合う手踊りは、次第にテンポが速く激しくなる。三味線の即興的な演奏も聴きどころ。舞台の楽しさはこの上なく、このまま時間が止まってほしいと思うほどだ。平成9（1984）年12月パリ・シャトレ劇場で13回も上演された、四世中村雀右衛門と五世中村富十郎の名コンビの『二人椀久』は、「歌舞伎の永遠の神々」と激賞された。

The *tsuremai* (two-man dance) is the biggest highlight of *Ninin Wankyu*. Wankyu and Matsuyama dance so perfectly in sync, it's as though a pair of identical twins are performing! As their *te-odori* progresses, the tempo quickens and the music becomes more intense. The improvised shamisen performance here is a highlight in its own right and will surely have you wishing time would simply stop and allow you to bask in the moment. The play was performed 13 times at Paris' Theatre du Chatelet in December of 1984, where Nakamura Jakuemon IV and Nakamura Tomijuro V were praised as "eternal gods of kabuki."

4. 本当にいた椀久
—— The Historical Wankyu

椀屋久兵衛は実在の豪商。同時代の井原西鶴作『椀久一世の物語』にその豪遊ぶりが描かれている。花見船に12人の禿（かむろ）を若衆姿にして乗せてバカ騒ぎ。季節外れに正月遊びを思い立ち、昼下がりから急に廓に松を飾らせ女郎たちに鞠羽子板で遊ばせる。節分の真似には豆替りに一分粒銀（一分＝一両の4分の1）を蒔く…。ついには破産して座敷牢に押し込められ33歳で水死したとも、実はひそかに松山と幸せになったとも伝わる。

Wan'ya Kyubei was a wealthy merchant whose extravagant adventures were chronicled in Ihara Saikaku's *Wankyu Issei no Monogatari*. He once dressed twelve young *kamuro* girls as men and had a flower-viewing party on a boat. Another time, he decorated the pleasure quarters with pine branches even though it was not the new year season. He then had the geisha play an ancient badminton-like game with him from the early afternoon. Yet another time, he imitated the end-of-winter *setsubun* tradition of tossing beans about, but instead of beans he used *ichibu* coins, a unit of currency at the time. He eventually went bankrupt and was imprisoned, however. By some accounts, he drowned to death at the age of thirty-three, while others say he lived happily ever after with Matsuyama.

『色彩間苅豆』
2011年6月　新橋演舞場
(左から) かさね (五代目中村時蔵)、
木下川与右衛門 (七代目市川染五郎)

Iromoyo Chotto Karimame
(Shinbashi Enbujo Theatre, June 2011)
(from left) Kasane (Nakamura Tokizo V), Yoemon (Ichikawa Somegoro VII)

あらすじ　　　　　　　　　　Synopsis

色彩間苅豆

流れ着いた髑髏（どくろ）が語る、過ぎし日の惨劇。
しっとりとした色模様から一転、
因果が絡むサスペンスの舞踊劇へ

雨上がりの木下川堤、恋の逃避行へと向かう与右衛門とかさねのもとへ流れ着いた、
いわくありげな卒塔婆。その謎解きから忌まわしき因縁と与右衛門の悪事が露見する。
その祟りからかさねは形相が変わり足も痛める。
恐ろしさから与右衛門はかさねを殺すが、怨霊はさらに与右衛門を苦しめる。

あらすじ

————　A skull appears to tell the tragic story of its past. This dramatic dance changes from a sweet love story to a suspenseful story of karmic bonds.

On the Kine Riverbank, Yoemon and Kasane are about to elope when an ominous tablet floats by bearing the skull of a man long dead. Yoemon's past evils are revealed and a karmic curse is placed upon Kasane, disfiguring her face and legs. Yoemon murders Kasane in fear, but her ghost returns to torment him.

舞台は下総羽生村の、木下川の堤。二人の捕り手が、百姓の助を殺した咎で、与右衛門を探索している。

やがて、清元の浄瑠璃が始まり、与右衛門が登場する。続いて腰元姿のかさねもやって来る。久保田金五郎という名の侍だった与右衛門は、武家奉公の時に同じ家中のかさねと恋仲になった。しかし不義密通はご法度のため、かさねに書置きを残し屋敷を抜け出したのである。

与右衛門に追いついたかさねは、一緒に死のうとまで約束をしたのに一人で出ていくとはと恨み言を言い、死を迫る。しかし、与右衛門は、かさねの養父が預かっている重宝・撫子の茶入れ紛失のため、殿の咎めを受けている折、不義の上、心中で死んでしまったら親への不孝になると宥める。
するとかさねは、去年の秋に初めて出会い結ばれたいきさつや、与右衛門の子を身籠もったことを明かす。これを聞いた与右衛門は、心中の願いを承諾する。

そこへ、卒塔婆と、草刈鎌が刺さった髑髏が川を流れてくる。卒塔婆には俗名助と書かれていた。髑髏は助のもの、鎌は与右衛門が助を殺した際に使った鎌であった。

The setting is Kine Riverbank in Hanyu Village, Shimousa Province. Two officials are searching for Yoemon who is accused of murdering the peasant Suke.

A *kiyomoto* accompaniment begins and Yoemon enters, followed by the chambermaid Kasane. Yoemon was once a samurai named Kubota Kingoro, but came to be a lowly servant serving in the same house as Kasane. There, the two fell in love, but Yoemon fled after being accused of illicit relations, leaving a note behind for Kasane.

Kasane catches up to Yoemon and scolds him for leaving her alone despite their previous promise to die together. Though she demands that they die together, Yoemon explains that he is responsible for the loss of his adopted father's heirloom tea container. On top of that, he has been accused of having illicit relations, and to commit lover's suicide with Kasane would show that he has no filial piety.
Kasane reminds him of how they met the previous fall and explains that she is pregnant with Yoemon's child, which persuades him to consent to a lover's suicide.

Just then, a skull with a scythe stabbed through it floats down the river on a wooden grave tablet. The tablet bears the name Suke, and the skull is that of the same man whom Yoemon killed with a scythe in the past.

与右衛門が卒塔婆を折ると、にわかにかさねが足を押さえ、髑髏を鎌で割ると顔を押さえて苦しみ始め倒れてしまう。

　そこに捕り手が現れ、与右衛門を捕まえようとする。立ち廻りのうち、与右衛門は捕り手の落とした書状を拾う。そこには与右衛門の悪事やその詮議に関わることが書かれてあった。

　この場を立ち去ろうとする与右衛門を、かさねが引き留める。かさねは片目が潰れ、さらに片足も不自由になった様子。与右衛門はかさねと共に行くふりをし、隙を窺い、髑髏に刺さっていた鎌でかさねに斬りつける。
　そして嫌がるかさねに鏡を見せ、かさねと自分の因果話を聞かせる。
　与右衛門に殺された助は、かさねの実父であった。しかも与右衛門は助の女房・菊とも関係があり、そのため助を殺害したのであった。かさねにとって与右衛門は実は親の敵。その仇と心中しようとしたかさねに報いが現れたのである。

　かさねは、鬼女のように変わり、与右衛門と激しい立ち廻りとなるが、ついに土橋の上で鎌で殺されてしまう。与右衛門は急いでこの場を去ろうとするが、かさねの恐ろしい怨念により逃げることができず、引き戻されてしまう。

When Yoemon breaks the tablet, Kasane suddenly seizes her legs, and when he breaks the skull, she grasps at her face and falls in agony.

Just then, the officials pursuing Yoemon appear and attempt to capture him. As a *tachimawari* fight ensues, Yoemon picks up a letter dropped by his pursuers. The note bears a description and discussion of Yoemon's crimes.

Yoemon attempts to flee but is stopped by Kasane, who is missing an eye and now has a lame leg. Yoemon pretends to take her with him but slashes at her at an opportune moment with the very scythe he used to kill Suke.
Kasane is shocked, but Yoemon hands her a mirror and tells her about their karmic connection.
It is revealed that Suke is Kasane's true father whom Yoemon killed after having an illicit affair with Suke's wife Kiku. The curse now placed on Kasane is karmic retribution for her wish to die together with the man who killed her father.

Kasane transforms into a demon and a violent *tachimawari* begins between her and Yoemon. Eventually, Yoemon kills her with his scythe and attempts to flee. Kasane's enraged spirit appears, however, determined to punish him.

作品の概要

演目名

色彩間苅豆

作者

作詞 = 松井幸三
作曲 = 初世清元斎兵衛

概要

　鬼才・四世鶴屋南北による、深い因縁の男女のもつれを描く舞踊劇。清元の哀切な浄瑠璃が、理不尽極まる異様な物語に砂糖をまぶすかのような情緒を付け、思わず知らず引き込まれる名作となっている。舞台は下総国木下川の堤。悪事が露見して逃げようとする薄情な色男・与右衛門を、うら若い屋敷勤めの女・かさねが追いかけてくる。与右衛門とかさねの登場には両花道を使うこともあり、同じ花道を後先に出ることもある。彼女は与右衛門の子を身籠っている身。男は一度は女の情けにほだされるが、ある事実を悟ると、豹変して女に斬りつける。南北の『法懸松成田利剣（けさかけまつなりたのりけん）』の二番目序幕として初演された。南北は生涯に五度、かさねと与右衛門の怪談劇を書いたといわれるが、本作は単なる怪談趣味だけでなく、男女の思いの落差を鋭く描き出し、近代の観客にも受け入れられたともいえるだろう。美男美女コンビとして知られた十五世市村羽左衛門、六世尾上梅幸で大正3（1914）年に上演されて以来、人気作品となった。

初演

文政6（1823）年6月江戸・森田座で、かさねは三世尾上菊五郎、与右衛門は七世市川團十郎。作詞は松井幸三、作曲は初世清元斎兵衛。

Overview

Title

Iromoyo Chotto Karimame

Writer

Lyrics: Matsui Kozo
Music: Kiyomoto Saibei I

Overview

　Tsuruya Nanboku IV shows his genius in this masterful buyo piece about the deep karmic bonds between a man and a woman. The melancholy *kiyomoto joruri* opening gives audiences a sweet impression before plunging them into the deeply disturbing truth of the story. Set on the Kine Riverbank, the heartless playboy Yoemon is fleeing after his misdeeds are revealed. His young lover, a chambermaid named Kasane, chases after him. (Some productions utilize two *hanamichi*, while some have the two lovers standing on the same *hanamichi*.) She reveals she is pregnant with Yoemon's baby, which makes him feel deep pity for her. When he tells her the truth about his past, however, everything changes and he murders her. Originally performed as a prologue to Nanboku's *Kesakakematsu Naritano Riken*, it is said that Nanboku wrote five ghost stories involving Yoemon and Kasane. *Kasane*, however, is not merely a ghost story, but a dramatic dance which depicts the difference in a man and woman's love. This may be the very reason that even modern audiences are captivated by the story. *Kasane* has enjoyed great popularity since the 1914 performance starring Ichimura Uzaemon XV and Onoe Baiko VI, a duo well-known for depicting the handsome man and beautiful woman.

Premiere

June 1823, Moritaza Theatre. Feat. Onoe Kikugoro III as Kasane, Ichikawa Danjuro VII as Yoemon. Lyrics by Matsui Kozo. Music by Kiyomoto Saibei I.

登場人物　　　　　　Characters

与右衛門 実は 久保田金五郎
よえもん じつは くぼたきんごろう

与右衛門は百姓となっているが元は侍で久
保田金五郎といった。その昔、菊という女
性と不義密通しその夫の助（すけ）を鎌で殺
しているが、なんと今はその助の娘であるか
さねと深い仲になっている。かさねが与右
衛門を追って来たところに助のどくろが卒塔
婆に乗って流れ着き、その祟りからかさねは
顔が醜く変貌し足を病む。やがて与右衛門
はかさねを鎌で殺すが、執念に燃えたかさ
ねの霊に強く引き戻される。

Yoemon / Kubota Kingoro

Once a samurai named Kubota Kingoro, Yoemon
has fallen in the world and is now a peasant. In
the past, he fell in love with a married woman
named Kiku and killed her husband Suke, the
father of his current lover Kasane. One day as
Kasane chases after Yoemon, she finds the skull
of her father drifting toward them, cursing her
with a disfigured face and lame legs. In the end,
Yoemon kills Kasane with a scythe as he had
killed Suke, but her spirit comes back due to
their profound karmic bonds.

腰元かさね
こしもとかさね

下総の国羽生村の助の娘だが、絹川家の
養女となり腰元となった。そのとき与右衛門
と深く馴染み、子を宿している。書置きをし
て居なくなった与右衛門を追って一緒に死
のうとするが、折しも流れ着いた助のどくろ
に祟られ、俄かに顔は醜く足も引きずるよう
に変貌する。実は父を殺した敵（かたき）こそ
与右衛門であった。与右衛門は恐ろしさに
震えてかさねを殺すが、その怨霊は与右衛
門を決して逃がしはしない。

Chambermaid Kasane

The daughter of Suke from Shimousa Province,
Kasane is adopted by the Kinugawa house and
becomes a chambermaid. There, she falls in
love with Yoemon and becomes pregnant. When
Yoemon leaves one day, leaving only a note, she
chases after him begging him to let her die with
him. At that moment, however, her father Suke's
skull drifts toward them, cursing Kasane's face
and legs. It is revealed that Yoemon is the man
who killed her father, leading to this karmic
curse. Though Yoemon kills Kasane, her ghost
returns, determined to punish him for his evil
deeds.

みどころ
Highlights

1. 累とは、因果な名前
—— "Kasane"—a Karmic Name

累物（かさねもの）と呼ばれる怪談の系統がある。累という名には本来悪い意味はないが、累物の主人公には大変気の毒なことが重なってしまう。俗に「親の因果が子に報い」というが、このキャラクターには親や恋人の悪縁がダブルでつきまとう。しかも本人はその因果を知らないという不条理感が肌をざわつかせる。また、鎌（かま）が足に刺さる場面があるのが累物のお約束。本作で、鎌を骸骨から抜くとかさねの足が悪くなるのはその約束を踏まえている。

There is a sub-genre of ghost stories referred to as *kasanemono*. Though the name "Kasane" didn't originally have a negative meaning, fictional characters with this name often have pitiful lots in life. It is said that the karma of a parent is visited upon the child, but characters named Kasane are said to be burdened with twice as much bad karma. What's more, these sad characters are not even aware of their bad karma. A trademark of *kasanemono* is a death by sickle.

2. 累伝説と、除霊スペシャリスト祐天上人
—— The Legend of Kasane and the Exorcist Priest Yuten

17世紀の中頃のこと、下総国羽生村（現在の茨城県常総市水海道羽生村）での出来事である。醜い生まれつきの累という女が嫉妬に狂ったあげく、夫・与右衛門に殺され、その怨念が残って一族に祟りが続いていたのだが、その頃下総国を廻っていた高僧・祐天の祈祷で、累の怨霊が解脱したという。多くの除霊伝説を持つ祐天は増上寺三十六世法主となり、五代将軍綱吉や母・桂昌院も厚く帰依した。目黒の祐天寺は、この祐天を開山とする。

This play depicts an incident from the 17th century that occurred in Hanyumura in Shimousa Province (present-day Ibaraki Prefecture). A disfigured girl named Kasane was driven mad with jealousy and eventually killed by her husband Yoemon. However, her angry spirit continued to curse the family after her death until a traveling monk named Yuten prayed for them and broke the curse. There are many legends associated with Yuten, who became the 36th high priest of Zojoji Temple. Shogun Tokugawa Tsunayoshi and his mother Keishoin were avid followers of his. Yutenji Temple in Meguro was built in his honor, and he was made the official founder.

3. 逃れられない連理引き
—— The Inescapable Bond Between Man and Woman

夫婦の縁の間には赤い糸があるなどと、人と人の間の因縁を見えない糸に例えることがある。逃げようとしたって、そうはさせない深い因縁の糸。その糸があたかも見えるかのような演出が「連理引き」。かさねの死体の腕が手招きすると、一度花道の向こうに走り去ったはずの与右衛門が、手や襟首を捕まれたように後ろ向きに舞台に戻ってくるのだ。まるでかかった釣り糸から逃れられない魚のように、男がたぐり寄せられていく。

The bond between husband and wife is often likened to a red thread that represents the invisible threads of karma that bond us. Such bonds are impossible to escape no matter what you do. Performances that show such bonds manifest in the physical world are called *renribiki*. In this play, for example, Kasane's corpse beckons to Yoemon, causing him to return from the *hanamichi*, moving backward as though being pulled by the back collar of his robes. He is reeled in like a fish caught by an invisible yet inescapable line.

4. 祐天上人と成田山
Priest Yuten and Naritasan

本作は、鶴屋南北が69歳のときに書いた『法懸松成田利剣』の一場面。「成田利剣」は、祐天上人が初め経文も覚えられない愚かさだったのが、成田山新勝寺で修行中に、不動尊から剣を呑まされる霊夢を見てから優れた能力を発揮するようになったと伝わることに当てている。文政6(1823)年の初演の折には、成田山と縁の深い七世市川團十郎が祐念(祐天)、与右衛門などを演じ、三世尾上菊五郎がかさねほかを演じた。

This play was originally a single scene from the larger work *Kesakakematsu Narita no Riken* written by Tsuruya Nanboku at the age of 69. "*Narita no Riken*" refers to a sacred dream that Yuten had when training at Naritasan Shinshoji Temple in which he was forced to swallow a sword by the deity Fudoson. Legend has it that he was given special powers after seeing this dream. Ichikawa Danjuro VII, who had a strong connection with Naritasan, played Yunen (Yuten) and Yoemon, while Onoe Kikugoro III played Kasane in this play's debut in 1823.

忍夜恋曲者
Shinobiyoru Koi wa Kusemono

『忍夜恋曲者』
2011年4月 京都南座
滝夜叉姫（五代目坂東玉三郎）

Shinobiyoru Koi wa Kusemono
(Kyoto Minamiza Theatre, April 2011)
Takiyashahime (Bando Tamasaburo V)

| あらすじ | Synopsis |

相馬の古御所には妖怪が棲むという。
だがその正体は奇怪な妖術を使う将門の娘・滝夜叉姫、
大宅光圀は敢然と闘う

かつて平将門が栄華を誇った館、今は荒れ果てた相馬の古御所に妖怪が出没するという。
その探索にやって来た大宅太郎光圀の前に現れたのは、美しい島原の傾城・如月。
しかし本性を現してみれば平将門の娘・滝夜叉姫、
崩れ落ちた御所の屋根で蝦蟇（がま）の妖術を使い、光圀と激しい立廻りを見せる。

——— Rumor has it an apparition haunts the ruins of the Soma Palace. This phantom turns out to be Masakado's daughter Takiyashahime, who possesses powerful magic. Will Oya Mitsukuni be able to defeat her?

The palace where the once-prosperous Taira no Masakado lived. A monstrous apparition is now said to haunt the old palace, and Oya Taro Mitsukuni has come to confirm these rumors. There he finds Kisaragi, the beautiful courtesan of the Shimabara pleasure quarters, but soon her true identity is revealed: Takiyashahime, the daughter of Masakado. The princess uses her magic to summon a great toad that engages in a *tachimawari* fight with Mitsukuni from the half-collapsed roof.

幕が開くと舞台は相馬の古御所。平安時代中期に朝廷に反旗を翻した平将門の本拠地であるが、将門が討ち取られた後は荒れ果てている。

常磐津の浄瑠璃につれ、傾城如月実は将門娘滝夜叉姫が登場し、まどろむ大宅太郎光圀に声を掛ける。大宅太郎は、源頼信から命を受け、妖怪変化が棲み、人々を悩ませているという古御所にやってきているのである。

傾城如月は、曲者と疑う光圀に、自分は島原の遊女で、いつぞや都で光圀を見染めたのだと話す。

嵯峨や御室の花盛り
浮気な蝶も色かせぐ
廓の者に連れられて
外珍らしき嵐山
それ覚えてか　君さまの
袴も春の朧染め

The curtain opens on the Soma Palace Ruins. Taira no Masakado made his headquarters here during the mid-Heian Period when he led a rebellion against the ruling powers, but since his defeat, the palace grounds lay in ruins.

Masakado's daughter Takiyashahime enters disguised as the beautiful courtesan Kisaragi, accompanied by a *tokiwazu* tune. She calls out to the apprehensive Oya Taro Mitsukuni, who is looking into rumors of evil apparitions sighted at the old palace at the behest of his master Minamoto no Yorinobu.

Kisaragi tells the suspicious Mitsukuni that she is a courtesan of the Shimabara pleasure quarters and that she fell in love with him after seeing him in the capital.

(See Japanese lyrics on left)

朧気ならぬ殿振りを

　その話を聞いた光圀は打ち解けた様子を装いながら、話を転じて将門の最期の様子を物語る。

　　平親王が最期の一戦
　　見よや見よやと夕月の
　　鹿毛なる駒に打ち乗って
　　向う者をば拝み打ち
　　立割り　ほろ付　車切
　　かくと見るより上平太が
　　放つ矢先に将門は
　　こめかみ篦深（のぶか）に射通され
　　馬よりどうとあえなき落命

　すると将門の討死の話を聞いた如月が涙ぐむ。光圀がそれを問い質すと、如月はこれは後朝の別れの涙だと取り繕い、廓の様子を話し始める。

　　ほのぼのと雀囀る奥座敷
　　灯火しめす男とも
　　屏風一重の彼方には、
　　まだ睦言の聞ゆれど
　　我は見足らぬ夢をさき
　　早後朝と引締める

　話のうちに、如月は相馬錦の旗を取り落とす。慌てて話をそらす如月。

　　一つ一夜の契りさえ
　　二つ枕の許しなき
　　三つ三重四重まはり気は
　　いつまで解かぬ常陸帯
　　六つむごいと思いはせいで
　　七つの鐘の恨めしや

　しかし相馬錦の旗は将門の印。光圀は如月を将門の遺児・滝夜叉と悟り、正体を明かすよう詰め寄る。

　如月は正体を現し、蝦蟇の妖術で光圀と激しく戦い、相馬の古御所は屋体崩しとなり、幕となる。

Mitsukuni pretends to let his guard down, but soon changes the topic of conversation to the death of Masakado.

　(See Japanese lyrics on left)

Kisaragi, hearing of her father's death, is moved to tears. When Mitsukuni inquires as to why she is crying, she lies and says she is sad that she will never see Mitsukuni again, changing the subject to life in the pleasure quarters.

　(See Japanese lyrics on left)

As she is talking, Kisaragi accidentally drops a brocade flag that betrays her connection to the Soma palace. She hurriedly changes the subject.

　(See Japanese lyrics on left)

Mitsukuni, however, knows that the flag is Masakado's and realizes that Kisaragi is in fact Takiyashahime.

Kisaragi shows her true form, summoning a magical toad to fight with Mitsukuni. The roof of the old palace collapses, signaling the end of the play.

作品の概要

演目名

忍夜恋曲者

作者

作詞 = 宝田寿助
作曲 = 五世岸沢式佐

概要

　妖艶で怪奇趣味あふれる常磐津舞踊の名作。一番目狂言『世善知鳥相馬旧殿（よにうとうそうまのふるごしょ）』の大詰として初演された。舞台はかつて平将門が住んだ相馬の古御所。反逆者・将門の忘れ形見である滝夜叉姫が、復讐のため、勇者たちを味方に引き入れようと暗躍している。怪異を聞きつけた源頼信の家臣・大宅光圀（おおやのみつくに）がまどろんでいると、花道のすっぽんから傾城姿の滝夜叉が現れる。恋文なのか天紅を付けた手紙を読む仇な姿が、妖しい灯りに照らし出されるが、かんざしを挿した髪は乱れ、傘は破れたまま。いぶかしむ光圀に滝夜叉が迫ってくる。この場の浄瑠璃「嵯峨や御室の花盛り　浮気な蝶も色かせぐ」は常磐津第一の艶やかな一節として知られる。将門物は人気で、遺児の姫の名は色々創作されたが、山東京伝が読本『善知鳥安方忠義伝（うとうやすかたちゅうぎでん）』で滝夜叉姫としてからは、この名前が定着した。一度は出家し如月尼と名乗ったが還俗。弟・良門（よしかど）と共に、妖術を遣って復讐を誓う身となった姫に相応しい凄艶な名である。

初演

天保7（1836）年7月江戸・市村座で、滝夜叉姫は二世市川九蔵、光圀が十二世市村羽左衛門。作詞は宝田寿助、作曲は五世岸沢式佐。

Overview

Title

Shinobiyoru Koi wa Kusemono

Writer

Lyrics: Takarada Jusuke
Music: Kishizawa Shikisa V

Overview

　A resplendent yet ghastly example of *tokiwazu* buyo, this play was first performed as the climax to the *ichibanme-kyogen* piece *Yoni Utou Soma no Furugosho*, set at the former palace of Taira no Masakado. Masakado's daughter Takiyashahime is secretly gathering allies to avenge her treasonous father. She appears before Minamoto no Yorinobu's retainer Oya Mitsukuni, who is investigating suspicious rumors of apparitions at the palace ruins. Takiyashahime seems to be reading a love letter, and an eerie light reveals her disheveled hair and a broken umbrella. She approaches the now apprehensive Mitsukuni as a famous *tokiwazu* tune begins. Plays about Masakado are quite popular, and there were once many names given to the princess of this story, but the name Takiyashahime was established with Santo Kyoden's *Utou Yasukata Chugiden*. The princess supposedly took the name Kisaragi after becoming a nun, but eventually returned to secular life. The somewhat otherworldly name is an appropriate one for a woman using magic to avenge her father.

Premiere

July 1836, Ichimuraza Theatre. Feat. Ichikawa Kuzo II as Takiyashahime, Ichimura Uzaemon XII as Mitsukuni. Lyrics by Takarada Jusuke. Music by Kishizawa Shikisa V.

登場人物 — Characters

傾城如月 実は 滝夜叉姫
けいせいきさらぎ じつは たきやしゃひめ

平将門の娘だが、艶やかな傾城の姿で相馬の古御所に現れる。ここはかつて将門が栄華を極めた館だが今は廃墟と化している。その古御所の様子を探りに来ていたのは大宅光圀。滝夜叉は都の島原の傾城で如月と名乗るが、光圀と共に舞ううち大切な相馬錦の御旗（平将門の形見）を落とし、正体を見破られる。そして光圀と激しい立廻りの末、覚えた妖術で大きな蝦蟇（がま）を使い、崩れかけた大屋根の上から威嚇する。

Keisei Kisaragi / Takiyashahime

Taira no Masakado's daughter, Takiyashahime (Takiyasha Princess) appears as the beautiful courtesan Kisaragi at the Old Soma Palace, where Masakado himself lived in prosperity once upon a time. Now an abandoned ruin, Oya no Mitsukuni has come to see what has become of the old palace. There he dances with the disguised princess, but she drops a brocade flag (a memento from her father), revealing her true identity. After a *tachimawari* fight with Mitsukuni, Takiyashahime uses magic to summon a great toad that glares down menacingly from the collapsed roof.

大宅太郎光圀
おおやのたろうみつくに

文武に優れた武士で、相馬の古御所に妖怪変化が出るというのでその様子を探りに主君の源頼信から遣わされてきた。館の内でしばしの眠りから覚めると目の前には何やら怪しき傾城姿の女性。そこで平将門の合戦の様子や最期の姿を物語ると女性が涙を浮かべ、さらに相馬錦の御旗を所持していたことから将門の娘・滝夜叉姫と見極める。やがて大勢と共に戦うが、しかし恐ろしい蝦蟇の妖術に苦戦する。

Oya no Taro Mitsukuni

A master of both martial and literary arts, Mitsukuni comes to inspect the old Soma Palace on behalf of his master Minamoto no Yorinobu after hearing rumors of evil spirits and apparitions there. After falling asleep in the palace, he awakens to see a beautiful but suspicious courtesan there. When he begins to speak of Taira no Masakado's battles and his final moments, the woman begins to cry and drops a brocade flag of the Soma house, revealing her true identity: Masakado's daughter Takiyashahime. A fight ensues, but Mitsukuni may have found his match in the magical toad Takiyashahime summons.

みどころ
Highlights

1. 怪しさが浮き出た裲襠（うちかけ）
— A Suspicious *Uchikake* Robe

滝夜叉姫の裲襠（うちかけ）。鼠色の繻子地に蜘蛛の巣と几帳の絵柄を吹き寄せに刺繍している。傾城を装うが、衣裳の柄に妖気を漂わせる。これに黒の蛇の目傘を差し、手紙を手にする花道の姿を面灯りが妖しく照らす。

Takiyashahime wears an *uchikake* robe with spider webs and *kicho* screens embroidered on a gray satin background. Though she is a gorgeous courtesan in fine robes, these patterns give her an otherworldly air, especially when seen illuminated on the *hanamichi* holding a black parasol in one hand and a letter in the other.

2. 今も生きる平将門伝説
— The Legend of Taira no Masakado, Still Alive Today

平将門は、平安前期に新皇を名乗り一時関東を独立統治した武将。朝廷から差し向けられた将門追討の軍勢にこめかみを射抜かれ、あえなく滅ぼされたが、追討軍には従兄弟にあたる平貞盛（清盛・重盛ら伊勢平氏の祖）もいた。京の都に晒された将門の首は空を飛んで、現在の東京大手町付近に落ちたといわれ、現在も大手町には将門の首塚が祀られている。徳川幕府は将門を関東鎮守として大切に扱った。将門が祀られる神田明神は、江戸城の鬼門にあたる場所に鎮座している。

Taira no Masakado was a warrior of the early Heian Period who seized power and temporarily unified the Kanto region of Japan. He was pursued by a party sent from the Imperial Court (which included his own cousin Taira no Sadamori) and was tragically killed. It is said that his head, which was displayed as an example in the streets of Kyoto, flew through the air all the way to the Otemachi area of Tokyo where he has been enshrined ever since. The Tokugawa Shogunate considered Masakado the guardian deity of Kanto, and Kanda Shrine, where he is enshrined, was appropriately located in the northeast corner (the direction from which misfortune comes) of Edo Castle.

3. 姫は蝦蟇(がま)の妖術遣い
—— A Toad Princess Wielding Black Magic

歌舞伎には将門の世界を扱った作品群がある。反朝廷の旗頭として歴史に名を残す将門はいつしか江戸の守護神になって畏敬されたわけだが、芝居に将門本人が登場することはほぼない。忘れ形見の滝夜叉姫やその弟・良門が再び天下を覆そうとするイメージのほうが定着している。妖術を自在に操る滝夜叉姫が着物の下に着込んでいる鎖帷子(くさりかたびら)は野望の象徴。傾いた古御所の屋根に蝦蟇を従えて闇を見据える姫の姿は、錦絵の題材ともなっている。

There is a subgenre of kabuki plays dealing with the world of Masakado. He famously rose up against the imperial court and is now respected as the guardian deity of Kanto, but he very rarely appears in these plays. Instead, it is often his daughter Takiyashahime and her younger brother Yoshikado who are shown attempting to take over the world. The chainmail worn under the black magic-wielding Takiyashahime's robes is a symbol of her twisted ambitions. The image of the princess gazing into the darkness while a great Toad sits on the roof of the ruined palace is an image often depicted in woodblock prints.

4. 歌舞伎が屋体崩しの元祖
—— Kabuki, Originator of the Collapsed Roof

大道具として舞台いっぱいに立てられた屋体が、次第に崩れていく大仕掛けが「屋体崩し」。かつて子供に人気があった生放送のコント番組でもよく使われた手法だが、歌舞伎の仕掛けにルーツがある。今にも崩れそうな古い御所が、妖術を遣った争いの果てに屋根までが崩れ落ちる。CGや特撮ではない生の舞台での、土埃が立ちこめそうな古びた建物の屋体崩しは、歌舞伎大道具の仕掛けの技が光る、迫力ある見どころだ。

In kabuki there is a large-scale stage mechanic called *yatai-kuzushi* (literally "roof-collapse") that depicts a roof gradually collapsing. It is a widely used technique that was even used in a popular children's program in Japan, but some may not be aware that it originated in the kabuki theatre. The thrilling depiction of a house collapsing during an intense battle of black magic offers a sense of intense realism without the use of CG we often seen in movies. This is one of the biggest highlights of the performance, and one that shows off one of the greatest techniques of kabuki.

黒塚
Kurozuka

03 下の巻

『黒塚』
2001年2月　大阪松竹座
老女岩手実は安達原の鬼女（三代目市川猿之助）

Part III

Kurozuka
(Osaka Shochikuza Theatre, February 2001)
Rojo Iwate / Demon of Adachigahara
(Ichikawa Ennosuke III)

| あらすじ | Synopsis |

安達原には恐ろしい鬼女が棲むという。
阿闍梨（あじゃり）の尊い仏の教えに心洗われた鬼女だが、
裏切られた怒りは凄まじい

夜道を行く阿闍梨祐慶の一行が一軒のあばら家を見つけ、一夜の宿を乞うと老女が快く迎えた。
老女は身の上話から自らの罪深さを顧みるが、阿闍梨の説く仏の教えに救われ心清らかになる。
だが本性は人を喰う鬼女、仏門の者に約束を破られ恐ろしい姿と化すも祈禱の力には敵わず、
ついに屈する。

━━━━━━ ## There are rumors of a terrible female demon in Adachigahara. Though she is nearly saved by the Buddhist teachings of Ajari, her anger at being betrayed wins out.

Ajari Yukei leads a group of monks on a pilgrimage which brings them to a lone house where they hope to take lodgings. The old woman who lives there welcomes them and regales them with sad stories of her past transgressions. Ajari's teachings seem to reach the sorrowful old woman but soon the monks find out that she is a demon who preys on travelers. Enraged at the betrayal of these holy monks, she attacks them but is no match for the power of their prayers.

01　上の巻

　芒原（すすきはら）を背景に、能の様式を取り入れた小家の作り物がある。奥州安達原にある、荒れ果てた一つ家である。上手には長唄連中、下手には囃子の連中が居並んでいる。
　この家には岩手という老女が一人で住んでいたが、諸国行脚の僧・阿闍梨祐慶一行の願いを聞き入れ、家に招き入れる。
　話の内に祐慶が、そばにある糸車に興味を示す。所望に応え、糸繰り唄を唄いつつ糸を取り、涙する岩手。その様子は、由緒ある出自のようにも見え、祐慶らの問いに答えるまま、岩手は我が身の上を語る。
　岩手はもと都の者であったが、流罪となった父と共に奥州に下ったことや、夫となった男は、都に行くと言って出ていったきりであることなどを話す。夫を恨み、世を恨み、浅ましい姿になり果てたと我が身を嘆く岩手に、祐慶は仏の道に入ったら罪も消え、来世は成仏すると説く。
　一念発起したら罪が消える。その言葉に力を得た岩手は、

01　Part I

　Amid a field of pampas grass sits a small house, a *tsukurimono* in the noh style. The house sits in ruin in Adachigahara in the Oshu region. On the right side of the stage is a *nagauta* accompaniment, on the left side is a *hayashi* accompaniment.

　The elderly woman who lives alone in the house welcomes a group of Buddhist monks, led by the priest Ajari Yukei, who come seeking lodgings.

　As the old woman and the monks talk, Yukei expresses interest in the spinning wheel the woman has in her house. At his request, the woman begins spinning while singing a melancholy song. As tears stream down Iwate's face, Yukei, who realizes she must come from a noble family, asks about her past.

　Iwate explains that she once lived in the capital but came to Oshu with her father who was banished. She is

後夜の勤めをする一行のもてなしのために山に薪を取りに出かけていく。しかし行きがけに、閨の内を見ることを固く禁じ、一行は承諾する。

　ところが、太郎吾が諫めを無視し、閨を覗いてしまう。そこには一面血の海、死骸の山。

　実は岩手は、安達ケ原に住むといわれる鬼女であった。

02　中の巻

　場面は一面の芒原。上の巻の長唄に加え、上手には箏曲と尺八、下手には囃子の連中が居並ぶ。

　舞台奥より岩手が柴を背負って登場する。最前の祐慶の言葉で、長年の妄執も成仏できると知った岩手は、足取りも軽い。月明かりの下、無邪気な心で余念なく踊る岩手。月影に映った我が影に戯れていると、太郎吾が血相を変えて逃げてくる。

　その様子から閨の内を見られ、正体を悟られたと知った岩手。見ぬと約束した一間を覗かれ、信頼した祐慶たちにも偽りがあることに、改めて怒りと悲しみを覚え、成仏の願いもこれまでと、鬼女の相を顕して姿を消す。

　太郎吾は、命からがらその場を逃げ去ってゆく。

03　下の巻

　舞台は一面の芒原。上手に長唄囃子連中が居並ぶ。やがて、古塚が現れる。

　祐慶と大和坊、讃岐坊は、老女が鬼女と知り、法力で鎮めようとやってくる。そこに声がして、古塚の中から現れる鬼女。鬼女は、裏切った祐慶らを嚙み殺そうと襲いかかる。これに対し、数珠を押し揉み対抗する祐慶ら。

　さしもの悪鬼も法力には敵わず、通力も次第に弱り、足元も危うくなってしまう。やがて、おのれの浅ましい姿に恥じ入った鬼女は、闇に紛れて何処かに消え去っていく。

married but was abandoned by her husband who returned to the capital and has not contacted her since. She bears deep resentment to her husband and to the world for her miserable lot, but Yukei explains that if she gives her life to the path of the Buddha her past sins will vanish and she can find peace in the next life.

Iwate is invigorated by Yukei's words and the promise that her sins can be cleansed. She decides to go out to collect firewood for the monks who will stay with her tonight but expressly forbids them from entering her room while she is away.

The curious Tarogo ignores Iwate's warning and looks in her room to find a great heap of bones and a pool of blood.

It is thus revealed that Iwate is the fearsome female demon who lives in Adachigahara.

02　Part II

Koto and shakuhachi players are added to the *nagauta* band on the right side of the stage, while a *hayashi* orchestra sits on the left side.

Iwate appears in the great field of pampas grass bearing a bunch of firewood. There is a certain spring in her step after hearing from Yukei that even one who has lived many years on the wrong path may achieve enlightenment. She dances in the moonlight with an air of blissful innocence. Just then Tarogo comes running, a terrible expression on his face.

Iwate takes one look at his face and realizes that he has been in her room and now knows her true nature. A renewed anger and disillusionment take over Iwate at learning that even devout men like Yukei and his monks lie and betray their fellow man. Thinking that the promise of salvation is but another lie, she transforms into her demon form.

Tarogo barely manages to flee with his life.

03　Part III

In the field of pampas grass sit the *nagauta* and *hayashi* musicians. Finally, Iwate's house reappears.

Yukei, Yamatobo, and Sanukibo, now aware that Iwate is a demon, have come to calm her through prayer to the Buddha. A voice is heard from inside as the demon emerges and bites at Yukei. Yukei and his men knead their prayer beads in resistance.

The evil demon is ultimately no match for the sacred power of Buddha, and her power gradually weakens as she loses footing. Ashamed of her reduced state, she flees into the night.

02 中の巻
『黒塚』
2001年2月　大阪松竹座
老女岩手実は安達原の鬼女（三代目市川猿之助）

Part II
Kurozuka
(Osaka Shochikuza Theatre, February 2001)
Rojo Iwate / Demon of Adachigahara (Ichikawa Ennosuke III)

作品の概要

演目名

黒塚

作者

作詞 = 木村富子
作曲 = 四世杵屋佐吉

概要

　みちのく安達原の鬼婆伝説を題材にした昭和の新作舞踊劇。能『黒塚』(観世流では『安達原』)が原作。二世市川猿之助(初世猿翁)が初演して一世を風靡し、猿翁十種の一つとなっている。古典を題材としているが、洋行を経験した猿翁ならではの知的で斬新な味わいがあり、舞台装置にも衣裳にも当時のモダンさが窺える。旅の阿闍梨一行に乞われ老婆が侘しい暮らしを聞かせる糸繰り唄、仏に救われると信じて浮かれる月夜の影遊び、しかし裏切られて猛々しい本性を顕しての祈りとの対決と、侘しさ、喜び、そして怒りの三つの山場がある。特に一面の芒原で月光を受けた自身の影と、童心に帰ったように戯れる場面が秀逸で、ロシアンバレエの手法が取り入れられているという。昭和38(1963)年5月に猿翁襲名の演目としても予定されたが休演となり、23歳だった孫の三代目猿之助(二代目猿翁)の本役となったことも知られる。以後三代目の代表作ともなり、四代目猿之助も再演を重ねている。

初演

昭和14 (1939) 年11月東京劇場で、鬼女に二世市川猿之助(初世猿翁)、祐慶に七世澤村宗十郎、太郎吾に三世市川段四郎。作詞は木村富子、作曲は四世杵屋佐吉。振付は二世花柳寿輔。装置は松田青風。

Overview

Title

Kurozuka

Writer

Lyrics: Kimura Tomiko
Music: Kineya Sakichi IV

Overview

Based on a legend from Adachigahara in the Michinoku region, this Showa-era buyo was based on the noh play of the same title (*Adachigahara* in the Kanze tradition). First performed by Ichikawa Ennosuke (En'o I), *Kurozuka* became one of the *En'o Jusshu* (10 Varieties of En'o). Though based on ancient Japanese legends, En'o's experience abroad gave the dance a more intellectual flavor. The stage and costume design, too, were rather modern at *Kurozuka*'s debut. When an old woman offers lodgings to a traveling group of Buddhist monks, she laments her poor lot in a woeful tune sung while spinning silk. Hearing of the mercy of Buddha, she believes she is overjoyed as she begins to think that she might be saved, but her true nature is revealed after one of the monks betrays her trust. Thus, the dance is divided into three distinct sections, each expressing a different emotion--misery, joy, and anger. The playful scene in the meadow is particularly moving, showing the old woman frolicking, childlike after hearing that she might be saved through Buddha's mercy. It is said that this scene incorporates techniques from Russian ballet. *Kurozuka* was meant to be performed to commemorate *En'o*'s succession to his stage name in May 1963, but this was ultimately canceled. Instead, 23-year-old grandson Ennosuke III (En'o II) performed as the lead. It went on to become his trademark role, and Ennosuke IV has taken up his predecessor's tradition, reprising the role many times over the years.

Premiere

November 1939, Tokyo Gekijo Theatre. Feat. Ichikawa Ennosuke II (En'o I) as the female demon, Sawamura Sojuro VII as Yukei, and Ichikawa Danshiro III as Tarogo. Lyrics by Kimura Tomiko. Music by Kineya Sakichi IV. Choreography by Hanayagi Jusuke II. Stage design by Matsuda Seifu.

登場人物 — Characters

老女岩手 実は 安達原の鬼女
ろうじょいわて じつは あだちがはらのきじょ

奥州安達原の古びた一軒家に住む老婆だが、実は旅人を喰うと人々から恐れられている鬼女である。一夜の宿を求めた僧・阿闍梨祐慶の一行を快く泊め、仏の道を諭されて身も心も清らかになり童心に帰って野に戯れる。留守の間、寝所を覗いてはならぬときつく言い置いたにもかかわらずそれを破られ、人間の裏切りに激しく怒り本性を顕して襲い掛かる。しかし祐慶の祈りには敵わず、やがて力尽きてゆく。

Rojo Iwate / Adachigahara no Kijo

Disguised as an elderly woman living in her humble home in Adachigahara in Oshu, Iwate is actually an evil demon who preys on passing travelers. When a group of monks arrives, led by Ajari Yukei, she welcomes them happily, and they even convince her that perhaps she too can be saved from her evil ways. While she is away, however, one of the priests looks in her room despite her forbidding them to do so. When she finds out about this, she is enraged by the dishonesty of men and transforms into her demon form. She attacks the priests, but she proves to be no match for Yukei's prayers, which weakened her greatly.

阿闍梨祐慶
あじゃりゆうけい

熊野那智大社の高僧で、山伏の従者と共に諸国を巡り修行の旅を続けている。人里離れた奥州の安達原を行くうち陽も沈み、一軒のあばら家を見つけて一夜の宿を所望する。そこに住む老女の昔話に耳を傾け仏の道を説いて光明を与えるが、老女が出かけた後、一間の惨状を見て実は鬼女であったと気付く。やがて凄まじい姿となった鬼女と対決するが、数珠を揉んで祈りを続け仏法の力で封じ込める。

Ajari Yukei

A high priest of the Kumano Nachi Taisha Shrine, Yukei leads a group of itinerant monks on a pilgrimage throughout the country. They come to a lone house in Adachigahara, Oshu requesting lodgings as the sun has begun to set. The old woman who lives there tells them of her past and Yukei preaches the way of the Buddha. Though his words seem to have struck home with her, the priests find out that she is actually a female demon when she leaves the house momentarily. Yukei faces off with the demon, praying fervently to the Buddha and finally sealing away her power.

大和坊・讃岐坊
やまとぼう・さぬきぼう

阿闍梨祐慶に従い共に修行の旅を続ける二人の山伏。煩悩を振り払い仏の道に忠実に従うが、同行してきた太郎吾の邪心から老女の本性が暴かれると、祐慶と共に鬼女と対決し法力でこれに対抗してゆく。

Yamatobo and Sanukibo

Two itinerant monks who are traveling with Yukei, Yamatobo and Sanukibo are faithful observers of their faith, but their fellow porter Tarogo has a wicked streak that ultimately allows them to find out the truth about the old woman who has given them lodgings. They join with Yukei in opposing the demon, relying on the power of the Buddha.

強力太郎吾
ごうりきたろうご

強力とは旅に付き添う荷物持ちで、時に案内役ともなる。阿闍梨祐慶の一行に伴い安達原の一軒家に泊まるが、主（あるじ）の老女が出がけに言い置いた「決して閨（ねや）の中を覗いてはならぬ」という言葉に背き、はやる好奇心から部屋の中を覗き見る。なんと中は散乱する沢山の骨と血の海、さては噂に聞く安達原の鬼女と知れ、太郎吾は暗い野道を一目散に駆けて行き老女と行き合って恐ろしい目に合う。

Goriki Tarogo

Tarogo is the porter and navigator of the group of monks who are on a religious pilgrimage around the country. When an old woman agrees to give them lodgings for the night, he goes against her wishes and peeks into her room. He finds a mountain of bones and blood there and realizes that she is the infamous demon of Adachigahara. His curiosity does not go unpunished, as he runs from the house in fear only to run into the demon on the road...

みどころ
Highlights

1. 鬼に遭遇したい
—— For Those Who Want to Meet a Demon

「みちのくの安達が原の黒塚に鬼こもれりと聞くはまことか」の古歌は、安達原伝説に引っかけた恋歌だという。安達ヶ原の一つ家（一軒家）に鬼女が棲み、旅人を殺して喰らうという噂は古くから知られていた。灯りに安堵する旅人、そこには凶暴な老婆が…という空想は何故かとても刺激的。鬼女に遭遇したいという気持ちが、どこかにある。苦しい人生を生きた人間は一度は鬼に憧れる、だから鬼伝説は人気があると言った人もいる。

There is an old love song that is said to be based on the Adachigahara legend. This legend tells of a famous female demon who eats unwary travelers who are fooled into a sense of relief by her disguise as an old woman living alone. There is something about such a story that almost makes one hope to meet with the demon oneself. Some say that stories of demons are popular because those who live difficult lives sometimes hope to meet with such monsters.

2. 月夜に、ダンス
—— A Moonlit Dance

芒一面の野原に、薪を拾いに行く老婆の心は軽い。己の罪障も消えると信じた哀れな鬼女は、月夜に浮かれて踊り始める。この場面を初演した初世市川猿翁は、洋行して観たロシアンバレエの手法を取り入れている。月光の下の、ソロダンスなのだ。自分自身の影を踏みながら、喜びを表現する場面は極めて近代的で、いつも大きな拍手が生まれる。埋め尽くす芒を照らす月は限りなく巨大、という背景も印象深い。

The old woman goes about her task of picking up firewood in a field of pampas grass without a care in the world. Though she is a demon, her sincere belief that her sins can be forgiven is manifest in her lighthearted dance in the moonlight. Ichikawa En'o I, who first played this role, incorporated techniques he had learned from Russian ballet. This solo dance bathed in moonlight is strikingly modern, particularly the dancer's way of stepping into his own shadow. This part of the performance never fails to receive a big round of applause. The pampas grass on stage is the real thing, and the massive moon in the background is truly breathtaking.

3. ダメと言われれば、覗きたい！
—— We All Want What We Can't Have

「けっして中を覗かないでくださいね」。ダメと言われれば、覗き見したいのは人間の常。この手の話は民話の定番である。鶴の本性を見られてしまう「夕鶴」が代表的な例だ。しかし『黒塚』の場合は、「食い散らかした死骸が積まれた閨を見ないでほしい」なのであって、そこには恥ずかしさのようなものも潜んでいるように感じられる。『黒塚』の老女は、高僧でも約束を破ることに絶望して、自ら鬼の本性を露わにしている。

We always want what we are denied, a facet of human nature often depicted in fairytales. The tragic tale of the opera *Yuzuru*, where the crane's true form is finally revealed, is a perfect example of this. But the revelation in *Kurozuka* is that the old woman is a demon who eats humans. Her forbidding the monks to look in her room is partly out of embarrassment at her terrible ways, but she eventually reveals herself in a rage after being betrayed by the monks who break their promise to her.

4. 追われた人間が鬼になる
—— Hounded Humans Become Demons

鬼という中国語と、和語の「おに」は全く同じ意味ではないらしい。日本の鬼は、目に見えない荒ぶる神や、もののけを指すこともある。夜叉や羅刹は仏教説話の鬼である。そのほか鬼は、朝廷に従わない集団、山の民など社会からはみ出した人間、恐怖を感じる相手を指す言葉でもあった。『紅葉狩』、『土蜘』、『黒塚』のほか『大江山酒呑童子』など鬼退治をテーマとする題材は、古代に起きた異民族との争いの名残とも考えられる。

The Chinese and Japanese words for a demon, which share a common Chinese character, do not actually have the same meaning. In Japan, "oni" can have a wide range of meanings. It can refer to a malevolent god or a phantom. "*Yasha*" and "*rasetsu*" are demons of Buddhist origin. The word has also been used to refer to social outcasts who are feared by society, such as traitors to the imperial court or groups who live in the mountains. *Momijigari*, *Tsuchigumo*, and *Kurozuka* are just a few of the many works of theatre and literature that detail demons and their defeat, and it is easy to see how they could have their origins in ancient conflicts that took place between different races and communities in Japan.

三社祭
Sanja Matsuri

『三社祭』
2014年10月 歌舞伎座
悪玉（三代目中村橋之助）

Sanja Matsuri
(Kabukiza Theatre, October 2014)
Akudama (Nakamura Hashinosuke III)

あらすじ　　　　　　　　Synopsis

浅草観音の縁起とは
漁師が川底から拾い上げた観音像だとか。
その二人の漁師が明るく軽妙に語り踊ってみせる

三社祭の山車人形が屋台から飛び出し、浜成・武成という二人の漁師姿で踊る。
観音様のご加護による魚河岸の賑わいなどを明るく陽気に踊るうち、
降りてきた黒雲から「善玉」「悪玉」が二人に乗り移り、男女の恋模様などを軽妙に描いてみせる。
やがて元の姿に立ち返り、舟の上で極まる二人。

Legend goes that a pair of fisherman brothers found a kannon statue at the bottom of the riverbed long ago, and that this is the origin of Asakusa Kannon. Watch as these two brothers tell stories through their nimble dancing.

Two puppets representing Hamanari and Takenari jump down from a festival float and begin dancing. As the two perform a dance depicting scenes of a riverside fish market, two spirits, Zendama and Akudama descend from the clouds and possess the two dancers. The possessed fishermen now perform a dance showing a story of love between a man and a woman. Finally, the two fishermen return to themselves and return to their boat, marking the end of the show.

　浅草の宮戸川。宮戸川は浅草周辺の隅田川の古称で、いにしえ、漁師の檜前浜成（ひのくまのはまなり）と武成（たけなり）の兄弟が、浅草寺の本尊である観音像を網で拾い上げたという伝承のある地。
　その川を背景に、網と櫂を持った浜成・武成兄弟が揺れている。三社祭の山車の人形が踊り出すという趣向である。

　　弥生なかばの花の雲
　　鐘は上野か浅草の
　　利生は深き宮戸川
　　誓いの網の古えや
　　三社祭の氏子中

舟から降りた二人は、清元の軽快な節に乗り踊る。

　　もれぬ誓いや網の目に　今日の獲物も信心の
　　おかげお礼に朝参り　浅草寺の観世音

Asakusa, along the Miyato River, the ancient name for the Sumida River where the fishermen brothers Hinokuma no Hamanari and Takenari are said to have discovered the Asakusa Kannon statue in the riverbed.

Puppets of the two brothers are set atop a Sanja Matsuri float, net and oars in hand. Suddenly, they come to life and begin dancing.

(See Japanese lyrics on left)

The brothers alight from their boat and begin dancing to the rapid *kiyomoto* rhythm.

(See Japanese lyrics on left)

網の光りは夕あじや　昼あみ夜網に凪もよく
乗込む河岸の相場にしけば
生貝生鯛生鰯　なまぐさばんだばさらんだ
わびた世界じゃないかいな
撞いてくりゃるな八幡鐘よ
可愛いお人の目をさます　お人の人の
可愛いお人の人の目をさます
サッサ何としょか　どしょかいな
帰りましょ　待たしゃんせ
憎や烏が啼くわいな

　折からそこに黒雲と共に悪玉と善玉が空から降り、二人に憑りつき、悪尽くしの踊りや玉尽くしの踊りを踊る。

悪にとっては　事もおろかや
悪七別当　悪禅師　保元平治に悪源太
梶原源太は梅ヶ枝を
蛭の地獄へ落したためしもありとかや

それが　いやさに気の毒さに
おいらが宗旨はありがたい
弘法大師のいろはにほへと
かわる心はからくり的
北山時雨じゃないけれど
振られて帰る晩もあり
それでお宿の首尾もよく
とかく浮世は儘にはならぬ
善に強きは コレ善の綱
牛に曳かれて善悪は浮かれ拍子の一踊り

早い手玉や品玉の
品よく結ぶ玉だすき
かけて思いの玉櫛笥
開けて口惜しき玉手箱
かよう玉鉾　玉松風の
もとはざざんざでうたえや
うかれ鳥の烏羽玉や

唄うも舞ふも法の奇特に善玉は
消えて跡なく失せにけり

　再び二人は舟に乗り込み、幕となる。

The spirits Akudama and Zendama descend from a black cloud and possess the brothers, their dances evoking the evil and good which they respectively represent.

(See Japanese lyrics on left)

Finally, the brothers return to their boat, marking the end of the show.

『三社祭』
2014年10月　歌舞伎座
（左から）悪玉（三代目中村橋之助）、善玉（二代目中村獅童）

Sanja Matsuri
(Kabukiza Theatre, October 2014)
(from left) Akudama (Nakamura Hashinosuke III),
Zendama (Nakamura Shido II)

作品の概要

演目名

三社祭

作者

作詞＝二世瀬川如皐
作曲＝初世清元斎兵衛

概要

　浅草の風物詩である三社祭の名がついた清元舞踊。しかし本作は、三社祭そのものを描くのではない。かつて祭に繰り出された山車人形の題材を変化舞踊に綴った『弥生の花浅草祭』の一場面が残ったものなのである。江戸時代の三社祭は、5月ではなく3月に催されたので題名に弥生が入っている。本作は浅草寺の本尊となった観音様を網で引き揚げた漁師たちを主人公にした二人の踊りである。大変に動きの速いリズミカルな振りの連続で、観客が眠くなる暇はない。後半は、空から降りてきた黒雲にくっ付いた善玉・悪玉に二人が魅られるという不思議な展開で、善と悪という文字が書かれた小さめの丸い面を被っての踊りになる。この趣向は、当時流行した心学という学問から来たもので、人間の心を、文字を書いたお面で見せるとてもユニークな舞踊である。すでに文化年間に悪玉踊りが流行したといい、文化8(1811)年初演の『浮かれ坊主』にも、悪の文字を手桶の底に使った踊りがある。

初演

天保3 (1832) 年3月江戸・中村座で、善玉が四世坂東三津五郎、悪玉が二世中村芝翫 (四世歌右衛門)。作詞は二世瀬川如皐、作曲は初世清元斎兵衛。振付は二世藤間勘十郎、松本五郎市。

Overview

Title

Sanja Matsuri

Writer

Lyrics: Segawa Joko II
Music: Kiyomoto Saibei I

Overview

　Sanja Matsuri is the quintessential festival of Asakusa, but this *kiyomoto* buyo piece is not actually about the festival. It is actually just a small portion of the *henge-buyo* dance that was once performed at the festival, called *Yayoi no Hana Asakusamatsuri*. It features the two fishermen who retrieved the kannon statue from the river (establishing Sensoji Temple's principal object of worship) as its main protagonists. The quick, rhythmic dances repeated one after another leave no time for the audience to nod off! The latter half of the dance shows the two spirits Zendama and Akudama descend from the clouds and possess the fishermen brothers, their possession expressed by masks with the characters for *zen* (good) and *aku* (evil). Expressing the heart of man through words on masks was a common feature of buyo dances in the past, and was inspired by the study of *shingaku* (a set of teachings from the Edo period which blend Buddhism, Shinto, and Confucian ideas). Dances featuring Akudama were already popular by the time of the Bunka Era (the early 1800's), and the buyo dance *Ukarebozu* (1811) featured the character *aku* written on the bottom of a bucket.

Premiere

March 1832, Nakamuraza Theatre. Feat. Bando Mitsugoro IV as Zendama and Nakamura Shikan II as Akudama. Lyrics by Segawa Joko II. Music by Kiyomoto Saibei I. Choreography by Fujima Kanjuro II and Matsumoto Goroichi.

登場人物

善玉
ぜんだま

宮戸川（今の隅田川）で漁をする漁師兄弟の兄で、名を浜成（はまなり）という。浅草観音の縁起伝説では二人の漁師が川底から観音像を引き揚げ、それをご本尊としたと伝えられるが、それに由来する山車（だし）人形に魂が宿って踊り出すといった趣向。二人が魚河岸の様子などを踊るうち、空から善悪二つの玉を乗せた暗雲が降りてきて、浜成には善玉が乗り移り様々な躍動的な踊りを軽妙に繰り広げる。

Zendama

Two fishermen brothers who plied their trade along the Miyato River (now the Sumida River) appear in this dance, the older named Hamanari. According to legend the brothers once fetched a sacred kannon statue from the riverbed and came to worship it. Because of this, the spirit of Kannon is said to descend upon the festival floats, causing puppets representing the brothers to dance. At first, the brothers' dance evokes images of a riverside fish market. Amid this performance, two spirits, one of good and one of evil, descend upon the scene. The spirit of good (Zendama) possesses Hamanari, causing him to dance nimbly upon the stage.

悪玉
あくだま

漁師兄弟の弟で、武成（たけなり）という。今日も朝に晩にと漁に励めるのも浅草観音ご信心のお蔭と、感謝を抱きながら網にかかった魚の様子などを踊るうち、降りてきた雲の中から悪玉が憑りつき、悪七別当、悪禅師、悪源太と悪づくしの踊りを披露する。そして善玉となった浜成と共に男女の恋模様を描いた踊りとなり、とかく浮世はままならぬと語ってゆく。やがて元の漁師の姿となり舟へと戻ってゆく。

Akudama

The younger of the two fisherman brothers is named Takenari. He dances fervently in honor of Asakusa Kannon, his movements depicting fish caught in fishing nets. As the two spirits of good and evil descend, the evil one (Akudama) possesses Takenari and causes him to perform a number of malevolent dances. Eventually, Takenari and his older brother Hamanari come to perform a dance depicting a love story between a man and woman that perfectly encapsulates the caprices of life before the two regain control of their bodies and return to their boat.

みどころ
Highlights

1. 浅草寺のご本尊
—— Sensoji Temple's Principal Deity

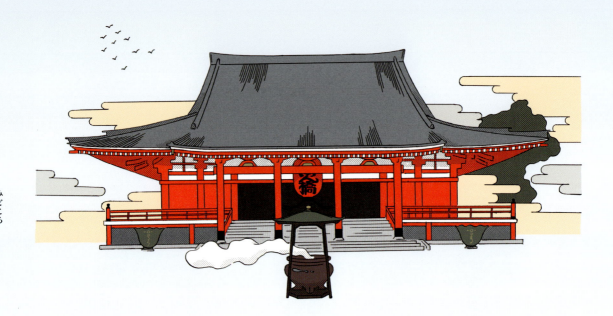

浅草寺のご本尊は秘仏で、人形のように小さい観音様といわれる。推古天皇の御代に、近くの隅田川がまだ浦辺であった頃、漁師の網に観音像がかかったと伝わる。引き揚げた二人の漁師・檜前浜成（ひのくまのはまなり）と檜前武成（たけなり）と、観音様を祀った土師真中知（はじのまつち）の三人を祀ったのが、境内にある三社様（正式名は浅草神社）。三社祭は毎年5月に盛大に行われるが、江戸時代には旧暦弥生の祭だった。

The secret image of Sensoji Temple's principal deity is said to be a small *kannon* figure. Legend has it that this figure was caught in a net and taken from the Sumida River by two fishermen in the time of Emperor Suiko (593–628). The fishermen Hinokuma no Hamanari and Takenari, as well as Hajinomatsuchi (who deified the *kannon* figure) are themselves deified at Sanjasama (officially named Asakusa Shrine). The Sanja Matsuri is held every May, which was the third month (*Yayoi*) by the old lunar calendar.

2. 体育会系の踊り —— A Sporty Dance

現在見られる歌舞伎舞踊中もっとも動きが激しいもののひとつ。体育会系とでもいおうか、情緒とか風情みたいなヤワな評価は似合わない。純粋に踊りの面白さを追求しているようだ。漁師二人がリズミカルに足を踏み、大胆で動きの速い振りを競いあう。こういうDNAが江戸っ子にはあると感じさせてくれる踊りだ。若い俳優でなければなかなか勤まらないが、もちろん未熟でも勤まらない。エネルギーのほとばしりと、確かな技術の安定が必要なのである。

This is one of the most energetic dances in the modern kabuki buyo repertoire. The word "sporty" may not be entirely appropriate for the vigorous movements of this dance, but neither do softer words such as "sentimental" or "elegant." It is as if this buyo is simply seeking out the sheer fun of dance. The two fishermen brothers can be seen rhythmically stamping at the stage and trying to outdo each other with their grand yet nimble movements that make one feel that such energy is truly the essence of what it means to be an *edokko* (a child of Edo). Naturally, only younger actors can play these roles to their desired effect, but their technical difficulty make them an equal challenge to an inexperienced performer. A controlled hand is required to balance the sheer energy and technical finesse that this piece demands.

3. 空から降ってくる善玉・悪玉 —— Zendama and Akudama Descend from the Sky

善玉とか悪玉とかコレステロールに冠するが、そもそもなぜ〜玉というのか。それは江戸後期の戯作者で絵師の山東京伝が、黄表紙と呼ばれた洒落本で、丸に善、丸に悪と、「心」をイラスト化して描いたから。流行していた心学という学問が、人は悪い心と、善い心に支配されると説いたのをモチーフにしたもの。もちろん悪玉のほうが若者にもてはやされた。漁師に善玉悪玉が乗り移ると、踊りが若干グロテスクにエスカレートする。

The names Zendama and Akudama almost sound like we're talking about eggs (*tamago* in Japanese), but many viewers may want to know why we use the suffix "tama" (ball) at all. Actually, it comes from a late-Edo drawing by the writer and artist Santo Kyoden, who drew a circle with the word "zen" (good) and one with the word "aku" (bad) written inside as a representation of the new psychological concept of the human heart being controlled by both good and evil impulses. Of course, Akudama (the "evil" spirit) tends to be more popular with younger viewers. As the two spirits possess the fishermen brothers, their dance gradually gets more energetic and even grotesque.

4. 本当は四変化 —— Originally in Four Turns

本来は、二人で踊る起伏に富んだ題材の変化舞踊である。最初は三社祭の山車人形の趣向で、神功皇后と武内宿禰に扮した踊り。身重の神功皇后が新羅出陣から凱旋して皇子（後の応神天皇）を出産したという、遥か昔の古代神話が語られる。それが一転して漁師に変わり、善玉と悪玉の踊りが済むと、善玉が吉原通いの通人に、悪玉が田舎侍に変わって絡む洒落た場面があって、最後は揃って勇壮な石橋（しゃっきょう）の獅子になる。

The original play was a *henge-buyo* with many twists and turns. It began with dolls on a float of the Sanja Matsuri—one dressed as Empress Jingu and one as Takenouchi no Sukune. Their dance depicts some of the ancient myths of the empress, who conquered the ancient kingdom of Korea and returned to Japan to give birth to a son (who would go on to become Emperor Ojin). From here the play shifts to the story of the fishermen / Zendama and Akudama. After this, Zendama becomes a regular customer of the Yoshiwara pleasure quarters while Akudama becomes a rural samurai warrior, and finally the play ends with a depiction of the mythical *shishi* lions of Shakkyo on Mt. Seiryo.

お祭り
Omatsuri

『お祭り』
2011年11月　平成中村座
鳶頭（十八世中村勘三郎）

Omatsuri
(Heisei Nakamuraza Theatre, November 2011)
Tobigashira (Nakamura Kanzaburo XVIII)

あらすじ   Synopsis   Omatsuri

ここは赤坂日枝神社、明るい山王祭の風景。
賑わう中へほろ酔いの鳶頭が進み出て、
気分はすっかり祭りの主役

山王祭は江戸の顔、将軍様が拝礼する天下祭。祭りの華といえば芸者衆や手古舞、それにもちろん
粋でいなせな鳶頭。頭（かしら）がほろ酔い気分で現れると「待ってました！」と飛び交う声。
すかさず「待っていたとはありがてえ」と受けて立ち、
絡む若い者たちを軽くいなし何処へともなく去ってゆく。

──────── **Akasaka Hie Shrine's exciting Sanno Matsuri Festival. As the festival is in full swing, a tipsy *tobigashira* arrives—he is the most anticipated participant, the life of the party.**

A festival celebrated by the Shogun himself, Sanno Matsuri Festival was one of the most important festivals of the Edo capital. Highlights of the festival included the stunning geisha and *tekomai* guards who protected festival floats. And then, of course, there was the stylish *tobigashira* (head of the *tobi* firefighters). As the tipsy *tobigashira* arrives, the crowd shouts joyously, "we've been waiting for you!" In response, the *tobigashira* shouts back, "'Preciate that!" deftly moving around the boisterous young festival participants and moving onward.

Synopsis

江戸時代、天下祭といわれた、赤坂日枝山王神社の祭礼である「山王祭」の当日。
清元の置き浄瑠璃のあと、ほろ酔いの鳶頭が登場する。

　　申西の
　　花も盛りの暑さにも
　　負けぬ気性の　見かけから

　　言わずと知れたお祭りの
　　なりもすっかりそこら中
　　行き届かせてこぶもなく
　　ここではひとつあそこでは
　　頭々とたてられて
　　御機嫌じゃのと　町内の
　　家主方も　夕日影　風も嬉しく戻り道

ここで客席から「待ってました」と声がかかり、それを受

The day of Sanno Matsuri Festival at Akasaka Hie Sanno Shrine, a grand event called "festival of the realm" during the Edo Period. After a *joruri* narration accompanied by *kiyomoto* music, the tipsy Tobigashira appears.

(See Japanese lyrics on left)

At this point, the audience shouts, "We've been waiting

けて「待っていたとはありがてえ」と鳶頭の台詞となる。

　そして、鳶頭は、昨年の大山詣の帰りに馴染みとなった女との惚気話を踊る。

じたい去年の山帰り
言うは今さら過ぎし秋
初の一座の連れのうち
面白そうな口合いに
好いたが因果好かれたも
心に二つはないわいな

　その後、字余りの都々逸を歌ったり、座敷での狐拳の様子を踊る。

あきらめて何のかのと
ありゃただの人
あか凡夫のわれわれなりゃこそ
減法界に迷いやす

お手がなるから銚子のかわり目と
上がって見たれば
お客が三人
庄屋ぼんぼん狐拳
とぼけた色ではないかいな

　そこへ若い衆が打ちかかるので、あしらいながら、引き物尽くしの踊りになる。

引けや引け引け
引くものにとりては
花に霞よ子の日の小松
初会の盃馴染みの煙草盆
おしやらく娘の袖たもと
したばの履き物
内裏女郎の召し物
座頭のまわし
あやめに大根
御神木のしめ縄
又も引くものは色々ござる
湯元細工のけん玉ぶりぶり
そ様故なら心の丈を
しめし参らせ候べくの
人形筆売この首を長く出したり縮めたり
何とのろいじゃあるまいか

　そして頭と若い衆の賑やかな所作ダテのうちに幕となる。

for you!" (*mattemashita*), and Tobigashira responds, saying "Preciate that you waited!" (*matteita to wa arigate*).

Next, the Tobigashira performs a dance depicting the touching story of a man who meets and gets to know a girl on his way back from a visit to a mountain temple.

(See Japanese lyrics on left)

Next, as a *dodoitsu* love song is sung, the dance changes to a depiction of a game played in a tatami room.

(See Japanese lyrics on left)

A crowd of youngsters now appears, causing a change in Tobigashira's dance. His dance now depicts a scene of gift-giving to everyone in the crowd.

(See Japanese lyrics on left)

Amid this boisterous dance between Tobigashira and the youthful crowd, the curtain finally closes, indicating the end of the play.

『お祭り』
2013年4月　歌舞伎座
(左から) 芸者 (三代目中村扇雀)、鳶頭 (十世坂東三津五郎)、芸者 (九代目中村福助)、鳶頭 (三代目中村橋之助)

Omatsuri
(Kabukiza Theatre, April 2013)
(from left) Geisha (Nakamura Senjaku III), Tobigashira (Bando Mitsugoro X), Geisha (Nakamura Fukusuke IX), Tobigashira (Nakamura Hashinosuke III)

作品の概要

演目名

お祭り

作者

作詞 = 二世桜田治助
作曲 = 初世清元斎兵衛

概要

　天下祭と呼ばれた日枝神社の山王祭の舞踊。主人公はお江戸の水で産湯を使った江戸っ子の鳶頭。幕が開くと祭礼の町中をすっきり描いた背景装置が目に飛び込み、良い気分で鳶頭の登場を待つことになる。初演は三変化舞踊で、本名題『再茲歌舞妓花籬（またここにかぶきのはなだし）』。歌い出しの文句が「申酉の花も盛りの暑さにも負けぬ気性の…」なので、通称『申酉（さるとり）』ともいう。山王祭に一番に出る山車の作り物が鶏、二番目が猿だったことに拠るが、祭りの頃に咲く猿捕茨（さるとりいばら）という花の名にも掛けている。娯楽の少ない江戸の町では、祭りは今よりももっと熱が入ったものだったらしい。鳶頭は祭りの先導役として一番の花形だった。首抜きという、首周りの柄を合わせた着物にたっつけ袴、黒足袋に、豆絞りの手拭い。髷は魚の鯔（いな）の背のように少し曲げるという粋な姿で衆目を集めた。本作はよく上演されるが、鳶が二人になったり、芸者を登場させたりすることもある。終盤にカラミを出し喧嘩の様子を見せるのが定番になっている。

初演

文政9（1826）年6月江戸・市村座で、三世坂東三津五郎による。作詞は二世桜田治助、作曲は初世清元斎兵衛。振付は松本五郎市。

Overview

Title

Omatsuri

Writer

Lyrics: Sakurada Jisuke II
Music: Kiyomoto Saibei I

Overview

　A buyo dance depicting Hie Shrine's Sanno Matsuri Festival, also known as *Tenkamatsuri*. The star of the show is the *tobigashira*, a born-and-raised child of Edo. The audience is bound to be dazzled as the stage opens to show a gorgeously rendered backdrop depicting the streets of Edo during the festival which also expresses the anticipation of the star of the show: the *tobigashira*. The first performance of this piece was in the *henge-buyo* style, and it was billed under the title *Mata kokoni kabuki no hanadashi*. It is also called *Sarutori*, taken from the opening lines. This also makes a pun on the fact that birds (*tori*) and monkeys (*saru*) were the most common float pieces in the festival. The *tobigashira* is the star of the show and the festival, wearing a stunning *kubinuki* robe with *tattsuke-bakama* trousers, black *tabi* socks, and a spotted handkerchief. This piece is often performed today, but some productions take artistic liberties, adding a second *tobi* firefighter or having geisha appear. The finale which features a heated quarrel has now become a standard part of any production of *Omatsuri*.

Premiere

June 1826, Ichimuraza Theatre. Produced by Bando Mitsugoro III. Lyrics by Sakurada Jisuke II. Music by Kiyomoto Saibei I. Choreography by Matsumoto Goroichi.

登場人物　Characters

鳶頭
とびがしら

赤坂日枝神社の山王祭、多くの人で賑わう中へほろ酔い気分でやって来たのは鳶頭。鳶は江戸の町火消や神社の氏子として町の人からの信も厚く、また鳶頭は粋でいなせなその姿から祭りの花形となる。首から肩にかけて大きく紋を染め抜いた「首抜き」という衣裳で登場し、大向こうから「待ってました！」と掛け声がかかると、「待っていたとはありがてえ」と返す、そんな段取りもお約束。

Tobigashira

As Hie Shrine's Sanno Matsuri Festival is in full swing, a somewhat drunken *tobigashira* arrives. As head of the *tobi* firefighters in the Edo period, who were also shrine parishioners, such a person would have been a deeply loved and trustworthy man to the townsfolk. This stylish and dashing man, therefore, is the very life of the party. He arrives wearing a "*kubinuki*" robe which features a large crest extending from the neck all the way across the shoulders. As he arrives, the crowd joyously shouts, "we've been waiting!" "'Preciate that!" the *tobigashira* shouts back in an exchange that is a must-have for this exciting buyo piece.

みどころ
Highlights

1. 江戸の天下祭
── The Premier Festival of Edo

江戸っ子は祭りが大好き。江戸三大祭といえば、山王日枝神社の山王祭（6月）、神田明神の神田祭（5月）、そして浅草神社の三社祭か、深川富岡八幡宮の八幡祭を指すだろう。地域が重なる山王祭と神田祭は交互に隔年に行われ、山王祭は西暦偶数年に行われる。日枝神社はもとは江戸城内に祀られ、徳川幕府成立後城外に移されたのだが、その後も祭りの山車や神輿が城内に入ることを許され、将軍の上覧に達したので、天下祭といわれた。

The residents of Edo loved festivals to a fault. If you had to list the three most important festivals of Edo, they would have to be the Hie Shrine's Sanno Matsuri in June, Kanda Shrine's Kanda Matsuri in May, and either the Sanja Matsuri at Asakusa Shrine or the Hachiman Matsuri at Tomioka Hachiman Shrine. The Sanno and Kanda Festivals are held every other year in the same area, the Sanno Festival taking place on every even-numbered year according to the western calendar. Hie Shrine was originally located within Edo Castle, but it was moved outside of the castle precincts after the Tokugawa shogunate was established. Even so, the floats and portable shrines of the festival were given permission to enter the castle, giving them the honor of the shogun's audience. Because of this, the Sanno Matsuri is often referred to as the premier festival of Edo.

2. 待っていたとは
—— "I 'Preciate Your Waiting"

この踊りには、ひとつのお約束がある。粋な鳶頭がほろ酔いで登場し、舞台中央にすっと形良く立ち止まると、大向こうから「待ってました」と声がかかる。と、鳶頭はにんまりと笑い、「待っていたとはありがてぇ」と返す。すると客席に笑顔がふわっと広がる。この客席と俳優の粋な交歓が、『お祭り』という一幕の楽しいお約束なのである。役を離れて、俳優が客席に応えるやりとりが、一種の型のようになるのも歌舞伎ならでは、である。

The one indispensable part of this dance is the banter between crowd and *tobigashira*. The tipsy firefighter stumbles onto the stage and, with an irresistible charm, stands center stage as the audience shouts, "We've been waiting for you!" In response, the *tobigashira* shouts back with a smile, "I 'preciate your waiting for me!" This fun call and response is one of the greatest pleasures of watching *Omatsuri*. Breaking the fourth wall like this is also one of the unique charms of kabuki.

3. 鳶は江戸の花形職業
—— *Tobi*—A Beloved Profession in Edo Japan

火事の多い江戸で、町火消を担う鳶は花形の職業だった。命を惜しまない鳶たちは半纏姿も勇ましく、髷もいなせに結い、普段は建築現場などで働きを見せた。大店の坊ちゃんが鳶になろうとして家を勘当されたり、お嬢さんが一目惚れしてしまったりという話が落語や芝居の種になっている。芝居では、町内での揉め事に駆けつけたり、金持ちが花見などに出るときにボディーガード的にお供したりする鳶頭の姿がよく見られる。

The *tobi* firefighters of Edo were beloved by the people due to the proliferation of fires in the city in those days. They were respected for their bravery in the face of deadly fires, and could also be seen at construction sites where they wore their hair in a stylish *mage* topknot. There is a popular story seen in *rakugo* stories and plays of the young son of a wealthy family who decides to become a *tobi*. He is subsequently disinherited by his family, but his gallant ways earn him the love of a beautiful young woman. In plays, *tobi* are often depicted rushing to quell fights that have broken out in the streets or accompanying wealthy patrons as bodyguards as they enjoy the cherry blossoms of spring.

4. 快気祝い
—— Celebrating a Full Recovery

体調を崩してしばらく休んでいた俳優が、めでたく舞台復帰するときに、この『お祭り』が出ることが多い。大病だったならば、再び舞台姿を見られる喜びもひとしお。少しほっそりとしたかと、涼しげな姿を見つめる客席も熱を帯びて、「待ってました」のかけ声が観客すべての期待の代弁になる。それに応える「待っていたとは〜」も、俳優の気持ちそのまま、ということになる。ホッと安堵のため息の、あたたかい波が場内を駆け抜ける。

It is common for an actor to return to the stage after an illness with a performance of *Omatsuri*. The more serious the actor's illness, the more joyous the performance is. This play particularly allows for the audience to shout with real vigor, "We've been waiting for you!" And of course, the actor's response is at once act and reality as he tells the audience directly, "I 'preciate your waiting for me!" The audience's sense of relief and warmth can be felt in the theatre on day's this play is performed by an actor who has taken ill.

Appendix

付録

Dramatic Dances —————— 舞踊

付録

歌舞伎の歴史

歌舞伎の歴史

日本の伝統芸能と歌舞伎の特徴

　日本には伝統的な音楽・舞踊・演劇などが数多く伝承されています。

　成立した順に挙げると、まず雅楽があります。現在伝わる形が整ったのが、10世紀頃。1000年以上の歴史がある音楽と舞で、宮廷音楽として、また寺社で受け継がれました。貴族たちの芸能といっていいでしょう。

　次が能楽。能と狂言を合わせた呼び名で、室町時代に大成し、650年近い歴史があります。江戸時代は武家式楽、武士の儀式に使われる音楽となりました。いわば武士たちの芸能。

　そして、歌舞伎。

　それから、人形浄瑠璃、文楽。浄瑠璃という音曲の語りに合わせ人形が動く人形浄瑠璃の内、現在、義太夫節を使用する「文楽」が代表的です。義太夫節の成立は300年ほど前。

　また、沖縄には、宮廷の音楽として作られ、300年近い歴史を有する「くみおどり」が伝わっています。

　今上げた五つの芸能は、ユネスコの無形文化遺産にも登録され、日本を代表する古典芸能です。さらに、落語や講談などの大衆芸能、琴や三味線を使った音楽、舞などの古典舞踊などもあります。これらは、国も専用の劇場を設け保護育成に力を入れている音楽・舞踊・演劇であり、それぞれ専門の実演家、プロフェッショナルがいる芸能、いわゆる人間国宝が出るジャンルともいえます。

　実はこれほど古い芸能が数多く残っているのは世界的にも珍しいのです。

　西欧では、新しい芸術が起きると、先行するものは淘汰されてしまうことが多い。それは芸能も同じで、先行の芸能は衰退してしまうのがほとんどです。ところが日本では、先行する芸能も大事に伝承してきました。いくつものジャンルがあって、それぞれ歴史が古い、これが日本の古典芸能の大きな特徴です。

　さらにもう少し大きく見ていくと、民俗芸能といわれるものがあります。地域の祭りや行事などの際、普段は別の仕事をしている人たちにより演奏され、演じられます。この中にもアイヌの民俗音楽など、無形文化遺産に登録されている芸能があります。

　また、声明などに代表される宗教音楽、さらに、民謡、盆踊り、太鼓、また、津軽三味線、沖縄の三線など、地方独自の音楽もあります。

　少し周りを見渡してみると、現代でも伝統的な音楽や舞踊は意外と身近にあるのです。

　そして、明治から取り入れた西洋の音楽や舞踊、これもまた、当たり前のように身近にある。どころか、世界中で活躍している音楽家やダンサーも輩出しています。

　つまり、日本には伝統的な音楽や舞踊も、西洋的な音楽や舞踊も身近にあり、我々はその中で生活している。なかなか気が付かないことですが、これは日本の文化の大きな特徴なのです。

　宮中や寺社で継承された雅楽、武家に庇護された能楽、宮廷音楽として発生した組踊と違い、人形浄瑠璃と歌舞伎は庶民が支持した芸能です。歴史をみても権力者による庇護はおろか、むしろ弾圧をうける方が多く、その網の目をかいくぐってきました。

　次からはその歴史を見てみましょう。

歌舞伎の歴史①―野郎歌舞伎まで

　慶長8（1603）年、京都でお国（出雲阿国）という女性が始めた「歌舞伎踊り」が歌舞伎の発祥とされます。

　これは歴史の教科書にも載っていることなので、ご存知の方も多いでしょう。

　では、なぜ女性の始めた芸能が、現在は男性だけによって演じられているのでしょう。実は現在の歌舞伎に至るまで、様々な紆余曲折があったのです。ここでは現在の歌舞伎の直接的な始まり「野郎歌舞伎」までの道のりをたどります。

　さて、お国の「歌舞伎踊り」は男女混交の一座により、歌と踊りを中心に、時に滑稽な寸劇が上演されました。お国は当時流行していた「かぶき者」の男に扮し、茶屋の女に扮した男性のもとに通う、茶屋遊びの踊りを見せたと言われています。この芸能は「お国歌舞伎」とも呼ばれ大流行。そのスタイルはすぐ全国に追随者を生み出しました。

　類似の集団に加え、人気に目を付けた遊女屋が抱えている遊女を舞台に上げ、歌や踊りを見せ始めました。遊女も含めた女性が登場する「女歌舞伎」は人気を博しましたが、風紀を乱すという理由で幕府は女性芸能を禁止してしまいます。

　かわりに台頭してきたのが、若い少年たちが歌舞を見せる「若衆歌舞伎」。これは「女歌舞伎」全盛時代から並行して行われてきていましたが、「女歌舞伎」衰退により一世を風靡しました。しかしこれも風紀を乱すという理由で禁止されます。

　一旦消えかけた歌舞伎の火は、関係者の熱意により、若衆

176

たちの若さと色気のシンボルである前髪を剃り落とし、野郎頭で演じる「野郎歌舞伎」として再興しました。

この「野郎歌舞伎」が現在の歌舞伎につながります。前髪を剃り落とされ、容色だけで売ることができなくなったこと、また、「狂言尽くし」として、歌舞でなく、演劇を主体とするように制限されたことが、現在の歌舞伎への道を切り拓いたのです。

お国が演じたレビュー的な「歌舞伎踊り」は、度重なる禁令と圧力を巧みにかわし、やがて男性のみで演じる演劇として姿を変えたのです。

「歌舞伎」と「傾(かぶ)き」

現在用いられる「歌舞伎」の表記は、音楽的(歌)で、舞踊の要素(舞)、芝居の要素(伎)もある演劇という特徴をよく表していますが、これは、後世の当て字。「かぶき」という言葉は、並外れたもの、常軌を逸するものという意味の「傾く(かぶく)」という動詞から来ています。

お国が歌舞伎踊りを始めた当時、「かぶき者」と呼ばれる一団がいました。わざと珍しい、人の目を驚かせるような奇抜な扮装や髪型をしたり、わざわざ目立つような行動を取ったりする若者たちでした。お国はかぶき者の男性に扮して、かぶき者たちの行動を舞台に取り入れました。

発生がかぶき者たちの姿を取り入れてできた芸能ゆえか、歌舞伎には常に同時代の流行を取り入れたいという傾向があるのです。

歌舞伎の歴史②──野郎歌舞伎から現在まで

野郎歌舞伎として再出発した歌舞伎は、江戸から現在にいたるまで様々に発展してきました。長い期間にわたる話なので、駆け足になりますが、後の「歌舞伎の言葉」で説明する用語を中心にざっと見ていきましょう。

元禄時代、江戸で「荒事」、上方で「和事」という対照的な芸が生まれました。また、この時代の作者としては近松門左衛門が知られています。やがて、人形浄瑠璃(現在の文楽)が、ドラマ性の優れる数多くの作品を生み出し人気を博したので、それらの作品を取り入れ上演するようになります。これらの作品を「義太夫狂言」と呼び、レパートリーの大きな位置を占めています。

文化文政期には、江戸で四世鶴屋南北が作者として活躍。

南北が得意としたのは、それまでの「世話物」をさらにリアルにした、後に「生世話」と呼ばれるジャンルでした。

江戸の終わりには「歌舞伎十八番」が制定されました。天保の改革では当時辺鄙であった浅草猿若町に劇場移転を命じられたり、人気俳優の追放などの弾圧をうけました。また、明治にかけては作者の河竹黙阿弥が活躍しました。

一方、舞踊も「三味線音楽」とともに目覚ましく発達を遂げました。天明期の舞踊や、江戸中期以降に流行した「変化舞踊」。江戸の終わりに端を発し、明治以降多く作られた「松羽目舞踊」など、様々な演目が今に伝えられています。

そのほか、舞台機構も発達。「花道」「廻り舞台」「セリ」など現在でも多用される機構が発達しました。

やがて明治維新を迎えると、歌舞伎も大きな転機を迎えます。高尚な作品を上演するようにという明治新政府の意向を受け、歴史に忠実であることを目指した、後に「活歴物」と呼ばれる作品群や、新たな時代の風俗をそのままに取り入れた「散切物」などの作品が生まれました。その後、外部の劇作家による、西洋戯曲に倣った「新歌舞伎」が新たなレパートリーに加わりました。

その後も軍部の統制、空襲による劇場の焼失、占領軍による封建的演目の上演禁止などの危機を乗り越えましたが、生活の急激な変化などにより、一時は公演数も少なくなります。しかし関係者の不断の努力もあり現在は隆盛が続いています。

また、海外公演を積極的に行い、日本だけでなく、広く世界の歌舞伎として認知されています。

以上駆け足で概要を紹介しましたが、歌舞伎の歴史は決していつでも順調だったわけではありません。激動する時代に適応し、たくましく歴史を重ねていることがおわかりいただけたのではないかと思います。

歌舞伎のように発生当時から今に至るまでショウビジネスとして成り立っている芸能というのは、ユネスコの無形文化遺産に登録されている世界の芸能の中で類を見ないことなのです。

The History of Kabuki

Traditional Japanese Performance Arts and the Characteristics of Kabuki

In Japan, there are many a great number of traditional styles of music, dance, and drama, each of which has been carefully passed down from generation to generation.

Gagaku music is the very first of these art forms to develop, the style as we know it today having been established in the 10th century. This thousand-year-old tradition of court music was passed down directly from the court and through temples and shrines. It is a high form of music originally meant for the aristocracy.

The next performance art to develop in Japan is *nogaku*. A general term that includes both noh and *kyogen* dramatic forms, *nogaku* was popular during the Muromachi Period of Japan (1336–1573) and has a history of over 650 years. In the Edo Period (1603–1868), samurai started using this style of music for ceremonies. It thus became very closely associated with the warrior class.

And finally, we come to kabuki and the puppet theater, *bunraku*.

The puppet theater involves the use of puppets which are skillfully manipulated in sync with the music and actors' spoken word. "*Bunraku*" which uses *gidayu-bushi* music is the most commonly known form of puppet theater and was established about 300 years ago. There is also a style of puppet theater music used by the royal court in Okinawa that has close to 300 years of history. This tradition is called "*kumi-odori*."

The above five performing arts are inscribed by UNESCO as intangible cultural heritage elements, and as such are the most representative of Japan's classical performing arts. There are, of course, many other performance arts, such as *rakugo* and *kodan* storytelling, *koto* and *shamisen* music, and traditional dances like *buyo*. These all fall under the categories of music, dance, or drama. The Japanese government has erected specialized theaters and supports the training of professionals in each field. These arts forms require specially trained professionals, and often produce living national treasures.

The number of ancient arts that have been preserved in Japan is actually quite high when compared to countries around the world. In western Europe it is common for new technologies to supersede the old, and the same goes for performance arts: when a new performance art is born, the previous one inevitably goes into decline. In Japan, however, the older traditions are passed on just as diligently as newer art forms. The most unique characteristic of Japanese arts is that there are so many genres, each with its own rich history.

There are also a number of folk art forms that have not been mentioned yet. These include the music played during regional festivals, often by locals who have normal day jobs. Another prime example is the folk music of the Ainu (native people of northern Japan), which has been inscribed as an intangible cultural heritage element.

Another example is Buddhist chants called "*shomyo*," a type of religious music. *Min'yo* folk songs, *bon-odori* dance, taiko drums, *Tsugaru-shamisen* and Okinawan *sanshin* music are just a few examples of Japan's rich tradition of unique regional arts.

Look around Japan and you'll find traditional art forms all around you. Our country has also absorbed a great number of Western art forms, and they, too, can be found everywhere in Japan. What's more, Japan boasts a great number of musicians and dancers who enjoy international acclaim.

The Japanese live amongst this rich intermingling of traditional Japanese and modern Western arts. Easy to overlook, this is one of the unique characteristics of Japanese culture.

Gagaku was preserved by shrines and temples, nogaku by samurai, and *kumi-odori* by the court. The puppet theater and kabuki, however, were popular arts supported by the public. Historically, these arts received no support from the government. In fact, they were often suppressed. Despite this, however, these dramatic art forms persevered.

Let's take a closer look at the history of the puppet and kabuki theaters.

History of Kabuki 1 —Beginnings to *Yaro-kabuki*

As commonly noted in history books, kabuki originated as a style of dance called *kabuki-odori,* which was developed in Kyoto in 1603 by a woman named Izumo no Okuni.

Now, how did this art created by a woman turn into a dramatic form performed exclusively by men? Well, there were a lot of twists and turns along the way before kabuki became what it is today. First, let's look at the early history leading up to *yaro-kabuki*, a form which more closely resembles modern kabuki.

Okuni's *kabuki-odori* featured a mix of both women and men depicting often comical sketches through song and dance. Okuni herself would dress as a male "*kabuki-mono*" and a male actor would dress as a female tea-shop worker. The two would perform a dance called "*chaya-asobi*," or "tea-house fun." Also called "*Okuni-kabuki*," *kabuki-odori* gained incredible popularity all around the country.

Soon rival troupes were formed, and brothels also began having their prostitutes perform songs and dance in this new style. "*Onna-kabuki*," for which prostitutes were used, gained enormous popularity, but was soon banned by the shogun because of its negative effect on public morality.

With the decline of onna-kabuki came the rise of "*wakashu-kabuki*," which had young boys perform instead of women. Despite its popularity, however, wakashu-kabuki was likewise prohibited due to its negative effects on public morality.

In response to these prohibitions, a new form of kabuki was developed which eliminated boy actors and the sexually suggestive bangs that female roles often called for. This new form of kabuki was called "*yaro-kabuki*."

Modern kabuki is derived from *yaro-kabuki*. With this new form of kabuki, actors who could no longer wear bangs were forced to rely on more than physical features to charm audiences. Furthermore, instead of song and dance, performers were made to use their dramatic skills in a form called "*kyogen-tsukushi*." These developments are what paved the road for modern-day kabuki.

Okuni's kabuki-odori evolved in response to the numerous prohibitions which threatened to stifle it, and thus it became a dramatic art performed exclusively by men.

Etymology of "Kabuki"

The modern-day word "kabuki" uses three Chinese characters meaning "song," "dance," and "skill," but these do not indicate kabuki's original meaning. The word "kabuki" derives from a verb meaning "to slant," and used to referred to an off-beat or eccentric person.

In Okuni's time, there were people known as "*kabuki-mono*," who donned strange clothes and hair styles, and conducted themselves in a strange fashion deliberately to shock other people. Okuni herself chose to dress as these *kabuki-mono* and incorporate their ways into her *kabuki-odori*.

It may be because kabuki originally sought to incorporate eccentricity that it continued to integrate modern fads into its performances through the ages.

History of Kabuki 2 — From *Yaro* to modern-day kabuki

The reborn *yaro-kabuki* underwent many changes from the Edo period (1603–1868) to the modern day. Since we will now cover a long period of history, this will be an abridged explanation. We recommend referring to the "Kabuki Glossary" for more detailed information about kabuki terms.

During the Genroku years (1688–1704), two contrasting performance styles developed: "*aragoto*" in Edo (Tokyo) and "*wagoto*" in Kyoto. The renowned writer Chikamatsu Monzaemon is also from this period. He and his contemporaries wrote a great number of masterful dramatic works for the puppet theater

(*bunraku*), making it the premier dramatic form of the time. These plays are commonly called "*gidayu-kyogen*" and constitute a large part of the repertoire.

The Bunka-Bunsei years (1688–1704) saw the works of Nanboku Tsuruya IV, who developed the "*nama-sewamono*" which brought a deeper realistic element to the everyday genre of "*sewamono*."

The Eighteen Great Kabuki Plays was established at the end of the Edo Period. The Tenpo years (1830–1844) saw various reforms resulting in the banishment of many actors from Edo and the relocation of theaters to Asakusa on the outskirts of the city. The dramatist Kawatake Mokuami was active during these final years of Edo and well into the Meiji Period (1868–1912).

While the dramatic arts were dampened, buyo dance thrived alongside *shamisen* music. The *buyo* style of dance from the Tenmei years (1781–1789) developed into the henka-buyo dance popular from the mid-Edo period, and the *hatsubame* style of dance was born at the end of the Edo period, continuing to thrive during the subsequent Meiji period.

Great developments were also made in staging and mechanics during this period, including the *hanamichi* platforms, the *mawari-butai* (rotating stage), and the *seri* lift.

With the Meiji Restoration, kabuki once again saw a great shift. Under orders from the Meiji Government to produce plays of high artistic value, writers now focused on plays that were historically accurate, now called "*katsureki-mono*." Another new form, called "*zangimono*," were meant to integrate aspects of modern thought and ways. Furthermore, a new style of kabuki that attempted to imitate Western theater was developed by non-kabuki writers. This new form was called "*shin-kabuki*" (new kabuki).

Later during the war, a number of playhouses were burned down in air raids, and during the occupation all feudalistic plays were prohibited. Kabuki persevered through this, but even after the occupation, due to the aftershock of the war kabuki plays were scarce for a time. Despite this, the art form was faithfully preserved and now enjoys great popularity again.

Nowadays kabuki is not only performed in Japan, but in countries all around the world.

This ends our abridged overview of kabuki's history. As you can see, kabuki did not always enjoy the popularity it has now but evolved with the violent changes of history to become what it is today. We hope that our readers have gained an appreciation for this rich history.

Kabuki started and developed until the modern day as a show business that exhibited great innovation and adaptability to survive to the modern day. We believe it is a performance art unlike any other inscribed as a UNESCO intangible cultural heritage element.

付録

歌舞伎の見方

もとより歌舞伎に「正しい」見方や作法、堅苦しいルールなどはありません。それぞれの心のままに見て楽しんでもらえればそれで十分であり、観客の数だけ見方があるともいえます。

しかし中には、心のままに、と言われても不安が残る方もいるようです。難しいのではないか、勉強しないと理解できないのではないか、などと見ない前から思い込んでいる方もいます。見たことがない方ほどその傾向は強く、堅苦しいものと決めつけてしまう人も多い。こうした思い込み、不安が先に立ち、歌舞伎の魅力に触れることができないとしたら、これは大変にもったいないことです。

歌舞伎は「商業演劇」

歌舞伎は400年を超す歴史を持ち、日本を代表する古典芸能の一つとして、ユネスコの無形文化遺産にも登録されていることはご承知の通り。それと同時に、発生から現在に至るまで、観客の入場料ですべてを賄う「商業演劇」でもあり続けています。これは大きな特徴です。

観客の支持なくしては立ち行かないのですから、観客の喜ぶものは何でも取り入れてきました。その集積が現在の歌舞伎です。400年以上お客様を喜ばせ続けてきた芸能、とも言えましょう。

現在隆盛の歌舞伎ですが、世間でよく言われるように、難しく退屈なだけの芸能だったら、果たしてこれほど多くの観客を集められるでしょうか。400年にもわたり続くでしょうか。

しかも、一度でも劇場に足を運んでいただけばわかるのですが、多くの観客が舞台を見ながら、笑ったり、涙を流したり、と舞台を楽しんでいます。現代においても十分「楽しめる」演劇なのです。「古典」や「伝統」と肩書がつくと、まるで博物館に展示されている骨董品であるかのように思えますが、現代の俳優が演じ、現代の観客が見て楽しんでいる、現代のエンターテインメントなのです。

もちろん長い時間をかけ磨き抜かれ、古典というにふさわしい大きさと深さを持つ戯曲や役も数多くあります。古典ならではの豊かな世界に身を任せ、深い感銘を抱く、これも楽しみの一つであることはいうまでもありません。

歌舞伎といってもいろいろある

歌舞伎を初めて観劇した人から、思っていたよりも「〇〇」だった、という声を聞くことがあります。「〇〇」の内容は様々

ですが、いずれも観劇前に抱いていた印象——綺麗だとか華やかなどのプラスの印象もあれば、退屈そうだとか寝てしまいそうだというマイナスの印象もある——とは違っていた、といいます。

観客の喜ぶものを取り入れ成長した歌舞伎は、実は大変に幅が広く、バラエティーに富んでいます。ひと口に歌舞伎といってもいろいろとあるのです。

一般によく言われる歌舞伎のイメージがあります。例えば顔や体に色の線を描く独特の化粧「隈取」や、男性が女性の役も演じる「女方」、大きくポーズを決める「見得」、独特の発声と台詞まわし、などです。誇張されたものではありますが、これらは確かに歌舞伎の一部。しかしすべてではありません。

隈取は歌舞伎を特徴づけるものですが、歌舞伎の演目に必ず隈取の化粧をした人物が登場するわけではなく、隈取の人物が一人も登場しない演目も数多くあります。劇場に行くと隈取が見られるだろうと思っている人がそうした演目を見ると、これは私が想像していた歌舞伎とは違う、となるかもしれません。

『勧進帳』という演目はよく知られていますが、この演目には女性の役はありません。普段女性を演じている女方の俳優が、源義経の役で出演することはありますが、これは男性の役。『鈴ヶ森』と呼ばれる演目も登場人物は男ばかり。つまり、女方といえども、すべての演目に登場するわけではありません。

独特の発声と台詞まわしも、実は様々な演技様式のうちの一つであり、様式が違えば台詞の印象も大きく違います。また、難しいと思われがちな言葉にしても、平易な現代語による脚本も数多くあります。

なかには、見終わって、これ《が》歌舞伎なの、と驚かれる作品もありますが、それ《も》歌舞伎。最初にこうしたもの、と思い込んでくると、大概そのイメージは覆される、それほど歌舞伎のレパートリーは広くて深いのです。

歌舞伎の幅広さを理解するには、「映画」に置き換えるとわかり易いかもしれません。ひと口に映画といっても様々です。ハリウッドの超大作、単館で上映される小品。ミュージカル、ホラー、スプラッタ。恋愛もの、アクション。アニメ、コメディー、ドキュメンタリー。歌舞伎も同じで、様々なジャンルの演目が揃っています。

幅広いレパートリーを持っていますので、華やかな世界を期待していったら、たまたまその月は渋い演目だった、とか、古典を期待していったら、新作歌舞伎の月だったなど、ミスマッチも起こります。ただそれで歌舞伎＝（イコール）つまらな

い、ということになってしまうのは残念、もったいない。

映画であれば、たまたまミュージカル映画を最初に見たからといって、映画には必ず歌や踊りがあるものとは思わないはず。たまたま見た映画が面白くなかったからといって、映画というジャンル自体をつまらないものと決めつけはしないでしょう。

ところが、歌舞伎は、最初に見たものが気に入らないと、歌舞伎そのものがつまらないと思われてしまう。いろいろとある中の一部分でしかないものをそれだけで判断されてしまうのです。

初めて歌舞伎を見たら、想像していた通りだったということもあるけれど、思っていたのと違うこともある。その時、思っていたのと違うけれど、これはこれで面白い、となる方もいるし、思っていたのと違うからダメだとなる方もいる。

もし、見たものが「私の考える歌舞伎」と違っても、ぜひ演目を選んで再挑戦してみてください。必ず「あなたの考える歌舞伎」が見つかるはず。逆に言えば何かしらお気に召す歌舞伎はあるはずです。

そしてそこから様々な歌舞伎に触れてみてください。あなたの考えていた歌舞伎以外にもきっと面白い歌舞伎が見つかるはずです。

歌舞伎の見方

「歌舞伎は商業演劇であり、今を生きているエンターテインメントである」ということと、「歌舞伎といってもいろいろある」この二点を覚えておいて、肩に力を入れず、気持ちを楽に持って、生の歌舞伎に触れてみてください。

歌舞伎には一言では言い尽くせないほどの魅力が詰まっています。

とにかく一遍実際に歌舞伎を「体験」してみてください。400年間エンターテインメントであり続けた歌舞伎は、様々な魅力や特徴を備えています。俳優の姿や演技、衣裳の華やかさ、音楽の楽しさ、お芝居の内容。きっとどこかで何かしら感じるところがあるはず。どこをどう面白いと思うか、素敵だと思うかはご覧になった方次第。そこを入り口にして、歌舞伎の世界を覗いてみてください。間口が広くて奥が深い、すばらしい世界が目の前に広がります。

同じ時間と空間を共有するのが、歌舞伎に限らずライブパフォーマンスの醍醐味です。その時、その場所で起こることを楽しむこと、歌舞伎の見方、というものがあるとしたらこの一言に尽きるだろうと思います。

ざっくりまとめると、歌舞伎の「多様性」と「商業性」の話で、あまり堅く考えすぎないで、ライブを楽しみに来てくださいね、というのが大意です。

ところでこの多様性、歌舞伎の特徴の一つでもあります。

歌舞伎に携わる人々には常にこの多様な演目とそれらの様式を身につけること、また、継承と創造との両方に精進することが課せられているともいえましょう。

一方で古典であり堅苦しく、敷居が高いと思われ、もう一方で、様々な新しい試みがマスコミで大きく報道されています。ややもすると現代的な試みばかりもてはやされがちですが、これらの試みも古典あってのこと。歌舞伎の俳優やスタッフは、そのことをよく知っています。どちらも歌舞伎であって、どちらも必要なことなのです。

「商業性」については、これが舞台の原動力であることは言うまでもありません。

ただし注意していただきたいのは、しばしば商業性と芸術性が対立しているかのように考えられることです。商業的になりすぎると芸術性が失われてしまう、むしろ芸術とは商業的であってはならないという考えすら見受けられます。確かに相反することもありますが、決して両立しないものではありません。商業的であることが芸術的ではないということは決してないのです。

歌舞伎を見たことがない人でも歌舞伎俳優の名前や顔を知っています。それは歌舞伎の俳優は映画やテレビにも出ているからです。時代劇はもちろん、現代を舞台にしたドラマなどにも出演しています。では、歌舞伎以外の伝統芸能の関係者で、ドラマに出演する人は何人ぐらいいるでしょうか。数人はいらっしゃいますが、歌舞伎ほど多くはいません。

歌舞伎の俳優は、舞台のみならず映画やテレビにも出演しており、歌舞伎を知らない人にも知られている。歌舞伎の俳優は、伝統の担い手であると同時に、現在でも一般的な知名度が高く、人気がある。これはほかの伝統芸能にはない、大きな特徴です。

また東京の歌舞伎座を国の施設だと勘違いしている人もいますが、歌舞伎座は松竹が経営しています。伝統芸能でもありながら、現代でも民間企業が公演する商業演劇でもあるのが現在の歌舞伎なのです。

How to Watch Kabuki

There is no such thing as a "proper" way to watch kabuki, nor are there any strict rules. The only thing a viewer has to do is watch and enjoy in his or her own way. You could say that there are as many ways to watch kabuki as there are audience members.

That being said, many still feel uneasy about watching kabuki, thinking that it will be too difficult to understand without studying beforehand. This is especially true of those who have never seen a kabuki play before. However, it would be a terrible shame if such preconceptions kept potential viewers from ever enjoying the many charms of kabuki.

Kabuki is Commercial!

One of Japan's representative classical art forms, kabuki boasts a history of over 400 years and is inscribed by UNESCO as an intangible cultural heritage element. At the same time, kabuki developed over the years funded entirely by its viewers who paid for entrance at theaters. This commercial element is a unique characteristic of kabuki. Since it couldn't survive without the support of its viewers, kabuki has constantly added new elements to please its audiences, and modern kabuki is the accumulation of that 400-year history of happy audiences.

Modern kabuki, too, is incredibly popular, and it is often argued that a boring, archaic art form couldn't possibly garner the audience that kabuki has, let alone survive off proceedings alone for 400 years. If you ever make your way to a performance, you'll see that kabuki audiences are incredibly engaged, laughing and crying throughout the program. When we use heavy terms like "classic" and "traditional" to describe kabuki, it may feel like an antique displayed at a museum. But in reality, contemporary actors stand on the stage and people just like you and me are in the audience watching. Kabuki really is a very modern form of entertainment.

Of course, many kabuki plays are old classics that have stood the test of time. Being able to enjoy these rich pieces of classical literature that have been polished over hundreds of years is naturally one of the many joys of the kabuki theater.

Kabuki is Multi-faceted

Many first-time viewers of kabuki say that it wasn't what they expected. Now, what they expected and how it was different varies greatly from person to person—some people expect brilliant stages and costumes, while others expect to be bored to death. This is because kabuki, which evolved by constantly incorporating new elements to bring joy to audiences, has an incredibly varied

repertoire. The word "kabuki" itself, therefore, cannot be summed up by any single image or expectation.

There are many well-known characteristics of kabuki, such as the bold kumadori makeup that is applied to the face and body of actors. Other characteristics of kabuki include *onnagata* (male actors who play female roles), bold poses called *mie*, and unique cadences and speech styles used by actors. These are indeed a part of kabuki, but it would be a mistake to think that any one of these applies to all of kabuki.

Kumadori is considered a staple of kabuki, but in fact kabuki plays do not all necessarily feature this unique makeup style. In fact, there are entire plays in which not a single actor wears *kumadori*. If you went to kabuki expecting *kumadori*, but happened to choose a play such as this, undoubtedly you will be surprised and even disappointed when the play ends.

Kanjincho is a very well-known play that features absolutely no *onnagata* parts. Sometimes an *onnagata* actor will play Minamoto no Yoshitsune, but the role is still that of a man. The play Suzu ga Mori is another play featuring all male characters. As you can see, kabuki does not necessarily imply the presence of *onnagata*.

The same goes for the unique cadences of kabuki. There are actually a number of different styles that can be used, and which is used may greatly affect the ultimate impression left on the audience. Furthermore, some old plays which originally used very antiquated and difficult language have been rewritten to be easier to understand.

It is very easy to see why some viewers get to the end of a play and think, is this really kabuki? The answer is yes, this too is kabuki. If you are convinced that kabuki must be this or that way, your entire view of it may be turned upside down by the time you get to the end of a play. That is just how deep and varied the kabuki repertoire is.

An easy way to think of this may be to compare kabuki to movies. The word "movie" encapsulates an unbelievable variety of genres, from big Hollywood blockbusters to independent films only shown at small local theaters, from musicals to horror films. Even within the horror genre there are subgenres such as splatter films. There are romantic, action, animated, comedy, documentary, and various other genres. Now, just think of kabuki the same way, with the same rich variety of genres.

It is because of this great variety that viewers are sometimes surprised at the plays they see. Some expect an opulent piece only to find they went to the theater during the run of a very dark play, while others may expect a classic piece only to find that the theater was producing a *shinsaku-kabuki* (contemporary kabuki) program that month.

However, it would be a shame for those viewers to think that all kabuki is uninteresting from just one such experience. If the first movie you saw was a musical, you probably wouldn't assume that all movies include singing and dancing. Neither would you assume all movies are boring just because of a bad movie you happened to watch.

When it comes to kabuki, however, this is exactly what some viewers do. Often times, viewers see a single play that only showcases a fragment of kabuki's variety, yet they proceed to cast judgement on the entire field. Some viewers may find that the play they watched was exactly what they expected, while others find it completely different. Some find kabuki interesting from the start, while others are displeased by their experience.

If you happen to see a kabuki production that didn't live up to your expectations, then try picking a different program next time. There are definitely plays that will live up to those expectations. To put it another way, I'm confident that, among the vast repertoire of kabuki, there is a play out there for you. Once you've found that, I encourage you to branch out from there. If you do, you are bound to find that some of the plays that don't quite match those initial expectations are quite enjoyable.

How to Watch Kabuki

Kabuki is commercial—a constantly changing, living form of entertainment. It also encapsulates an incredible depth of variety. From now on I ask that you approach kabuki with these two points in mind, and when you get to the theater, just relax and enjoy the story that unfolds before your eyes.

The many charms of kabuki defy attempts to define it in a single word, but I encourage everyone to go and see one live. It is a 400-year-old form of entertainment that has evolved and grown with audiences over the ages. The actors' stances and performance styles, the gorgeous costumes, the unique music, and the stories themselves—every aspect of kabuki is the product of years of tradition and evolution, and there is bound to be something that moves you. What it is that you find funny, stunning, or deeply moving, is entirely up to you. Whatever it is, use that as your gateway to the world of kabuki. An incredibly vast and deep world is just waiting for you to explore.

When watching kabuki, there is an incredible sensation of sharing in this moment, in this space. This isn't unique to kabuki; it is exactly what makes any live performance exciting. If I had to explain what the proper way to watch kabuki is, it would be simply that: experiencing the events unfolding before you, here and now.

In other words, as a multi-layered form of commercial entertainment, don't think too hard about what kabuki is. Rather, just sit back and enjoy the live performance.

The variety of experience is again another important aspect of kabuki. In the past, many have tried expounding on kabuki as though it could be expressed in so many sentences. But kabuki is something that defies such simple explanations. After all, by saying "kabuki must be thus," you run the risk of missing out on all the forms of kabuki that do not fit that description.

Those involved in the kabuki industry are constantly honing their skills to tackle the many different styles and forms that make up the industry. They are also charged two-fold with honoring long-standing traditions and creating new ones.

On the one hand, kabuki can be archaic, formal, and unapproachable, but on the other hand it can be an incredible cutting-edge experiment that spreads like fire through the media. Though we are prone to get caught up in these exciting new experiments, they are only possible because of the classics. Kabuki actors and crew members all know this, as should everyone. Both the classical and the modern are vital aspects of kabuki.

At this point it hardly warrants saying that the commercial aspect of kabuki is a driving force of the field. However, we must be careful when talking about this. It is often said that business and art are opposed to one another. Indeed, many believe that the more commercial art is, the less valuable it is as art. Some even believe that art must not be commercialized at all. I recognize that the two are at time opposed, but that does not mean that they cannot coexist. Just because art is commercialized does not take away its artistic value.

Have you ever wondered why it is that some people who have never watched kabuki nonetheless know the names of kabuki actors? The answer is simple: those actors also appear in movies and on TV. They often play in period pieces, and even in dramas set in modern times. Though there are a few artists from other traditional performance arts who appear in dramas like this, no other art boasts the number that kabuki does.

This is another important characteristic of kabuki—that many of its actors are popular figures who appear in other productions such as TV programs and movies.

Kabuki actors shoulder the heavy burden of a rich tradition but are at the same time highly popular figures widely known to the public. There are no other artists from other fields who appear on variety and quiz shows like kabuki actors do.

There are also some who come to the Kabuki-za Theatre in Tokyo and mistakenly assume it is a government-run establishment. It is in fact the Shochiku Company that runs Kabuki-za, making kabuki a truly unique hybrid—a traditional performance art and commercial show run as a private business.

付録

歌舞伎の言葉

歌舞伎の言葉

演目に関する言葉

【狂言】
能とともに上演される狂言。その狂言と全く同じ文字、同じ発音だが、歌舞伎関係者が狂言という時は、大概「演目」と同じような意味になる。「襲名披露狂言」「追善狂言」「狂言作者」など様々に使われる。

【みどり狂言】【通し狂言】
一日の内に数種類の演目を並べて上演する興行方法を、「みどり」「みどり狂言」という。見せ場を抜きだし並べることで、歌舞伎の持つ多彩な魅力が味わえる。漢字をあてれば「見取」で、より取り見取りのみどりだと言われている。これに対し、最初から最後まで、ストーリーを通して上演することを「通し狂言」「通し上演」という。

【純歌舞伎狂言】【義太夫狂言】【舞踊】
歌舞伎の狂言は、成立によって「純歌舞伎狂言」「義太夫狂言」「舞踊」に大別される。「舞踊」は「所作事」ともいい三味線音楽とともに発達した。また、人形浄瑠璃から移入した作品群を「義太夫狂言」や「丸本歌舞伎」などと総称する。「純歌舞伎狂言」というのは、歌舞伎のために書きおろされた演目のことである。

【和事】【荒事】
演技の様式。元禄期、京・大坂を中心とした上方と、江戸とで、それぞれ異なる芸が生まれた。上方では、後に「和事」と呼ばれる演技術が生まれた。優雅でやわらかい身のこなしが特徴。「荒事」は江戸で発達した芸で、「隈取」をはじめとする扮装や、「六方」などの演技により表現される豪快で力強い芸。

【活歴物】【散切物】
明治維新以降、時代の流れに乗り、それまでの荒唐無稽な作劇法ではなく、時代考証を重視し、史実に忠実な作品、「活歴物」が作られた。また、髷を切った散切り頭の人物が登場する「散切物」も創出された。どちらも明治の新時代に合わせ、従来の歌舞伎にはない新たな活動であった。

【新歌舞伎】【新作歌舞伎】【スーパー歌舞伎】
明治中期以降、外部の文学者・作家によって書かれた戯曲作品のことを「新歌舞伎」という。欧米の演劇や小説の影響を受けた作品が、近代的な演出で上演された。また戦後に新たに書かれた作品は、「新作歌舞伎」として区別されるのが一般的。さらに現代でも「スーパー歌舞伎」をはじめ様々な新しい試みがされている。

【時代物】
公家や武家の社会で起こった事件を題材にした演目をいう。狭義には平安中期から戦国期までの武将を主人公にした演目を指すが、平安以前の貴族社会を題材にした「王代（朝）物」、江戸時代の武家のお家騒動を題材にした「お家物」も含むことがある。
時に史実に大胆な虚構を加え、正史でない、歴史の裏側を描き出す。いわば江戸時代の庶民から見た歴史フィクション。登場人物は、名前こそ歴史上の人物だが、姿も行動もすべて徳川時代の人間の投影である。
豪華な衣裳、誇張された台詞など、いわゆる歌舞伎らしい演出が見られる。

【世話物】
「世話」とは、「世」間の「話」というほどの意味であり、世上に起こることは善悪を問わず題材となる。盗賊が主人公になる「白浪物」や、落語や講談の人情話を脚色した作品など様々な演目が含まれ、登場人物もアウトローや名もなき市井の人々といった同時代人。いわば江戸時代の現代劇である。江戸と上方で地域色あふれる演目が生まれ、今に伝承されている。
衣裳や台詞、演技も誇張の少ないものとなり、演者には、リアルな味わいが求められる。今や失われてしまった江戸時代の風俗習慣が舞台上で再現されることも楽しみの一つ。

【舞踊】
「歌舞伎踊り」から現在に至るまで、舞踊はレパートリーの大きな位置を占め、俳優は踊りの修練が欠かせない。もとは女方の専門領域であったが、やがて立役も踊るようになり、伴奏音楽の発展とともにレパートリーが広がった。音楽にのせ躍動的な動きを見せる舞踊の魅力に溢れる作品に加え、演劇的な構成と内容を持ち、かつ音楽的舞踊的な見せ場もある「舞踊劇」ともいうべき演目もある。長さも小品から大作まで多彩である。一人の踊り手が様々な役を次々踊り分ける「変化舞踊」、能狂言の様式を取り入れた「松羽目舞踊」などがある。

【新作歌舞伎】
古典の継承と新作の創造は現代の歌舞伎の大きなテーマである。一見相反するように見えるが、どちらも歌舞伎の発展には欠かせない両輪である。新作は内容や表現に新たな地平を拓くとともに、新たな客層を開拓する役目をはたし、現代においても様々な新作が試みられている。古典様式に則った擬古典的な作品、現代の作家・演出家と組んだ作品、原作をマンガなどに求めた作品もある。埋もれた過去の作品を現代に合わせ再創造することも大きな意味での新作である。優れた新作は再演を重ね、やがて新たな古典となっていくのである。

俳優に関する言葉

【名跡】【襲名】【追善】
代々継がれていく名前を「名跡」という。名優の「名跡」はことに大切にされ、継いだ俳優も、名前にふさわしい名優にならなければならないとされる。名を名乗ることを「襲名」という。襲名披露の公演はことに華やかである。また亡くなった名優を偲ぶことを「追善」とよび、追善狂言もまた華やかである。みどりのうちの一本を追善狂言として上演することもある。襲名や追善は歌舞伎の活性化につながっている。

【屋号】【俳名】
歌舞伎の俳優はそれぞれ屋号を持っている。市川家の「成田屋」が始まりといわれ、初代團十郎が成田山を信仰したことに由来するといわれる。
また「俳名」を持つ俳優もいる。俳名とは俳句の号。俳句の趣味はなくても俳名を持つ俳優もあり、名跡同様継承されることもある。また、俳名を芸名として襲名することも多い。

【女方】【立役】【敵役】
女性の役、またはその役を演じる俳優を「女方」という。対して、男性役全体、または善人の役を主に演じる俳優、またはその役を「立役」という。本来は「敵役」に対する、善方の役を指す言葉だが、後に男性の役全般を表す言葉になった。

【家の芸】
俳優の家に代々伝えられた得意芸や演目を集めたもの。市川團十郎家の「歌舞伎十八番」「新歌舞伎十八番」が知られている。他に尾上

184

菊五郎家の「新古演劇十種」などがある。また、俳優一代の当たり役を集めることもあり、初代中村鴈治郎の当たり役を集めた「玩辞楼十二曲」、初代中村吉右衛門の「秀山十種」などがある。最も新しいものは平成22年に選定された「三代猿之助四十八撰」である。

演技に関する言葉

【見得】
演技のクライマックスで、一瞬動きを止め、その演技を誇張する手法。多くにらみを伴う。形により「元禄見得」「柱巻の見得」などの名前がある。

【立廻り】【立師】【とんぼ】【所作立】
劇中の戦いの場面を「立廻り」、立廻りを考案する担当者を「立師」と呼ぶ。立廻りの途中、切られたり投げられたりした者が空中で回転する動きを「とんぼ」、また、舞踊の中で、曲に合わせ演じる立廻りを特に「所作立」という。

【だんまり】
登場人物が暗闇の中で探り合う動きを様式的に表した場面。暗闇の場面であるが、照明は暗くせず、明るい中で演技される。

扮装に関する言葉

【隈取】
顔の筋肉を誇張したものとも血管を表したものともいわれる。役柄により色や形が異なり、主に赤（紅色）、青（藍色）、茶（代赭色―たいしゃいろ）の三色が用いられる。赤い隈は、若さや正義、力、激しい怒りなど発散する陽の力を表し、青い隈は邪悪や怨霊など陰の力を表現。茶色の隈は、人間に化けた妖怪変化などに使用される。隈取は、筆や指で直接顔に描く。これを「隈を取る」、という。

【ぶっかえり】【引き抜き】
「引き抜き」は、衣裳を一瞬にして変える仕掛け。舞踊で曲調の変わり目に、場の雰囲気を一変させたい時などに使われる。「ぶっかえり」は隠していた正体を現したり、性格が一変する際などに使われる技法。衣裳はその役の性格や境遇を表しているので、性格が変わったり、本名を名乗るなど境遇が変わると、当然衣裳も変わるというのが歌舞伎の考え方。その大胆なデザインや色遣いで、世界的にも評価されている歌舞伎の衣裳は劇的効果を高める役割も果たしている。歌舞伎では衣裳も芝居の一部なのだ。

【黒衣】
全身黒ずくめの着衣、またはそれを着ている人を「黒衣」という。歌舞伎では、黒で無を表すので、黒く塗られている、また、黒布で覆われたり、隠されているものは、ないもの、見えないものとする、という約束がある。ゆえに黒衣姿で舞台に登場しても、その人物はいない、見えないということになる。なお、通常「くろご」と濁って発音される。

音に関する言葉

【三味線音楽】
歌舞伎には三味線音楽が欠かせない。舞台に溢れる音のほとんどは、三味線の音色だ。戦国時代に琉球から伝来したというが、「お国歌舞伎」の後に取り入れられた。当時最先端の楽器だったのだ。やがて江戸時代の音楽は三味線抜きでは語れないくらいに広がりをみせる。ひと口にいっても、様々な流派があり、音域や表現方法、用いる楽器の大きさなども違う。歌舞伎では、「長唄」「義太夫節」「常磐津節」「清元節」などが多く用いられる。

【黒御簾音楽】
舞台に向かって左手、下手にある黒御簾と呼ばれる場所で演奏される音楽。中には、長唄や囃子の担当者がいて、舞台に合わせて音楽を演奏している。ここで演奏される音楽を黒御簾音楽といい、芝居を盛り上げるバックミュージックや、雨の音や雪の音などの効果音を演奏している。水、雨、雪、幽霊の出現などを太鼓で打ち分け表現するなど優れた工夫が伝承されている。

【柝（き）】
幕開きなどに鳴る拍子木。この拍子木は「き」と呼ばれ、舞台進行の合図である。開幕、閉幕、道具の転換などはこの「柝」の合図で行われる。ゆえに、舞台進行を担当する「狂言作者」が打つことになっている。

【ツケ】
上手、舞台に向かって右側で、拍子木のような棒を板に打ち付けてバタバタという音を出すのがツケ。立廻りや見得を引き立てる、一種の効果音。

【掛け声（大向こう）】
演技の途中に客席から掛かる声。観客が演者をほめる掛け声で、大向こうと通称されるが、本来大向こうというのは客席の一部を指す言葉である。掛け声は屋号のほか、代数などを掛ける。観客も一体となって芝居を作り上げているのだ。

舞台機構の言葉

【花道】
歌舞伎に欠かせない舞台機構の一つ。舞台の一部が客席を貫いて張り出し、主要な役の登退場に使われる。観客のすぐ近くを俳優が通ることで、客席と舞台に一体感が生まれる。時にはこの花道での演技が大きな見せ場になることもある。

【セリ】
舞台を四角に切り、昇降するようにした機構。上に人物や大道具を乗せて上げ下げする。花道のセリを特別に「スッポン」と呼ぶ。「セリ」「スッポン」を使用する演出も多い。

【廻り舞台】
舞台を円形に切り、回転するようにした機構。今では外国のミュージカルなどでも使われるが、発祥は日本。現在のような大掛かりな機構は250年ほど前の大坂で、世界に先駆けてつくられた。

【揚幕】
花道の突き当たりに吊ってある幕。この幕を開け閉めして、人物が登退場する。劇場の座紋などが染め抜かれていることが多い。

【定式幕】
黒色、柿色、萌葱色の三色の引幕。歌舞伎をイメージする色としてよく知られている。色の並びは劇場により異なる。江戸時代には幕府から認められた「大芝居」のシンボルであった。

Kabuki Glossary

Performance Terms

"kyogen"
Though "kyogen" originally refers to short skits performed together with noh plays, it is also often used in a kabuki context. In this case, "kyogen" simply refers to a program. Shumeihiro-kyogen, for example, refers to a program featuring an actor who is succeeding to another actor's stage name.

"toshi-kyogen" and "midori-kyogen"
A program which takes scenes from various plays to perform in a single day is called "midori-kyogen." The term "midori" refers to the action of selecting the best out of a pool of candidates, making a midori-kyogen program the perfect way to get a taste of the kabuki's great variety. "Toshi-kyogen," on the other hand, refers to a program that showcases scenes from a single play in a way that shows audiences the full story.

"jun-kabuki kyogen" / "gidayu-kyogen" / "buyo"
Kabuki plays can be classified into three broad categories: jun-kabuki-kyogen, gidayu-kyogen, and buyo.
"Buyo" is a type of dance-drama that developed in conjunction with shamisen music. Several sub-genres are included in the category of buyo. "Henka-buyo" is a variation in which a single actor performs multiple roles, while "matsubame-mono" are Noh plays that were adapted for kabuki. Kabuki plays that have been adapted from bunraku scripts are called "gidayu-kyogen" or "maruhon-kabuki"
"Jun-kabuki," or "pure kabuki," refers to plays originally written specifically for the kabuki theater.

"aragoto" / "wagoto"
These are contrasting acting styles that developed during the Genroku Period (1688–1704) in Kyoto/Osaka and Edo (Tokyo). The graceful wagoto style was developed in Kyoto and Osaka, while the rough aragoto style was developed in Edo. The wild kumadori makeup and dramatic roppo exit are characteristics of the vigorous aragoto style.

"katsureki-mono" / "zangiri-mono"
During the Meiji Restoration, the writing of bunraku and kabuki plays shifted from the absurd and comical to the historical, and these plays were called "katsureki-mono." Plays featuring characters sporting the zangiri-atama ("cropped head") hairstyle also appeared. These were called zangi-mono. Both forms were innovations to kabuki that had never been seen before the Meiji Period.

"shin-kabuki" / "shinsaku-kabuki" / "super kabuki"
"Shin-kabuki" (new kabuki) refers to plays written by non-kabuki writers from the mid-Meiji Period onward. These pieces were influenced greatly by western theater and novels and strived for a modern performance style. Plays written after the war are commonly called "shinsaku-kabuki" (contemporary kabuki) while "super kabuki" refers to experimental plays written very recently.

"jidai-mono"
Broadly defined as a play featuring historical events involving nobles or warriors, a "jidai-mono" is narrowly defined as a piece featuring a warrior hero from the Heian through the Warring States period. Pieces featuring nobles from before the Heian Period are called "odai-mono" or "ocho-mono," and those involving family disputes of warriors from the Edo period are called "oie-mono."
A feature of some jidai-mono is the inclusion of elements that are not true to history. This historical fiction of the people often features historical names whose appearance and actions are made to reflect those of the Tokugawa Period.

"sewa-mono"
"Sewa" refers both to "taking care of" someone and "worldly talk." Thus "sewa-mono" plays depict real-life events in the world without drawing conclusions about good and evil. Including "shiranami-mono" in which the knave is the hero, and dramatizations of heartwarming rakugo / kodan stories, sewa-mono feature casts of common folk and outlaws. Sewa-mono were created during the Edo Period and have been passed down to the modern day.

"buyo"
"Buyo" dance constitutes a large part of the kabuki repertoire and has been a feature of kabuki since the original kabuki-odori. Therefore any aspiring kabuki actor must practice dance. Originally only required of onnagata actors, eventually leading roles came to require dancing, expanding the repertoire together with developments in music. Over time more dramatic elements were added to kabuki along with the lively movements of the buyo dance. Still, there are "buyo-geki" which feature striking scenes in the buyo style. The length of a buyo-geki can vary from a short sketch to an epic, from the "henka-buyo" featuring a single actor playing multiple parts to the "matsubame-buyo" which take their cue from noh plays.

"shinsaku-kabuki" (contemporary kabuki)
A major issue in modern kabuki is the balance between traditional methods and the creation of something novel. Although these two may seem contradictory at first glance, they are both vital to the development of kabuki. The creation of new works paves the way for kabuki in the modern world and attracts new audiences. Some modern dramatists conform to classical formats, while others experiment by working together with other writers and actors. There are even cases of kabuki plays based on manga! Reproductions of forgotten plays is yet another form of shinsaku ("new production"). The best of these shinsaku-kabuki plays, after all, will eventually become the classics of tomorrow.

Terms Relating to Actors

"myoseki" / "shumei" / "tsuizen"
A name that is passed down from generation to generation is called "myoseki." Myoseki of great actors are particularly important, and their successors are under a lot of pressure to live up to that name. "Shumei" refers to the act of succeeding to another's stage name. Performances honoring such a succession are often particularly lavish to denote the occasion. "Tsuizen" refers to the memorial of a great actor who has passed away. Tsuizen performances are also very lavish, and occasionally portions of a midori-kyogen will be dedicated as a tsuizen performance. As such, shumei and tsuizen are often important catalysts for kabuki performances.

"yago" / "haimyo"
All kabuki actors have a yago, or stage name. The Ichikawa family, for example, used the name "Narita-ya" presumably because the first Danjuro believed in the faith of Mt. Narita.
There are also actors who possess a haimyo. Originally meaning a pen name for haiku poets, some actors also have a haimyo, which is sometimes passed on to a successor like myoseki.

"onnagata" / "tachiyaku" / "katakiyaku"
Both female roles and the actors who play them are referred to as "onnagata." Male roles in general and the actors who play them are called "tachiyaku." In a narrow sense, "tachiyaku" can also refer specifically to male protagonists. Tachiyaku was originally meant to contrast the term "tekiyaku" (villain) but is more often used to refer to male actors in general now.

"ie-no-gei"
Specialized arts and roles passed down within an acting family are called ie-no-gei. The Eighteen Great Kabuki Plays and New Eighteen Great

Kabuki Plays of the Ichikawa Danjuro family, and Onoe Kikugoro's *Ten New and Old Plays* are just a few examples. In some cases *ie-no-gei* can be the a compilation of roles played by a single generation, as with the first Nakamura Ganjiro's collection, Ganjiro's Twelve Selections. The most recent example of this is Forty-eight Selections of Ennosuke III, which was compiled in 2010.

Performance Features

"Mie"
"*Mie*" refers to the dramatic pose taken by an actor at the climax of a play, often accompanied by a sharp glare. There are many varieties of mie, including *genroku mie* and *hashiramaki no mie*.

"tachimawari" / "tateshi" / "tonbo" / "shosa-date"
"*Tatemawari*" refers to fight scenes in kabuki plays, and "*tateshi*" refers to the actor who specializes in staging such scenes. When an actor is cut or thrown in a fight scene, the "*tonbo*" (flip) movement is used, and *tachimawari* scenes that are staged in sync with music are a type of *buyo* called "*shosa-date*."

"danmari"
"*Danmari*" refers to a scene in which characters are supposed to be in darkness. Though the stage lights are lit for the audience to see, the actors use a formal technique to seem as though they are groping in the dark.

Costumes and Cosmetics

"kumadori"
"*Kumadori*" makeup is meant to exaggerate facial muscles and/or blood vessels in the face. The color of *kumadori* can be red, blue, or green depending on the role. Red *kumadori* suggests youth, justice, power, and anger, and is used for righteous roles. Blue, on the other hand, is used to express vengeful spirits and evil. Green *kumadori* is used for spirits that have transformed into humans. *Kumadori* makeup is applied with brushes or directly with one's hand.

"bukkaeri" and "hikinuki"
"*Hikinuki*" refers to a dramatic, instantaneous costume change. A *hikinuki* occurs together with a musical shift to completely alter the mood of a scene. "*Bukkaeri*" also refers to a costume change in which a character reveals his/her true identity or undergoes a change in character. In kabuki, a costume is an expression of a character's personality, so it is common sense that a change in character or name would result in a costume change. This bold aspect of kabuki design serves an important role in productions and is widely acclaimed around the world. Costumes are thus an integral part of kabuki.

"kurogo"
"*Kurogo*" refers to an actor who wears all black or to the costume itself. Black represents nothingness in kabuki, and therefore any character or thing that is painted or clothed in black is meant to be invisible or nonexistent. Therefore, if you see a character wearing all black appear on stage, he is meant to be ignored as though he does not exist in the world of the play.

Musical / Audial Terms

"shamisen ongaku"
"*Shamisen ongaku*," or "shamisen music," is an integral part of kabuki that makes up most of the music in kabuki. This music which came from the Ryukyu Islands during the Warring States period, was incorporated after the original *okuni-kabuki*. It was the premier instrument of its time and had become completely inseparable from kabuki by the Edo period. There are several different styles of music and sizes of shamisen instruments, and kabuki uses a great number of these, including the "*nagauta*" and "*gidayu-bushi*."

"kuromisu-ongaku"
This refers to the music played in the pit ("*kuromisu*") located in a corner of the left-hand side of the stage. The conductor makes sure the music is in sync with the play, guiding both the dynamic background music and sound effects such as rain and snow. The orchestra uses a number of traditional techniques, such as the striking of the taiko drum when the weather changes or an apparition appears.

"ki"
"*Ki*" are simply wooden clappers used at the opening of the curtain and other pivotal moments during a play, such as the lowering of the curtain and changing of the set. The actor in charge of the "*ki*" is called the "*kyogen-sakusha*."

"tsuke"
"*Tsuke*" refers to the sound effect produced by striking wooden clappers against a board on the right-hand side of the stage. It is used to emphasize the *tatemawari* and *mie*.

"kakegoe" ("omuko")
"*Kakegoe*" refers to a shout by audience members in the middle of a performance. It is commonly called "*omuko*" (referring to a portion of the audience) and is meant as a form of praise to the actor. Calling an actor's *yago* or succession number is a common form of *kakegoe*. It is meant to include the audience as a participant in the production.

Stage Mechanisms

"hanamichi"
The "*hanamachi*" is an indispensable part of kabuki. It is a piece of staging that juts out into the isles between the audience's seats and is used for entrances and exits of important characters. By having the actors pass right through the audience, the hanamichi creates a sense of unity between the audience and the stage. Some plays even feature important scenes performed on the *hanamichi*.

"seri"
"*Seri*" simply refers to a rectangular lift used to raise and lower the stage or portions of the stage. A lift used for the *hanamichi* is called a "*suppon*," and many kabuki performances utilizes either one or both of these mechanics.

"mawari-butai"
"*Mawari-butai*" refers to a stage cut into a circular pattern to allow it to rotate. Many musicals around the world now use such a mechanism, but it originated in Japan. The first time a large-scale mawari-butai was ever used was in Osaka 250 years ago.

"agemaku"
The "*agemaku*" is the curtain that hangs down at the end of the *hanamichi*. It is opened and closed in conjunction with entrances and exits of important characters and often bears the theater's crest.

"joshiki-maku"
The "*joshiki-maku*" is a unique and well-known feature of kabuki. It is the main stage curtain and consists of 3 colors: black, reddish-brown (*kaki-iro*), and green (*moegi-iro*). The order of these colors differs depending on the theater. This style of curtain was officially recognized as a symbol of a major theater by the government of the Edo period.

付録　隈取一覧　　　　　　　　　　　　　　　　　　　Kumadori

筋隈 すじぐま / Sujiguma*

超人的な力強さを備え、激しいエネルギーを発する正義の側の人物にしばしば用いられる。梅王丸（『菅原伝授手習鑑 車引』）、曽我五郎（『矢の根』）など。赤い隈（紅隈）は、主に力強さ、若さ、血気などを表す。

This mask is often used for characters on the side of justice possessing superhuman power and energy. Used for Umeomaru ("Sugawara Denju Tenarai Kagami Kurumabiki") and Soga Goro ("Ya no Ne") etc. Red kuma (crimson kuma) mainly express power, youthfulness, and passion.

むきみ隈 むきみぐま / Mukimiguma

目元にのみ施す隈。血気、力強さなどとともに、二枚目の要素をもあわせもつ人物に用いられることが多い。桜丸（『菅原伝授手習鑑 車引』）、助六（『助六』）など。

Kuma are only found around the eyes on this mask. This kuma is used for characters who posess both passion and strength, such as Sakuramaru in Sugawara and the Secrets of Calligraphy.

一本隈 いっぽんぐま / Ipponguma

血気、力強さを備えた若い荒武者の役に用いられることがある。梅王丸（『菅原伝授手習鑑 賀の祝』）など。

This mask is sometimes used for the role of a young warrior with passion and physical strength. Used for Umeomaru in Sugawara and the Secrets of Calligraphy.

二本隈 にほんぐま / Nihonguma

比較的珍しい隈。松王丸（『菅原伝授手習鑑 車引』）に用いられる。

This mask is fairly unusual. It is used for Matsu Ohmaru ("Sugawara and the Secrets of Calligraphy").

猿隈 さるぐま / Saruguma

額に複数の横筋を描いた隈。力強さとともに、おどけた人柄を表している。小林朝比奈（『寿曽我対面』など）に用いられる。

This mask features several horizontal kuma lines on the forehead. It indicates a strong and jocular character such as Kobayashi Asahina in "The Soga Confrontation."

弁慶 べんけい / Benkei *2 kinds (1 and 2)

源義経の豪勇無双の忠臣・武蔵坊弁慶の隈。『御所桜堀川夜討 弁慶上使』『義経千本桜 鳥居前』で用いられる(1)。また別の演目では、やや異なる形の隈がみられることもある(2)。あごや口のまわりの淡い青は、濃いひげを表したものと考えられ、勇猛で男性的な弁慶の人物像を感じとることができる。

Minamoto Yoshitsune's courageous and matchless loyal retainer Musashibo Benkei's kuma. Used for *Gosho Zakura Horikawa Youchi, Benkei Jou no Dan*" and "*Yoshitsune and the Thousand Cherry Trees*" (1). In other programs somewhat different forms of kuma can be seen (2).The pale blue around the chine and mouth is meant to be a dark beard, giving audiences the impression that Benkei is truly a brave and masculine character.

1　　2

奴 やっこ / Yakko

武家の従僕である「奴」の役に見られる隈。左右へはね上げた「鎌ひげ」が特徴的。

The *kuma* for this mask is used for characters playing the role of an attendant or servant of a samurai. This mask is characterized by the sickle-shaped moustache turned up on the left and right.

火焔隈 かえんぐま / Kaenguma

炎を思わせる曲線を描いた隈。精霊などに用いられる。源九郎狐（『義経千本桜 鳥居前』）が代表例。

Kuma drawn as curves reminiscent of a flame. It is used for spirits and the like. Genkurou Gitsune ("*Yoshitsune and the Thousand Cherry Trees*") is a typical example.

公家荒 くげあれ / Kugeare (2 varieties)

天皇の位を奪おうともくろむ、皇族や公家の極悪人に用いられる隈。「公家荒」の青（藍）は、冷酷さ、邪悪さ、さらには妖気を表す。役や俳優により、いくつものパターンがある（1：藤原時平『菅原伝授手習鑑』）（2：蘇我入鹿『妹背山婦女庭訓』）。

This *kuma* is used for villains that are from the royal family or court nobles that endeavor to usurp the Emperor. The blue (indigo) of *kugeare* represents coldness, evilness, and even spirited vibe. There are several patterns depending on roles and actors (1: Fujiwara Tokihira "*Sugawara and the Secrets of Calligraphy*") (2: Soga no Iruka "*Imoseyama Onna Teikin*").

1 2

平知盛の霊 たいらのとももりのれい / Taira no Tomomori no Rei

『船弁慶』に登場する、平家随一の勇将・平知盛の霊に用いられる隈。平家一門の仇・源義経に、怨霊となって襲いかかる知盛の執念や妖気を表す。

Used for the spirit of the famous Heike warlord Taira no Tomomori (Funa Benkei). It evokes the otherworldly mood of the revengeful spirit that attacks Yoshitsune, the Taira clans enemy.

般若 はんにゃ / Hannya

鬼女と化した女性の、すさまじいねたみや復讐の念に燃えるさまを表した、能の面「般若」を思わせる。

This mask is reminiscent of the noh mask called "*Hannya*," which represents a woman turned into a devil, consumed by envy, and obsessed with revenge.

土蜘 つちぐも / Tsuchigumo

『土蜘』に登場する土蜘の精の隈。僧侶に化けていたところを見破られたのち、妖怪の本性を現した時に用いる。黛赭（たいしゃ・茶色）の隈は、主に妖怪変化に用いる。

This is the *kuma* of the ground spider that appears in *Tsuchigumo*. It is used to show the true nature of a phantom after its disguise as a monk is revealed. The mayuzumi (brown) *kuma* is mostly used when characters change into phantoms.

茨木 いばらき / Ibaraki

『茨木』に登場する妖怪・茨木童子の隈。切り落とされた腕を奪い返すため老婆に化けていた茨木童子が、本性を現した時に用いる。

This *kuma* is used for the phantom Ibaraki Doji that appears in "*Ibaraki*". This mask is used to show the true nature of Ibaraki Doji, who turns into an old woman to take back her arm that was severed.
* (the term "kuma" stands for the makeup seen on each mask)

189

付録

「歌舞伎名演目」主要参考図書

「名作歌舞伎全集」
郡司正勝・山本二郎・戸板康二・利倉幸一・河竹登志夫 監修（東京創元社）

「歌舞伎オン・ステージ」
（白水社）

「日本戯曲全集」
渥美清太郎 編（春陽堂）

「新版 歌舞伎事典」
服部幸雄・富田鉄之助・廣末保 編（平凡社）

「歌舞伎登場人物事典」
河竹登志夫 監修（白水社）

「演劇百科大事典」
早稲田大学演劇博物館 編（平凡社）

参考文献

「日本古典文学大辞典」
日本古典文学大辞典編集委員会 編（岩波書店）

「国立劇場上演資料集」
国立劇場調査養成部調査資料課 編（日本芸術文化振興会）

「松竹歌舞伎検定公式テキスト」
松竹株式会社 編（マガジンハウス）

「季刊 歌舞伎」
（松竹株式会社演劇部）

「歌舞伎衣裳図録」
（松竹株式会社事業部）

公演筋書および上演台本
（松竹株式会社）

Selected Bibliography

Meisaku Kabuki Zenshu (Anthology of Famous Kabuki Works)
Edited by Gunji Masakatsu, Yamamoto Jiro, Toita Yasuji, Toshikura Koichi, Kawatake Toshio (Tokyo Sogensha)

Kabuki On Stage
(Hakusuisha)

Nihon Gikyoku Zenshu (Complete Anthology of Japanese Gikyoku)
Edited by Atsumi Seitaro (Shunyodo)

Shinpan Kabuki Jiten (New Encyclopedia of Kabuki)
Edited by Hattori Yukio, Tomota Tetsunosuke, Hirosue Tamotsu (Heibonsha)

Kabuki Tojojinbutsu Jiten (Kabuki Character Dictionary)
Edited by Kawatake Toshio (Hakusuisha)

Engeki Hyakka Daijiten (Great Encyclopedia of Theatre)
Edited by Waseda University Theatre Museum (Heibonsha)

Nihon Kotenbungaku Daijiten (Great Dictionary of Classical Japanese Literature)
Edited by Nihon Kotenbungaku Daijiten editorial committee (Iwanami Shoten)

Kokuritsugekijo Joenshiryoshu (Documents of the National Theatre)
Edited by Survey Division of the National Theatre Survey and Training Department (Nihon Geijutsubunka Shinkokai)

Shochiku Kabuki Kentei Koshiki Tekisuto (Official Textbook of the Shochiku Kabuki Exam)
Edited by Shochiku Co., Ltd. (Magazine House)

Kikan: Kabuki (Kabuki Quarterly)
(Shochiku Co., Ltd., Theatre Dept.)

Kabuki Isho Zuroku (Illustrated Encyclopedia of Kabuki Costumes)
(Shochiku Co. Ltd., Multi Business Dept.)

Synopses and Scripts
(Shochikuk Co. Ltd.)

歌舞伎名演目
舞踊

監修　松竹株式会社
発行日　2019年6月30日　第1刷

デザイン	TAKAIYAMA inc.
イラスト	大津萌乃

執筆・原稿提供	松竹株式会社　演劇ライツ室 （概要・あらすじ・歌舞伎の言葉・隈取一覧） 金田栄一（演目紹介・登場人物） 関根和子（概要・みどころ） 元禄鯨太（歌舞伎の歴史・歌舞伎の見方）
執筆協力	熊野剛 懐遼舘主人
監修協力	松竹衣裳株式会社 歌舞伎座舞台株式会社
写真	松竹株式会社　演劇ライツ室
写真協力	公益社団法人　日本俳優協会
翻訳	クリストファー・E・ザンブラーノ
校正（日本語）	みね工房
校正（英語）	アーヴィン香苗
編集	碓井美樹（美術出版社）
印刷・製本	凸版印刷株式会社
発行人	遠山孝之、井上智治
発行	株式会社美術出版社 〒141-8203 東京都品川区上大崎3-1-1 目黒セントラルスクエア5階 Tel. 03-6809-0318（営業）、03-6809-0542（編集） 振替　00110-6-323989 http://www.bijutsu.press

禁無断転載
落丁、乱丁本、お取り替えいたします。

-

松竹株式会社
明治28（1895）年創業。映像事業、演劇事業、不動産・その他事業の3つを
主体とする、総合エンターテインメント企業。

KABUKI GREATS
Dramatic Dances

Supervised by SHOCHIKU
The First Edition Published on June 30, 2019

Designer	TAKAIYAMA inc.
Illustrator	Moeno Ootsu
Manuscript	SHOCHIKU Co., Ltd. / Play Rights Division (Overviews, Synopses, Kabuki Glossary / Kumadori explanation) Eiichi Kaneda (Introductions, Characters) Kazuko Sekine (Overviews, Highlights) Geita Genroku (The History of Kabuki, How to Watch Kabuki)
Manuscript Assistance	Go Kumano Master of Kairyokan
Editorial Assistance	SHOCHIKU COSTUME KABUKIZA BUTAI
Photography	SHOCHIKU Co., Ltd. / Play Rights Division
Photography Assistance	Japan Actors Association
Translator	Christopher E. Zambrano
Proofreader (Japanese)	Mine Kobo
Proofreader (English)	Kanae Ervin
Editor	Miki Usui (BIJUTSU SHUPPAN-SHA CO.,LTD.)
Printing and Binding	TOPPAN PRINTING CO., LTD.
Publisher	Takayuki Toyama, Tomoharu Inoue

Published by BIJUTSU SHUPPAN-SHA CO.,LTD.
MEGURO CENTRAL SQUARE 5F, 3-1-1
Kamiosaki, Shinagawa-ku, Tokyo 141-8203 Japan
Tel. 03-6809-0318 (Sales), 03-6809-0542 (Editorial)
Transfer account 00110-6-323989
http://www.bijutsu.press

All Rights Reserved
We will happily replace any copy of this book that contains missing pages
or pages bound out of order.

-

SHOCHIKU CO., LTD.
Est. 1895, Shochiku is a general entertainment enterprise consisting of the
three primary divisions of Motion Picture, Theater, and Real Estate among
other divisions.

ISBN978-4-568-43108-7 C0074
© Shochiku / BIJUTSU SHUPPAN-SHA CO., LTD. 2019
All rights reserved Printed in Japan